PATERNOSTER THEOLOGICAL MONOGRAPHS

Revelation and the Spirit

A Comparative Study of the Relationship between the Doctrine of Revelation and Pneumatology in the Theology of Eberhard Jüngel and Wolfhart Pannenberg

PATERNOSTER THEOLOGICAL MONOGRAPHS

A full listing of titles in this series
and Paternoster Biblical Monographs
appears at the end of this book

PATERNOSTER THEOLOGICAL MONOGRAPHS

Revelation and the Spirit

A Comparative Study of the Relationship between the Doctrine of Revelation and Pneumatology in the Theology of Eberhard Jüngel and Wolfhart Pannenberg

Graham J. Watts

Wipf and Stock Publishers
199 W 8th Ave, Suite 3
Eugene, OR 97401

Revelation and the Spirit
A Comparative Study of the Relationship Between the Doctrine of Revelation and Pneumatology of the Theology of Eberhard Jüngel and Wolfhart Pannenbery
By Watts, Graham J,

ISBN: 1-59752-770-x
Publication date 6/10/2006
Previously published by Paternoster, 2005

This Edition Published by Wipf and Stock Publishers
by arrangement with Paternoster

Paternoster
9 Holdom Avenue
Bletchley
Milton Keyes, MK1 1QR
Great Britain

PATERNOSTER THEOLOGICAL MONOGRAPHS

Series Preface

In the West the churches may be declining, but theology—serious, academic (mostly doctoral level) and mainstream orthodox in evaluative commitment—shows no sign of withering on the vine. This series of *Paternoster Theological Monographs* extends the expertise of the Press especially to first-time authors whose work stands broadly within the parameters created by fidelity to Scripture and has satisfied the critical scrutiny of respected assessors in the academy. Such theology may come in several distinct intellectual disciplines—historical, dogmatic, pastoral, apologetic, missional, aesthetic and no doubt others also. The series will be particularly hospitable to promising constructive theology within an evangelical frame, for it is of this that the church's need seems to be greatest. Quality writing will be published across the confessions—Anabaptist, Episcopalian, Reformed, Arminian and Orthodox—across the ages—patristic, medieval, reformation, modern and counter-modern—and across the continents. The aim of the series is theology written in the twofold conviction that the church needs theology and theology needs the church—which in reality means theology done for the glory of God.

Series Editors

For Susan, Joanna and David
with much love and thanks for your support

Contents

Abbreviations xiii
Introduction xv

PART 1
The Advent of God:
The Theology of Eberhard Jüngel

Chapter 1
Being and Becoming: The Self-revelation of God **3**
Introduction 3
Revelation as God's Self-interpretation 4
God's Self-revelation as Event 6
The Being of God in Becoming 13
The Triune God as the Mystery of the World 21
Being and Becoming: The Speakability of God 23
Critical Discussion 27

Chapter 2
Presence and Possibility: Eberhard Jüngel's Theology of the Spirit **35**
Introduction 35
The Presence of God and the Death of Christ 36
The Word of Address: The Presence of God and the Being of Humanity 43
The Priority of the Possible 53
The Death and Resurrection of Christ: The Presence of God in the Perishable 58
Jüngel's Ontology and its Implications for a Doctrine of the Spirit: A Critical Assessment 64

PART 2
The Presence of the Infinite God: The Theology of Wolfhart Pannenberg

Chapter 3
The Revelation of the Triune God: The Doctrine of God in the Theology of Wolfhart Pannenberg **77**
Introduction 77
The Doctrine of Revelation: Historical Process and the Person of Christ 78
The Doctrine of the Trinity: The Threeness of the One God 89
The Doctrine of the Trinity: The Unity of the Divine Essence 99
Critical Discussion 111

Chapter 4
Pannenberg's Doctrine of the Spirit and the Infinity of God **123**
Introduction 123
The Divine Essence as a Dynamic Field of Force 124
The Ontology of the Future: Anticipation and the Temporal Structure of Being 136
The Love of God: Person and Relation 143
Critical Discussion 148
Summary 162

PART 3
Revelation and the Spirit

Chapter 5
A Comparative Appraisal: Jüngel and Pannenberg on the Self-Revelation of God and the Doctrine of the Holy Spirit **167**
Introduction 167
The Doctrine of Revelation 167
The Doctrine of Creation 174
The Person of Christ 178
God and Humanity in Communion: The Spirit and the Nature of Faith 183
The Person of the Holy Spirit 188

Chapter 6
Participation in God **201**
Introduction 201
Revelation and Communion 203
God the Spirit: Participation and Public Personality 204
Inspiration and Trinitarian Pneumatology 209
Spirit of Life, Spirit of Truth 213
Conclusion 215

Bibliography **217**

Index of Names **225**

Subject Index **227**

Abbreviations

CD Karl Barth, *Church Dogmatics*, translated by G.W. Bromiley, edited by G.W. Bromiley and T.F. Torrance (Edinburgh: T&T Clark, 1936-1969)

GMW Eberhard Jüngel, *God as the Mystery of the World*, English translation by D.L. Guder, (Edinburgh: T&T Clark, 1983)

ST Wolfhart Pannenberg, *Systematic Theology*, English translation by G.W. Bromiley, Vols. 1-3 (Edinburgh: T&T Clark, 1991-1998

Introduction

There are many pressing questions facing the Christian church at the start of the twenty first century. In what way can we speak responsibly about God in the context of the postmodern rejection of the grand story? The Christian claim to knowledge of God is traditionally expressed in terms of the uniqueness of Christ; how do we understand that claim in relation to the concept of truth? In a culture that has become deeply suspicious of authority and increasingly mindful of competing claims to truth, how does the church understand its mission and proclaim the Gospel?

In response to the first question the Christian theological tradition makes reference to the doctrine of revelation; God is self-revealing. We speak about God in the light of a prior movement from God to humanity in certain historical events. The second question, which concerns the idea of truth in relation to experience, finds a focus in pneumatology. It is this God and none other, revealed in Christ, who comes to us in and through the Holy Spirit who is, biblically, the giver of life and the Spirit of truth.

The theological focus of this study can be summed up as an exploration of the relationship between the doctrine of revelation and pneumatology. The Christian confession of God as Father and Jesus Christ as Lord is both a summary statement grounded in the self-revealing character of God, and, in biblical terms, a belief engendered by the Holy Spirit. If God has revealed himself historically in Christ and continues to come to the world in the power of the Holy Spirit, then the expressly theological relationship between the concept of revelation and trinitarian pneumatology is a strong and vital, yet relatively unexplored one.

The main purpose of this study is a comparison of two contemporary Lutheran theologians, Eberhard Jüngel and Wolfhart

Pannenberg. Eberhard Jüngel's theology is a conscious interpretation and development of the work of Karl Barth. The structure and content of the doctrine of revelation is the ground of Jüngel's doctrine of the Trinity and underpins his lengthy exposition of the nature of God's relationship to the world.[1] Given the importance of the idea of revelation for this approach to the doctrine of God, the implications for a doctrine of the Spirit are significant. Yet Jüngel's theological preference for the short essay means that no systematic pneumatology has been produced. It will be argued that his considerable interest in theological language, particularly metaphor, is rich with possibilities for a doctrine of the Spirit, but in Jüngel's own writing this remains relatively underdeveloped. In short, here we have a theologian asking what it means to speak about God in the light of his self-revelation.

By contrast, Pannenberg's theology in both his earlier work and his Systematic Theology marks a significantly different approach to the doctrine of revelation.[2]. By understanding the concept of revelation in terms of God's self-revealing acts throughout the totality of the historical process, Pannenberg asserts that any Christian claim to truth must be provisional in nature. Yet, by utilising the idea of prolepsis, Christ is regarded as the anticipatory disclosure of the eschatological reality. The doctrine of the Trinity is expressed as a truth based on God's self-revealing acts. Yet Pannenberg is a realist and refuses to conduct the theological quest in isolation from a meaningful engagement with philosophy and modern science. He attempts to relate a doctrine of God, based on revelation, to an account of God as the true Infinite. This is because Pannenberg seeks a *via media* between the concept of God gained through revelation and the nature of God conceived by human reason. Here the relationship between the doctrine of revelation and a trinitarian account of the person and work of the Spirit is expressed more openly and in some original ways. Whether the resulting model of the Spirit is internally, logically coherent, and whether it accords with biblical testimony and theological orthodoxy, will be questioned.

The study is structured in such a way as to bring out three interrelated theological issues. Firstly, the comparative nature of the study will show alternative, contemporary approaches to the theological exposition of truth. How is it possible to speak of God in a way which is true to the Gospel in the context of a culture which is defined by radical individualism and the search for truth within ourselves, rather

---

[1] Jüngel's magnum opus in this regard remains *GMW*.

[2] W. Pannenberg, *ST*.

than in a universal focus; 'we no longer look beyond ourselves for what is true, good or beautiful.'[3] In this context talk about God becomes increasingly difficult, since it is no longer clear that there is a universal understanding of the word 'God.' Such God-talk has been termed an 'embarrassment for the human spirit.'[4]

Yet, by contrast, there appears to be an increasing interest in what might be loosely termed 'spirituality.' Individualism and the interior focus of the search for truth and reality are matched by a desire for transcendence. There is a renewed search for community together with the exaltation of the notion of tolerance in all things pertaining to religion. Pluralism has become the accepted popular dogma with the consequence that statements of belief are placed into the realm of subjective statements of opinion. When all religious confessions of faith are regarded as valid expressions of individual belief then the key motivation for religious involvement is the question 'does it work?' 'It is assumed that since all faith and morality are firmly in the area of opinion and that all opinions are equally valid, the only thing that really matters is whether or not they work.'[5] Pluralism engenders a market situation in which religious institutions are invited to offer their wares as consumer commodities. Accordingly there is an implicit rejection of 'any notion of the objective, what is true, what is real and any genuine understanding of revelation.'[6]

The response of our two theologians is markedly different. Jüngel's theology is a conscious and sustained working through of Barth's dictum that it is 'God alone, in the event of revelation, who creates the possibility of knowledge of God's Word.'[7] Pannenberg's response is to insist that 'every theological statement must prove itself on the field of reason;' 'theological discourse about God requires a relationship to

---

[3] C. Gunton, *The One, the Three and the Many*, Cambridge, 1993, p.16.

[4] Jüngel, *GMW*, p.3.

[5] L. Strobel, *Inside the Mind of Unchurched Harry and Mary*, Grand Rapids, Michigan, 1993, p.15.

[6] E.D. Cook, 'Truth, Mystery and Justice: Hick and the Myth of Christian Uniqueness,' in A. Clark and B. Winter (eds), *One God, One Lord in a World of Religious Pluralism*, Cambridge, 1991, p.187. Among many criticisms of the underlying philosophy of relativism is the coherence of making relativism the absolute criterion by which alternative views are judged. A commitment to pluralism must logically include an acceptance of its own relative value as a world view.

[7] K. Barth, *CD, I\2*, p.247.

metaphysical reflection if its claim to truth is to be valid.'[8] The extent to which these two approaches enable us to speak responsibly about God, out of the Christian experience of God's presence through the Spirit, will provide one focus for this study.

The second related theological concern is born from my own experience in local church life and reflects the extent of confusion surrounding the language of revelation and the Spirit. It is quite commonplace in some church circles to encounter sincere believers who claim to have some 'revelation' from the Spirit; sometimes this can take the form of an experience into which, it is argued, others need to be initiated. The relatively widespread appeal of the 'Toronto Blessing' and similar ecstatic phenomena illustrates the desire of some authentic and sincere Christians to enter into a direct, renewing experience of God's presence. Acute pastoral and theological questions are raised concerning the authenticity of such experiences, and the extent to which they might denote an act of God or, conversely, a 'spiritualising' of the 'spirit of the age.'

Neither is this problem confined to local church life. At the 1990 gathering of the World Council of Churches Chun Hyun Kung invoked ancestral spirits and called upon names from the Korean spirit world in the context of the invocation 'come Holy Spirit.' This is, at the very least, confusing, but led to some equally theologically naïve reviews. As one example, it is hard to discern the coherence in Boyd's remarks that 'syncretism is quite legitimate so long as it is centred on Christology and the Trinity.'[9] More recently, the nature of inter-faith relations has been highlighted in the light of the rise of religious fundamentalism and extremist sectarianism. Given these concerns, this study aims to consider in what ways we may express the reality of God's presence with us through the Spirit in such a way that is consistent with God's self- revelation in Christ.

The third related focus of this thesis, which gives direction to the argument, is to move towards a trinitarian doctrine of the Spirit which is not primarily grounded on the concept and structure of revelation alone, but which will give greater emphasis to our participation in

---

[8] W. Pannenberg, *Basic Question in Theology, Vol.2*, English translation by G. Kehm, London, 1983, p.102; *Metaphysics and the Idea of God*, English translation by P. Clayton, Edinburgh, 1990, p.6.

[9] R. Boyd, 'Come Holy Spirit. And we really mean come!' in *The Ecumenical Review*, 43.2, April 1991, p.181. See this issue for a number of reviews of the conference.

Christ. This would be consistent with the theology of Luther, the influence of whom is noted throughout our comparative study. It is argued that by grounding trinitarian pneumatology in the notions of participation and communion, a doctrine of the Spirit might emerge which is eschatologically oriented and christologically determined. It is further suggested that such a pneumatology would underpin an ontology of created and personal particularity within the concepts of communion and participation.

In seeking to shift the emphasis in our trinitarian understanding of the Holy Spirit it is hoped that we might further enable our speech about God to be responsible and thus serve in the wider sustaining of the truth of the Gospel.

PART 1

The Advent of God:

The Theology of Eberhard Jüngel

Chapter 1

Being and Becoming:

The Self-revelation of God

Introduction

> Insofar as it reflects upon the Christian faith, theology has to conceive of God as the one who came to the world in Jesus Christ and as such does not cease to come to the world.[1]

This programmatic statement demonstrates the orientation of Eberhard Jüngel's theological position. As one of the ablest interpreters of Barth, his doctrine of God is grounded in the trinitarian structure of the doctrine of revelation. Consistent with his Lutheran heritage there is considerable emphasis upon the Word, centred in the person of Jesus Christ, yet interpreted in terms of the language of encounter and address. Consequently Jüngel's is a theology that engages at length with the role of language in speaking about God; in part this reflects the influence of Ernst Fuch's who, in turn, was a pupil of Bultmann. The two main strands of twentieth century German Protestant theology, represented by Barth and Bultmann, intersect in Jüngel's work.[2] As we shall observe, this also draws him into considerable involvement with the existentialist philosophy of Heidegger.

Given these diverse strands within Jüngel's theological writing it is not surprising that he has admitted that 'truth does not yield immediate satisfaction;' as a leading critical interpreter of Jüngel, Webster states that 'Jüngel is by no means an easy thinker.'[3] In order to assess the

---

[1] E. Jüngel, 'Metaphorical Truth,' in *Theological Essays*, translation by J.B. Webster, Edinburgh, 1989, p.59

[2] Jüngel states that Barth and Bultmann are 'like two souls to me.' R. Garaventa, 'L'esito dell teologia: Dio e altro dall' uomo (intervista a E. Jüngel),' *Il Regno*, Vol. 2, 1987, p.38.

[3] J.B. Webster, *Eberhard Jüngel: An Introduction to his Theology*, Cambridge,

significance of his doctrine of the Spirit it will be necessary to outline Jüngel's doctrine of God as he expounds that in the context of God's self-revelation as event. This will prompt an investigation of Jüngel's approach to language in the light of God's address to humanity. These two loci will structure the present chapter. The pneumatological implications of Jüngel's doctrine of God will be explored in the following chapter where the underlying ontological presuppositions will be outlined. Particular attention will be paid to Jüngel's exposition of the presence of God in relation to the death of Christ and to his explication of the relationship between the actual and the possible within the context of the doctrine of justification. The particular implications of these for an understanding of the person and work of the Holy Spirit will then be critically evaluated.

Revelation as God's Self-interpretation

Jüngel's earliest account of the doctrine of God is arguably his most structured and rigorous. *The Doctrine of the Trinity: God's Being is in Becoming* (*Gottes Sein ist im Werden*) was written in the context of a debate between Braun and Gollwitzer in the early 1960's.[4] The focus in this dispute was the relationship between the being of God revealed in the economy of salvation (*ad extra*) and the immanent being of God (*ad intra*). The New Testament writer Braun, pursuing the implications of the theology of Bultmann, argued that speech about God as an independent, objective entity was better replaced by speech about God as a subjective reality; 'I can speak of God only where I can speak of man, and hence anthropologically.'[5]

Gollwitzer, a dogmatician deeply influenced by the thought of Barth, objected to this as an effective reduction of theology to anthropology.[6] The being of God must be understood as more than the subjective

---

1986, p.3. Webster's book remains the most comprehensive summary of Jüngel's theology and has been used extensively in the anaylsis offered here.

[4] E. Jüngel, *The Doctrine of the Trinity: God's Being is in Becoming*, English translation by H. Harris, Edinburgh, 1976.

[5] H. Braun, 'The Problem of a New Testament Theology,' in *Journal for Theology and Church* 1965, p.169. Bultmann interpreted Braun's position as close to his own.

[6] H. Gollwitzer, *The Existence of God as Confessed by Faith*, translation by J. Leitch, Philadelphia, 1965; originally *Die Existenz Gottes im Bekenntnis des Glaubens*, Munchen, 1963.

experience of God. Gollwitzer proposed a distinction between the essential being of God and the free encounter of God with humanity with the consequence that it is impossible for us to know everything about God on the basis of revelation. Yet, this brought him into dispute with Barth in his concept of the self-revelation of God. Thus while seeking to counter Braun's perceived reductionism, Gollwitzer was himself at risk of compromising his own indebtedness to Barth.[7] Jüngel perceived that Barth's doctrine of the Trinity moves beyond the polarity between God's being *ad intra* and *ad extra*. By neglecting the trinitarian basis of a Christian doctrine of God, he argues, Braun and Gollwitzer both opened up a gulf between God's being in himself and his being for us. Jüngel sees that Barth's understanding of God as triune denies such a gulf in asserting that, in the event of revelation, 'God corresponds to himself.' In actuality, Barth's Dogmatics is basically a detailed exegesis of this proposition.'[8] Lying behind this is Barth's understanding of God's being in the act of revelation so that this revelation 'has its basis and prototype in his own essence, in his own being as God.'[9] This means that 'God's being *ad extra* corresponds essentially to his being *ad intra* in which it has its basis and prototype.'[10]

Jüngel's use of the term 'correspondence' (*Entsprechung*) is quite distinctive in that he uses it to show how the history of the man Jesus is constitutive for the immanent trinitarian life of God; 'God's revelation of himself in Christ is not foreign to but identical with his own inner life' which is to say that 'God's way of being himself is by being God for us.'[11] As will become clearer in our discussion of revelation as an event in which God interprets himself, the term 'correspondence' is not intended to imply identity. It is rather a way of speaking of God's

---

[7] Schubert Ogden, while regarding the critique of Braun as significant asks whether Gollwitzer's own position 'can have sense.' S. Ogden, *The Reality of God*, London, 1967, p.26.

[8] Jüngel, *The Doctrine of the Trinity*, p.24.

[9] Jüngel, *The Doctrine of the Trinity*, p.23.

[10] Jüngel, *The Doctrine of the Trinity,* p.23. Expressed rather differently, Barth's doctrine of the Trinity serves to show how far God in his revelation can be 'our *God*, and '*our* God.' Thus the self- revelation of God cannot imply a separation between the being of God in his economy and in his essence. Throughout this interpretation of Barth, Jüngel makes constant cross reference to *CD* I/1.

[11] J. Webster, *Eberhard Jüngel: an Introduction to his Theology*, Cambridge, 1986, p.18.

intimate relation to the world without 'reducing "God" to a cipher for a human state of affairs.'[12]

This poses problems for Braun's doctrine of God since speech of God's being *ad intra* is essentially related to God's being *ad extra.* 'God's being as object is his being-revealed...that means that...God's being-as-object is not the result of human *extra* objectification of God...He is only objective as the one who has *made* himself objective.'[13] Thus proper talk about God's being-as-object (*Gegenständlich-Sein*) is the result of God giving himself to be known as such. This is counter to Braun's suspicion that talk of God's objectivity can be no more than a reification of human thinking into a divine order of being.

Yet Jüngel's exposition of Barth also serves to highlight the weakness of Gollwitzer's approach. In proposing a distinction between the will and the essence of God, Gollwitzer is seen as threatening the correspondence of God's being for us and God's being in himself. This in turn runs counter to Barth's whole conception of the being of God in the event of revelation.

The application of Barth's doctrine of the Trinity to the polarities inherent in the Braun-Gollwitzer debate demonstrates the interpretative power of Jüngel's approach and indicates the way in which the very diverse thought of Barth and Bultmann interweaves through Jüngel's distinctive theology. For the purposes of this chapter it is now important to examine how he interprets Barth's doctrine of revelation as event in terms of God's self-interpretation, since this is the foundation of his doctrine of the triune God.

God's Self-revelation as Event

From considerations so far it is clear that Jüngel perceives Barth to have made a substantive epistemological shift from questions about our subjective experience of God to the objectivity of God which is apprehended in the context of self-revelation. God is known as he gives himself to be known. Therefore, the essential question becomes 'in what sense *must* we speak of God, so that our speech is about *God*?'[14] Consequently the question of the being of God 'reflects on (*nachdenkt*)

---

[12] Webster, *Eberhard Jüngel*, Cambridge, 1986, p.18.

[13] Jüngel, *The Doctrine of the Trinity*, p.44. The implication of this for Jüngel is that the objectivity of God can only be understood because God gives himself as object to be apprehended within our human subjectivity.

[14] Jüngel, *The Doctrine of the Trinity*, p.ix.

the being of God;' it is a thinking in the light of God's free bestowal of himself in the act of revelation.[15]

Jüngel expounds Barth's doctrine of revelation from the foundational statement that 'God's being proceeds.'[16] By this Jüngel means God's free decision from eternity to take the path into 'the far country' in the person of Jesus Christ.[17] In that God freely chose to endure 'what is strange to him for the benefit of man' this is understood as an act of love; thus God's being is perceived as 'he who loves in freedom.'[18] Following Barth, revelation is seen as 'the Person of God speaking (*Dei loquentis persona*).'[19] In the act of revelation 'God's Word is identical with God himself...revelation is that event in which the being of God comes to word.'[20] Behind this conception lies the notion of revelation as the self-interpretation of God. God reveals himself and in the act of revelation God interprets himself. In this event of revelation, form and content cannot be distinguished; 'when revelation is an event according to the Bible, there is no second question as to what its content might be.'[21]

We are to conceive of God in the event of revelation as differentiated being. He is in the event of revelation, he is the revealed content of that revelation and he is manifest in us in the event of revelation; we have thus to conceive of the being of God 'in a threefold way;' following Barth's formulation, God 'in unimpaired unity is the revealer, the revelation and the revealedness.'[22]

---

[15] Jüngel, *The Doctrine of the Trinity*, p.xix. In this sense 'the being of God which is the subject of theological inquiry precedes the question...God's being precedes the theological inquiry after this being.'

[16] Jüngel, *The Doctrine of the Trinity*, p.1, drawing upon Barth's exposition of the movement of God's being to manifestation under the headings 'the Way of the Son of God into the Far Country' and the 'Homecoming of the Son of Man.' *CD* IV/3.

[17] It is of note that Jüngel speaks of the coming of Jesus in parabolic terms; in so doing he follows the structure of Barth's doctrine of reconciliation but also reflects his own thesis of God's coming to speech in parables, as first expounded in his doctoral thesis *Paulus und Jesus*, (1962).

[18] Jüngel, The Doctrine of the Trinity, p.3.

[19] Jüngel, *The Doctrine of the Trinity*, p.15.

[20] Jüngel, *The Doctrine of the Trinity,* pp. 15,16, quoting Barth *CD* I/1, p.304.

[21] Jüngel, *The Doctrine of the Trinity*, p.16.

[22] Jüngel, *The Doctrine of the Trinity,* p.16. Putting this in a different way, God is 'subject, predicate and object of the revelation-event.' The proposition which grounds the revelation-event is 'God speaks:' *'Deus Dixit.'*

The distinction within the being of God is grounded in an understanding of revelation as a 'reiteration of God.'[23] The significance of this is to establish that revelation is not something 'other' or 'over against' God, but rather grounded in the unity of the 'internally-distinguished being of God.'[24] Thus God's taking form in the event of revelation is interpreted as a self-unveiling which is grounded solely in the being of God. In the event of revelation God manifests himself and distinguishes himself in concealment and manifestation; this is 'God a second time in the form of something he is not: God the Son.'[25] This dialectic of revelation and hiddenness is characteristic of Jüngel and reflects the extent of his indebtedness to Barth and Luther. Whether is serves to clarify his doctrine of the triune God or create difficulty is open to question and will be discussed in a later chapter.

Revelation is understood as 'a matter of impartation, of God's being revealed...God's being revealed makes it...an effective encounter between God and man.'[26] In becoming God to specific individuals we say that 'God reveals himself as the Spirit.'[27]

It is axiomatic for Jüngel, as for Barth, that if revelation is the self-interpretation of God then God reveals himself as the one who *can* reveal himself. This constitutes the concept of the Lordship of God; the possibility of revelation, grounded in the being of God is the expression of the lordship of God.[28]

---

[23] Jüngel, *The Doctrine of the Trinity*, p.17.

[24] Jüngel, *The Doctrine of the Trinity*, p.17. In other words the doctrine of the Trinity considers the oneness and differentiation of God's being; the threefold mode of being constitutes the differentiation of God's being.

[25] Jüngel, *The Doctrine of the Trinity,* Jüngel correctly notes the christological grounding of Barth's doctrine of the Trinity. It is vital to note here that God in his 'hidden mode of being' is not alienated from his revelation. Utilising the Lutheran terminology of hiddenness and revelation, he states that is it as the '*Deus absconditus*' that God is the subject of revelation. 'The fact that this subject of revelation is the God who cannot be unveiled to man, heightens and secures the concept of revelation as Gods' self-unveiling...it is the *Deus revelatus* who is the *Deus absconditus*.' In expressing this Jüngel both maintains the distinction between God as the subject of revelation and the revelation itself; this is formally the way in which God reveals himself as the Father of the Son 'without ceasing to be the free ground and the free power of his being God in the Son.'

[26] Jüngel, *The Doctrine of the Trinity*, p.20.

[27] Jüngel, *The Doctrine of the Trinity*, p.21, quoting Barth *CD* I/1, p.232.

[28] 'God reveals himself as the Lord. That, for Barth, is the basic axiom of

The concept of event is pivotal for Barth and hence also for Jüngel. It is therefore vital to look in more detail at the nature of 'event' language, how this relates to the triune God and how Barth and Jüngel's use differs from alternative expressions of 'event' terminology.

In developing his doctrine of the Trinity out of the doctrine of revelation, Jüngel follows Barth in utilising the Patristic term 'mode of subsistence' (*tropos huparcheos*). The significance of this move for the understanding of trinitarian personhood will become apparent later; the purpose of this is to explicate the differentiation of God's being in terms of the relationships which constitute God's oneness. Barth's use of 'mode of being' is intended to express the mutual relations in which the being of God can be conceived as 'Trinity in Unity' as derived from God's self-revelation.

> If revelation is understood as the event of God's self-identification, then with the oneness of the distinctions between revealer, becoming revealed and being revealed which constitutes this event, revelation...allows us to … distinguish the being of God into three modes of being in the sense of different genetic relationships to one another.[29]

At heart this construction means that the being of God as differentiated being is constituted as such only by the trinitarian relationships. Yet these relationships are not impersonal; rather God's being is 'pure event...a reiteration in God...a *repetitio aeternitatis in aeternitate* by which the oneness of the revealed God is differentiated from everything else that may be called oneness.'[30] In theological terms this means that the essence of God is not conceived in isolation from the trinitarian relations. Hence 'being as event is only to be comprehended in its divine singularity as "threehood" (*Gedritt*), not as "fourhood" (*Geviert*).'[31]

---

revelation.' *The Doctrine of the Trinity,* p.21. It is of note that here Jüngel perceives an underlying ontological proposition in Barth regarding the relationship of the possible with the actual; 'where the actuality exists there is also the corresponding possibility.' See the discussion on this point in the following chapters.

[29] Jüngel, *The Doctrine of the Trinity*, p.27.

[30] Jüngel, *The Doctrine of the Trinity*, p.27 Jüngel notes that this distinguishes the idea of the divine unity from any other metaphysical idea of singularity.

[31] Jüngel, *The Doctrine of the Trinity*, p.28. In other words the essence of God cannot be understood as distinct from his relations; it is not a fourth mode of being behind the threeness. This responds to an often stated criticism of Barth's doctrine of the Trinity, that it is effectively modalistic because there is the suspicion of a fourth 'essence' behind the triune relations.

God in his threeness as Father, Son and Holy Spirit is one 'in the freedom of his being-as-event' as love.[32] The self-giving of God to the world corresponds to the self-giving in which he belongs to himself. 'In the self-relatedness of God's being the relational structuring of this being *eventuates*. As the mutual self-giving of the three modes of God's being, the being of God is event.'[33] The concept of event therefore serves to expound God's self- revelation as a historic event in the coming of Christ. God's being may only be known as a result of God's free self-disclosure in Christ. Further, event terminology serves to emphasise the disruptive nature of the encounter between God and humanity. It meshes with Jüngel's understanding of language in which God addresses humanity and confronts human existence with new possibilities. To speak of God revealing himself in an event implies change, a dynamic of movement.

It is of further importance to note that, following Barth, Jüngel sees that the language of event employed in this way serves to preserve the freedom of God as the one who 'exists in His act;' to speak of God as event in the specific way envisaged by Barth and interpreted by Jüngel is to recognise that God's being is entirely self-moved, 'His own conscious, willed and executed decision.'[34] Whether the language of event is theologically adequate to interpret the being of God in his revelation is questionable and in order to clarify Jüngel's use of the term a contrast must be drawn with alternatives. Jüngel's appropriation of the language of event can be distinguished from that associated with process philosophy, as typified in the work of Whitehead. Here natural processes are understood to consist of events of creativity which, when added together, make up the whole of created reality. God is posited as the sum of the events, the supreme actual entity or event. Thus God is understood to be dependent upon the creation for his own future. As God acts to influence all microevents he sets limits to their facility for creative change.[35] We will compare Jüngel's theology with process thought in

---

[32] Jüngel, *The Doctrine of the Trinity*, p.28.

[33] Jüngel, *The Doctrine of the Trinity*, p.29. Jüngel is quite clear that this must not be understood as a merely abstract formula separate from the conceptualisation of God as love. The use of the term 'eventuate' may be regarded as a rather obscure way of expressing the truth that the being of God is only to be understood in terms of the self-relatedness of God in his three modes of being; it speaks in rather abstract terminology of the relatedness of God's being.

[34] Barth, *CD II/1,* p.272.

[35] See especially, A. N. Whitehead, *Process and Reality: An Essay in Cosmology*, New York, 1929.

greater depth when considering the use of the term 'becoming.' It is sufficient here to note that process thought has been criticised on many counts, most commonly on the tendency to dissolve God into the world.[36]

To this point we have followed Jüngel's interpretation of Barth's doctrine of the Trinity as derived from the doctrine of revelation. Yet his own theology moves beyond that of Barth in his development of the concept of the address of God as a 'speech-event.'[37] In fusing Barth's concept of event with the idea of 'speech-event' Jüngel develops a particular view of language as performative. He argues that the language of the New Testament does not simply carry information, but actually conveys the presence of the realities which it addresses. For example, in the parables of Jesus the Kingdom of God is not simply described, but is brought into present existence; 'the eschatological Kingdom of God comes to speech in the forms of speech of Jesus' preaching.'[38] In this way God comes to speech in the Word; in this event humanity is addressed and reality is interrupted. The category of event is characterised by its interruptive nature. In disrupting creaturely reality, God addresses us in such a way as to define us anew. In this event 'man has a qualitatively new experience of being.'[39] In other words performative language is related to action.

J. L. Austin explains it as 'in saying what I do, I actually perform that action;' for example in saying that I name a ship 'X' I do not describe the ceremony of naming, I actually perform the ceremony. Similarly in saying 'I do' in a marriage service I am not merely reporting on a marriage, I am indulging in it.[40] We will consider later whether Jüngel's preference for understanding language as performative properly takes account of other semantic possibilities in describing the being of God.

The full exposition of Jüngel's understanding of the performative nature of theological language will be expounded later since it has considerable bearing on his doctrine of the Spirit. The purpose of

[36] We shall have cause to compare Jüngel with process thought on a number of occasions since they utilise common concepts; it will be seen that Jüngel carefully redefines his terminology in order to distance himself from process thought.

[37] He borrows this term from his teacher Ernst Fuchs and employed it in his doctoral dissertation *Paulus und Jesus*, Tubingen, 1962.

[38] Jüngel, *Paulus und Jesus*, p.292.

[39] Jüngel, *GMW*, 1983, p.32. The precise nature of this will be examined in a later section since Jüngel's use of speech event is ontological in form.

[40] J. L. Austin, *Philosophical Papers*, ed. J. Urmson and G. Warnock, Oxford, 1961, p.222. Austin describes 'performative' as 'a rather ugly word...but there seems no word already in existence to do the job.'

introducing the concept here is to indicate the way in which Jüngel has expanded the category of event in his own understanding of the being of God in the event of revelation.

An interesting comparison can be made with Jenson who has also employed Barth's language of event but in a different way. In *The Triune Identity* Jenson seeks to balance what he sees as Barth's tendency to look back to Christ as a primal reality by adding an eschatological dimension to the discussion of God's being as event. God's being in act supremely reveals Jesus Christ as the Lord who's final return will unveil the triumph of the man Jesus who was defined in his being for others in the events of his life, death and resurrection.[41] In the specific historicity of Jesus, God's being is uniquely revealed. God's being coheres in the history of Jesus of Nazareth; it will cohere as event in the final eschatological consummation. Yet God's being is more than an identity with a given historical event; it is an event in a unique way. To speak of God as event is to speak of God as relational within himself and in relation to his creation in such a way that does not reduce God to a dependence upon his creation. God is related to his creation precisely in his distinction from it. It is apparent that Jüngel's use of the language of event constitutes a distinctive development of Barth's doctrine of God; in particular the ontological implications of the performative nature of language will be explored in a later section. Before examining this it will be helpful to note the theological implications of Jüngel's doctrine of God as expounded thus far.

The first major implication is christological. Jüngel's early work which we have examined so far, focused on the Word of God as a uniting theme in theological debate between historical critical method and dogmatics; they have a 'common relation to the same Word.'[42] His later work focused on the relationship between the dogmatic confession of Christ and the historical accounts in the Gospel texts. By insisting on the essential unity of New Testament texts about God he provides a basis for an essential unity between the Christ confessed by faith and Jesus of Nazareth.[43]

---

[41] R. Jenson, *The Triune Identity*, Philadelphia, 1982. See also Jenson's two volume *Systematic Theology*, Oxford, 1997-99.

[42] E. Jüngel, *Paulus und Jesus*, p.v. 'As exegesis, theology inquires after the "Word of God as text;" as dogmatics, theology inquires after the same word "as truth to be reiterated."' Webster, *Eberhard Jüngel*, p.28.

[43] Jüngel expresses this rather idiosyncratically in stating that there is a '*communicatio idiomatum* between the earthly Jesus and the risen One' such that in the light of the Easter event 'the earthly Jesus becomes a hermeneutical aid to

This leads to a second implication. The practical significance of this is to see the theological task as 'historical (*historisch*) work...for the narrated past is effective in that it lays bare possibilities in the present.'[44] Hence at a hermeneutical level the task of theology is one of narration through which God will come to speech, bringing new possibilities out of past events.[45]

An important systematic question is suggested at this point. What is the relationship between the unique, historical Christ-event and the event by which God encounters humanity in a word of address? In what way does this language of event, grounded in a trinitarian structure of revelation, assist in distinguishing a distinctively Christian experience of God from any other spiritual experience? In order to respond to these sorts of questions it is necessary to pursue Jüngel's doctrine of God and, in particular, his idiosyncratic use of the term 'becoming.'

The Being of God in Becoming

One of the implications of understanding revelation as God's self-interpretation is that this enabled Barth to speak of the being of God without reference to a general category of being. Jüngel observes that Barth objected to any 'threatened development of the doctrine of God into a doctrine of being.'[46] Yet Jüngel perceives that Barth's doctrine of revelation provides a way of speaking ontologically about the being of God; 'God's revelation is the criterion of all ontological statements in theology. In the face of this criterion ontological statements in theology are not only legitimate but indispensable.'[47]

Starting from the concept of revelation as God's self- interpretation Jüngel sees that the being of God must be thought of as a oneness in three

---

the kerygma.' 'Jesu Wort und Jesus als Wort Gottes. Ein hermeneutische Beitrag zum christologischen Problem,' in E. Busch and J. Fangmeier (eds) *Parrhesia. Karl Barth zum 80. Geburtstag*, Zurich, 1966, p.92.

[44] Webster, *Eberhard Jüngel*, p.33. He quotes Jüngel: 'To narrate history means to examine its unique actuality...going back to the past possibility out of which it came, looking forward to its future possibilities....'

[45] This relates closely to Jüngel's ontological view of the importance of the realm of the possible which we shall examine in detail in the following chapter.

[46] Jüngel, *The Doctrine of the Trinity*, p.62, quoting Barth *CD II/1*, p.260.

[47] Jüngel, *The Doctrine of the Trinity* p.63. For Jüngel this is necessary if we are to speak responsibly about God's being.

modes of being in such a way that God's being is 'self-related being.'[48] These modes of being are so structured that each mode becomes what it is only in relation to the other two modes of being. In this sense, arising out of the trinitarian relations, God's being is 'a being in becoming.'[49]

With regard to God's relationship to the world, God's self-interpretation in the event of revelation is understood as being-in-act. Consequently God's being is actualised in the event of revelation but not in any way that God becomes subsumed in the relation of himself to the world. 'The concept of God is won anew from the interpretation of revelation as the self-interpretation of God.'[50] God is no other than who he is in his revelation, in his coming to us as event. In this sense 'God's being is in becoming.'[51] Jüngel's distinctive use of the term 'becoming' is that which is peculiar to God's being; it is a 'becoming which allows us to comprehend God's being as "being-in-act."'[52]

Webster identifies a key theological principle which grounds Jüngel's discussion. First, to describe God's being as becoming is to specify the ontological principle by which God in his freedom can become that which is other than himself. In particular it is an attempt to speak in ontological terms of how God's being can suffer death in the crucifixion of the Son without ceasing to be God.[53]

This conception rests on Barth's understanding of the freedom of God. In expressing the being of God as free, Barth distinguishes God from any other created being; 'He is the one, original and authentic person through

---

[48] Jüngel, *The Doctrine of the Trinity*, p.63.

[49] Jüngel, *The Doctrine of the Trinity*, p.63. Within the trinitarian life of God the doctrine of perichoresis by which the three modes of being interpenetrate each other forms the material, dogmatic basis for this use of the term 'becoming.' It is in the differentiation and perichoretic unity as 'threehood' that 'God's being is in becoming.'

[50] Jüngel, *The Doctrine of the Trinity*, p.64. This is the heart of the understanding of revelation as event. It is an actual, factual event in history; 'revelation is real, revelation takes place.' On the basis of revelation as event the being of God is also understood as event. The emphasis made by Barth is supremely upon the being of God as 'free event, free act...' (pp.65-66).

[51] Jüngel, *The Doctrine of the Trinity*, p.64.

[52] Jüngel, *The Doctrine of the Trinity*, p.100.

[53] 'The force of the concept of God's 'being in becoming' is to try to specify the voluntary nature of God's self- sacrifice in identifying himself with the crucified Jesus...the definition of God's being as "being-in-act" is not contradicted when suffering is predicated of God.' Webster, *Eberhard Jüngel*, p.21.

whose creative power and will alone all other persons are and are sustained.'[54] Expressed negatively, this is freedom from any external compulsion to act. Positively, it is freedom to communicate himself and even unite himself with the other. God, in his freedom, can be inwardly present to his creatures; he is 'free to be immanent, free to achieve a uniquely inward and genuine immanence of his being in and with the being which is distinct from himself.'[55] This freedom is uniquely fulfilled in God's union with the man Jesus. 'God is free. Because this is the case, we must say expressly...that the freedom of God is the freedom that consists and fulfils itself in his Son Jesus Christ.'[56]

Jüngel's use of the term 'becoming' rests substantially on this view of God's freedom and is very different from any concept of God's being developing in relation to events in the world. This distinction will become apparent by a brief comparison with process thought.

Whereas, for Jüngel, the becoming of God is unique to the being of God, Whitehead proposed a metaphysical view in which God was regarded as the chief exemplification of metaphysical categories.[57] For Whitehead, the basic constituents of reality are actual entities, each of which have two poles, the physical pole and the mental pole. The mental pole represents the entities desire for and realisation of an ideal form, while the physical pole represents the entities relationship to the environment from which it arises. An actual entity is formed out of the decay of other actual entities; as such it is a metaphysics rooted in an evolutionary view of reality. God is understood as an actual entity whose two 'poles' refer to a primordial nature and a consequent nature. God's primordial nature constitutes the realm of possibilities; God's consequent nature represents God's relationship to the world such that events within the world are received and objectified in him. The result of this is to posit a real sense in which God's being is in a state of 'becoming' or development as a result of events in creation; God suffers, grows and becomes that which, in some sense, he previously was not.[58]

---

[54] Barth, *CD, II/1*, p.301.

[55] Barth, *CD, II/1*, p.313.

[56] Barth, *CD, II/1*, p.321. The significance of this for Jüngel's view of the presence of God in the event of the cross will be pursued later.

[57] The following summary is drawn principally from Whitehead's *Process and Reality*.

[58] 'One side of God's nature is constituted by his conceptual experience. This experience is the primordial fact of the world, limited by no actuality which it presupposes...this side of his nature is free, complete....The other side originates with physical experience derived from the temporal world....it is determined,

Whitehead has been criticised on many grounds. Quite apart from making God's being dependent upon world processes there is the strong sense in which Whitehead fails to integrate the dipolar nature of God; 'it appears as if he is speaking of two gods rather than one.'[59]

The comparison with Jüngel is quite clear. There is no sense in which Jüngel understands the category of becoming in process terms. For Jüngel, becoming is not a general ontological category applied to God; it uniquely characterises God's being in his freedom.

Consequently we can see that Jüngel employs the term 'becoming' to signify the manner in which God's being may be understood ontologically as a being in relationship and rests upon the concept of the freedom of God to become ontologically localised.

Being in Becoming: The Triunity of God

The diverse nature of Jüngel's magnum opus *God as the Mystery of the World* does not conceal the importance of the central category of becoming in his further outworking of the being of God in trinitarian terms. Here the condensed conceptual language of his earlier work is expounded in the theological framework of the Trinity.[60] 'The doctrine of the Trinity is an attempt to think out the self-relatedness of God's being...the being of God as Father, Son and Spirit.'[61]

The conceptualisation of the being of God in becoming implies a real movement within God such that God 'comes out of himself when he comes to himself.'[62] In relation to the person of Jesus, God came in an event of self-identification. God the Father came to himself in the Son and yet God 'remained totally in the process of coming as the Holy

---

incomplete, consequent...' *Process and Reality*, p.524.

[59] J. J. O'Donnell, *Trinity and Temporality*, Oxford, 1983, p.74. Whitehead's thought was significantly adapted by Charles Hartshorne in his doctrine of God. For a comparison of this with Karl Barth's doctrine of God see C. Gunton, *Becoming and Being: The Doctrine of God in Charles Hartshorne and Karl Barth*, Oxford, 1978.

[60] Jüngel, *GMW*.

[61] Jüngel, *The Doctrine of the Trinity*, p.99; yet this is only possible when we understand God's self-relatedness in his modes of being as 'the power of God's being to become the God of another.'

[62] *GMW*, p.380. This is equivalent to saying that God is his own absolute origin as well as his own goal. 'God comes as God from God to God. God is his own mediation.'

Spirit.'[63] To speak of God as his own origin is to speak of God as one who 'lives totally out of himself.'[64] This is to speak of God as Father. 'As God comes from God, he is called Father. As God the Father, God is the origin of himself.'[65]

Yet God is not a 'solitary thing' (*solitarium*). The language of Father means that God, in his free sovereignty, 'permits participation in being.'[66] The eternal God reveals himself as Father in the sending of his Son. God is not only his own origin, he encounters himself out of this origin in such a way that he 'becomes his own partner.' In this sense God comes to God; 'God is God the Father as the Father of the Son.'[67] Consequently to say that God comes to God is to believe in God the Son. Yet this must be understood only within the context of the coming of God to man. In this event we find the ground of all Christian knowledge of God; the event of revelation constitutes the Christian concept of God. Yet the God who comes to man in the person of Jesus is no different from the God who comes to himself in his own being. God comes to man and thus comes to himself in the Son to realise his own goal.[68] Jüngel pursues this manner of argument with particular reference to the death of Christ. God comes to God even in the extremity of the cross of Christ. This death is 'the seal of that event in which God comes both to God and to man, of that event then in which God as man is his own goal.'[69] In this quite specific context God is revealed to be the eternally living one who is his own goal. This is critical in Jüngel's thought. It is out of God's entering into perishing in the cross of Christ that God may be understood as the origin and goal of all created being:

> With his 'Yes' to man God remains in the event of the...death of Jesus Christ true to himself as the triune God. In the death of Jesus Christ God's 'Yes,' which...constitutes all being, exposed itself to the 'No' of the

---

[63] *GMW*, p.381.

[64] *GMW*, p.387.

[65] *GMW*, p.381. Jüngel explicates this further by referring to the eternity of God. As the eternal Father 'God is the origin of himself, is earlier than being and nonbeing...to believe in the eternal Father means...to acknowledge God as the sovereign of all that exists.'

[66] *GMW*, p.382.

[67] *GMW*, p.382.

[68] This is the logical outcome of Jüngel's interpretation of the being of God in the event of revelation.

[69] *GMW*, p.383. The central theological importance of the presence of God in the death of Christ will be examined in the next chapter.

nothing. In the resurrection of Jesus Christ the 'Yes' prevailed over the 'No' of the nothing. And precisely with this victory it was graciously settled why there is being at all, and not rather nothing.[70]

The significance of this understanding of the cross for the doctrine of creation is of note and will concern us later. The present concern is to note how Jüngel articulates the correspondence of God with the historical event of the death of Christ. God comes to himself in the Son, through death; in entering into the nothingness of death, and in the raising of Jesus from the dead, God shows himself to be God. The correspondence of the man Jesus with God is historically localised. For God to become an existential reality for us the significance of the historical Christ event must become an event for us. We cannot attain this through our own effort. 'We do not press through to God; rather the Holy Spirit presses through to us.'[71] It is in the Holy Spirit that God 'has become expressible as God.'[72] It is through the Spirit that God draws humanity into relationship with himself and opens up new possibilities for the future; God 'remains in the process of coming...God comes as God.'[73] God does not cease to be God in his mediation between his own origin and his own goal. In trinitarian terms, God mediates between the Father and the Son in his third mode of being, the Holy Spirit.[74]

Here we reach the heart of Jüngel's understanding of the Spirit as the being of God in the unity of his origin and his goal. Jüngel finds his own interpretation of the filioque clause; if God comes to himself both from his origin and his goal then in the Spirit the Father and the Son affirm each other mutually. In this mode of being he is 'the Spirit who proceeds from the Father and the Son.'[75] In this context Jüngel expounds the Spirit

---

[70] Jüngel, *The Doctrine of the Trinity*, pp.107-8. This rather densely conceptual expression of the significance of the death of Christ effectively grounds Jüngel's doctrine of creation in a theology of the cross. The death of Christ is constitutive for the existence of the world and expresses in time and history the eternal being of God in his becoming. The ontological language will be explored in the following chapters.

[71] *GMW*, p.387.

[72] *GMW*, p.387. Jüngel understands this in terms of a 'drawing out' of the human person.

[73] *GMW*, p.387. In this sense God is not only his own origin and his own goal, but he remains related to himself as origin and goal.

[74] Typically Jüngel expresses the same thought in a number of different ways. So, 'the coming in which God's being is, is God himself.' (*GMW*, p.388)

[75] *GMW*, p.388.

in terms of love; it is as love that God's being is in coming. As the Spirit of love God is his own origin and his own goal. Jüngel affirms the basic Augustinian insight that the Spirit is the 'bond of love,' (*vinculum caritatis*), though his own development of this is quite distinctive.[76] The Holy Spirit is understood as 'the relation of the relations' who constitutes the being of love as event.' He is the 'relationship of the relationships and thus an eternally new relationship of God to God.'[77]

In this form the description of the Holy Spirit remains at a rather abstract level and is not theologically transparent; yet it is apparent that Jüngel is moving beyond the Augustinian position by affirming the ontological significance of the statement 'God is love.' In the context of the being of God as event, it is love which is the event which constitutes 'the essence of deity.'[78] The Father loves of himself and out of himself, the Son is beloved of the Father, the Holy Spirit is the 'constantly new event of love between the Father and the Son.'[79] Jüngel is quite clear that this must not be construed as simply an inner-trinitarian loving such that God might be described as 'the most sublime egoist.'[80] Rather, the Holy Spirit is simultaneously the eternally new event of love between the Father and the Son, and the gift in which God relates himself to humanity and takes us up into the event of divine love. God's being as love is thus an overflowing of the life of God; through the unique event of the cross God's love comes to humanity as a renewing gift. The Spirit actualises the selfless giving of God for us and radically realigns us towards God, our fellow human beings, and the future. In this sense the being of God is:

---

[76] *GMW*, p.388. An indication of the way in which Jüngel develops this may be inferred from his statement that the Spirit as the bond of love 'moves those who are bound eternally "toward something new."' The full implications of this are worked out in his separate explication of Luther's doctrine of justification which is understood in terms of God's free creation of the new. This will be examined in the following chapter. The implications of this for a theological understanding of life in the Spirit as the gift of new life are argued in his essay 'The Emergence of the New,' in J. Webster (ed.), *Theological Essays, Vol. 2*, Edinburgh, 1995, pp.35-58.

[77] *GMW*, p.375.

[78] *GMW*, p.375.

[79] *GMW*, p.375. Jüngel is here concerned to distinguish between human love between persons and the Spirit of God who is love. 'The person who is love is not possible. It is solely the Spirit of God...who constitutes the being of love as event.'

[80] *GMW*, p.375.

> nothing other than a self-relationship which in freedom goes beyond itself, overflows itself, and gives itself away. It is pure overflow, overflowing being for the sake of another and only then for the sake of itself. That is love.[81]

This is what Jüngel means when he speaks of God as an event of the Spirit.

At this point Jüngel interacts with Karl Rahner's formulation that the immanent Trinity is the economic Trinity.[82] Within the classical theological tradition the distinction between the immanent and economic Trinities was maintained as a way of securing God's ontological freedom from creation. Zizioulas has been critical of the tendency to conflate the two; while we may accept that the economic Trinity reveals God as he is in his immanent being, we cannot assume that the immanent Trinity is necessarily exhausted in the economy of salvation. By denying the reversibility of Rahner's axiom Zizioulas maintains that we may retain a concept of God who does not need his creation.[83]

Jüngel differs from Rahner and shares the concern expressed by Zizioulas in wishing to retain the freedom of God in his acts. Yet this is precisely the point of Jüngel's account of the being of God in becoming. In this sense Jüngel steers a different course from Zizioulas and from Rahner. The relationship between the economic and immanent Trinity is, for Jüngel, only to be understood in terms of the being of God as he comes to the world in the event of revelation. It is as the Spirit implements the selflessness of God for us, as we are drawn into the constantly new relationship of love in the trinitarian life of God, that Jüngel can say that the immanent Trinity is the economic Trinity.[84]

---

[81] *GMW*, p.369.

[82] K. Rahner, *The Trinity*, translation by J. Donceel, New York, 1974.

[83] J. Zizioulas, 'The Doctrine of God the Trinity Today: Suggestions for an Ecumenical Study,' in *The Forgotten Trinity*, pp.19-32.

[84] In *The Triune Identity*, Jenson articulates an alternative view. Working with a concept of God's freedom as 'freedom from oneself as given, yet for oneself as given' and as 'the power of the future to transcend what is' he states that to be God is 'to possess oneself only as the opportunity of being other than the possessed self.' (p.167). Consequently Jenson posits the identity of the immanent and economic Trinities at the Eschaton. It is of interest that he is assisted in this greater eschatological emphasis by giving greater weight to the resurrection of Christ, whereas Jüngel concentrates far more on the death of Christ.

The Triune God as the Mystery of the World

So far we have seen the extent to which Jüngel's doctrine of God is grounded on the concept of revelation as the being of God in his acts; God's being has come into the world in Christ and does not cease to come to the world in and through the Spirit. In the closing pages of *God as the Mystery of the World*, Jüngel expounds the concept of the invisibility of God which is manifested in revelation through the agency of the Spirit. For Jüngel it is as Spirit that God is the mystery of the world.[85] In this sense we might note a parallel with the New Testament exposition of the plan of salvation hidden in the past but now revealed; the content of that mystery is 'Christ in you, the hope of glory.' (Col. 1:27).

Jüngel seeks to articulate the concept of mystery by enquiring as to the anthropological correspondences to the concept of God as the mystery of the world. In other words, what are the 'human acts and modes of being which express...that they are concerned with something completely other than an unknown Invisible.'[86] Jüngel finds in faith, hope and love the modes of being of humanity in which we are 'so related to God...that his invisibility becomes concrete as the focusing of his knownness.' This is what it means for humanity to be 'addressed and defined' by the Holy Spirit.[87]

Faith is understood negatively as the opposite of self-possession. Positively, it is the experience of God in his coming to the world and drawing near to us. It is an existential experience in which one encounters self and is set free from the dominion of self-possession; 'in faith one goes beyond oneself and grounds oneself in God.'[88] In this event God liberates

---

[85] The purpose of Jüngel's use of the term mystery can be seen in relation to his debate with theism and atheism. There is a difference between 'the person who experiences the invisibility of God and the one who is content with the non-experiential statement that something like a God cannot be seen.' *GMW*, p.376. The point is that from the first perspective, the invisibility of God is part of the structure of the experience of God; from the second perspective this might only provide an introduction to atheism. Jüngel's formal purpose in the whole structure of this work is to explain by reference to the apparent invisibility of God in the cross of Christ how God is indeed 'the mystery of the world.' It is of interest to note here the similarity between Jüngel's use of the term mystery and Luther's concept of the *deus absconditus*. We will pursue this link in a later chapter.

[86] GMW, p.390.

[87] GMW, p.390.

[88] E. Jüngel, 'On Becoming Truly Human,' in Webster, *Theological Essays*,

humanity such that new ways of being become possible. Following Luther, Jüngel conceives this in an essentially passive way; the human person 'permits himself to be taken along by God.' In order to become 'acquainted with oneself as person, the achiever must be elementally interrupted.'[89] The initiative lies with God in his grace. Pneumatologically, it follows that Jüngel understands the work of the Spirit to be life giving and liberating.

The second anthropological mode of being in which we encounter God as the mystery of the world is love. This also demonstrates that humankind does not possess itself; we find ourselves in relation with an other. In the act of loving, humanity most closely corresponds to God as relational being; 'in the event of love, God and man share the same mystery.'[90] In this encounter with God, the human being is set free from self-possession to be able to live for another.

From a pneumatological perspective, through the overflow of the Spirit of love, humanity is taken up into the divine loving; we become intimately related to God as Father and united with Christ.

The third mode of being attributed to humanity is hope. Hope protects human beings from possessing themselves. It is grounded on the movement of God towards his own goal; without this hope humankind remains fixed in the 'ontologically false ideal of humanity as self-having and self-possession.'[91] By contrast, the one whose hope is in God can 'release himself...can let himself go - toward the God who is coming.'[92]

Once again the implications for the doctrine of the Spirit as clear. The Spirit aligns humankind eschatologically. Taken together, faith, hope and love express in human form that God's being is in becoming.[93]

In faith, love and hope, Jüngel defines the work of the Spirit in terms of freedom, relationship and eschatology. God is the mystery of the world in that in his invisibility he has given of himself to be known in the visible incarnation of his Son; the mystery is revealed. The doctrine of the Trinity

---

Vol. 2, pp. 216-240.

[89] *GMW*, p.390 and 'On Becoming Truly Human,' p.238.

[90] *GMW*, p.392. 'in the event of love, man corresponds to the God who has come to the world in both the most intensive and the most extensive ways...in the event of love man is at his most mysterious.'

[91] *GMW*, p.395.

[92] *GMW*, p.395.

[93] 'Returning in faith to the God who is coming from himself to the world. taken along in the love of the human God who is coming to himself even in death, and in hope going towards the God who is coming and who is helping love to its victory, man preserves God as the mystery of the world.' *GMW*, p.395.

essentially implies the self-differentiation of the invisible and visible God in such a way that they are united in the Spirit 'who produces in an invisible way, visible results in us...as Holy Spirit God is the mystery of the world.'[94]

Being and Becoming: The Speakability of God

The dense, conceptual language employed by Jüngel should not conceal the sense in which he finds in his interpretation and development of Barth's doctrine of the Trinity a way of speaking of the being of God that is far from abstract. Rather, his theological programme may be seen as 'an attempt conceptually to clarify how one historical episode - the life and especially the death of Jesus of Nazareth - can be determinative of our understanding of the ways and works of God.'[95]

From the outset Jüngel has been concerned to show in what way theology must speak responsibly of God in the light of God's self-revelation. Following Barth, he wishes to establish that speech about God is truly speech of *God.* It is speaking in the light of God's self-revelation; 'the theological question concerning the being of God reflects on (*nachdenkt*) - the being of God.'[96]

For Jüngel, this approach facilitates a way of speaking of God in response to his understanding of traditional theism and metaphysical atheism. By reflecting upon the contemporary difficulty or 'embarrassment' of talking about God he seeks to articulate a theological response to theism and atheism on the basis of a theology of the cross.

Speaking of God in the Context of the Contemporary Aporia

Jüngel analyses the perceived contemporary aporia, or 'situation of doubt' concerning speech about God in terms of a 'linguistic displacement of God; God has no place in our thought and thus has no place in our language.'[97] This results in an increasing inability to speak about God.[98]

---

[94] *GMW*, p.379.

[95] Webster, *Eberhard Jüngel*, p.24. Thus the criticism of Ott that Jüngel has indulged in a form of abstract conceptual play, a 'high scholasticism,' as we shall see, is wide of the mark.

[96] Jüngel, *The Doctrine of the Trinity*, p.xix.

[97] *GMW*, p.3. 'He does not occur, has no topos (place, position.')

[98] 'Theology is thus in a bad state.'*GMW*, p.4.

Jüngel sees this exemplified in the realm of science. In that God is mentioned within this sphere of discourse at all, it is only as a general, descriptive word which conveys little by way of defined meaning; 'within the horizon of contemporary scientific thought, God appears at best as a quotation.'[99]

Although Jüngel does not deal specifically with the issue of religious pluralism in the light of philosophical relativism, there is a sense in which this compounds the difficulty of speaking about God. The Psalmist's question 'where can I go and meet with God?' might well find the modern pluralist response that there are many places where God can be encountered.[100]

The theological question thus centres upon our ability to speak of God in the light of this linguistic displacement of God. There are two principal issues that concern Jüngel and which ground his discussion of what he terms the 'speakability' of God.

First, speech about God must be authentically human speech. While speech about God is only made possible by God's self- revelation, language about God is still human language.[101] Such speech is indeed demanded from beyond the normal horizon of discourse; 'language about God is certainly not immanent within the structures of ordinary human speech.'[102] Yet human talk about God is made possible on the basis of God's address to humanity; authentic speech about God is more than ordinary human speech since through it God speaks. 'Human talk about God merits being called responsible when its only intention is that God should be permitted to speak.'[103] This leads to a second principle that Jüngel employs with regard to human language about God.

Since proper speech about God brings God to speech, such human language is metaphorical; it uses familiar human language in unfamiliar ways by applying known words to new referents. There is an interplay

---

[99] *GMW*, p.3. Some such use of the word God might be discerned for example in Stephen Hawking's often quoted conclusion to *A Brief History of Time* that a thoroughgoing theory of everything in science might mean that we would at least come near to 'the mind of God.'

[100] Psalm 42:2. We shall consider in the later critical discussion whether Jüngel's emphasis upon the debate with atheism would be helpfully tempered by a more critical engagement with the issue of pluralism.

[101] This lies behind the discussion of the *vestigium trinitatis* as a hemeneutical problem in *The Doctrine of the Trinity*, pp.5-15.

[102] Webster, *Eberhard Jüngel*, p.40.

[103] *GMW*, p.227. In this sense human speech about God 'corresponds to God in that it lets him come.' Only this sort of speech is 'responsible talk about God.'

between the familiar and the unfamiliar that is expressed in metaphor and analogy.[104] We shall examine the concept of language as God's address in more detail in the following chapter. It is sufficient to note here that to speak of God coming to speech in human language is a way of describing the being of God in becoming in that act of address; this in turn is a further interpretation of the statement that God comes as God in and through the Spirit.

Speaking about God in the Context of the Debate between Theism and Atheism

In *God as the Mystery of the World* Jüngel strives to articulate the speakability of God on the basis of God's address to humanity within the context of the debate between metaphysical theism and atheism. This debate he interprets as grounded on the Cartesian structure of thought exemplified by Descartes.

For Descartes, the thinking 'I' is the foundational concept; 'the fact that *I* think when I *think* led, in Descartes to the self-establishment of thought in the "I think."'[105] Jüngel sees that this leads to a radical subjectivisation of our knowledge of God. Now Descartes regarded that which is true as that which is fully comprehended, that which is present to the thinking mind. Hence, 'the clearly and distinctly comprehending ego becomes the place of presence in general. Only the ego can be present in a total way.'[106] Consequently God can only be proven to exist beyond doubt to the extent that he is present.[107]

Yet Jüngel argues that Descartes saw the idea of God to be necessary for human thinking (*res cogitans*). 'Descartes understands God as a necessary essence, as a necessary being (*ens necessarium*).'[108] God is understood as the essence which is more perfect than humanity; he is the guarantor of coherent thought. 'God is a methodological necessity for the *res cogitans* which seeks to secure the continuity of its existence.'[109] God is thus a being of the highest perfection, the omnipotent, independent, infinite substance as traditionally expounded by metaphysical theism.

---

[104] Jüngel's extended essay 'Metaphorical Truth' is a reflection upon the hermeneutical function of metaphor as 'a fundamental characteristic of religious language.' Webster, *Theological Essays, Vol. 1*, p.19.

[105] *GMW*, p.111.

[106] *GMW*, p.124.

[107] Thus 'modern man is man appropriating God; man is responsible for God.'*GMW*, p.125.

[108] *GMW*, p.119.

[109] *GMW*, p.122.

Here Jüngel identifies an ambiguity in the thought of Descartes. God in his essence is thought as the almighty Creator, a necessary and perfect being. Yet his existence is secured through the thinking ego:

> in terms of his essence God is...necessary in and through himself and through whom I am...in terms of his existence, however, God is through me, in that his existence can be understood only as representedness through and for the subject, which 'I' am.[110]

Jüngel finds in this contradiction the seed bed of modern atheism as expounded by Feuerbach and Nietzsche. Following Descartes, if God is not perceived to be present then he cannot *be*; negating his presence becomes interpreted as negating his being. Hence Nietzsche's often quoted question in the face of the apparent absence of God at the cross, 'could ye conceive a God?'[111] Similarly, in Feuerbach's assertion 'Only when thou dost think of God as unthinkable, dost thou truly think, rigorously speaking,' Jüngel perceives a common heritage in the thought of Descartes.[112]

Jüngel's response to both the metaphysical, theistic view of God as perfect, unmoved being and modern atheism is to find a way of speaking of the presence of God in the event of the death of Christ and, further, the presence of God in his address to man. This represents a thoroughgoing attempt to think of the being of God beyond the polarities of subject and object, as a being who, in his freedom, enters into that which is other than himself, even to the point of death. The detailed exposition of this will follow in the next chapter; once again the point here is to note the methodological significance of the concept of the being of God in

---

[110] *GMW*, p.125. Webster criticises this analysis of Descartes as creating a 'false dichotomy' through a persistent confusion of the epistemological with the ontological. He 'does not distinguish between the claim that God is contingent upon the world and the claim that *knowledge* of God is dependent upon *knowledge* of the world.' (*Eberhard Jüngel*, p.54). This does not deny the full import of Jüngel's critique of Descartes in that the concept of God as shaped by, or filtered through, the ego may lead to a restrictive account of the being of God.

[111] F. Nietzsche, Thus Spake Zarathustra in *The Complete Works of Friedrich Nietzsche*, (English translation by G. Eliot) New York, 1957, p.36.

[112] Ludwig Feuerbach, *The Essence of Christianity*, as quoted by Jüngel in *GMW*, p.127. Jüngel makes the point that the focus of the two statements is the same, but the context of their writing means they are expressed differently. Feuerbach was writing against an attack on atheism; Nietzsche considered himself as prosecutor of Christianity.

becoming as the ontological place of God's being for Jüngel's theological strategy.

Becoming as a Pneumatological Category

When understood in terms of the place of God's being, the language of becoming clearly has pneumatological implications. To speak of God as Spirit is to refer to the being of God in terms of the possibility of God crossing ontic boundaries. It is to reflect upon the being of God who is free to become ontologically localised as the creative, life-giving presence of God. Through the Spirit, God comes to the world and is active within the world. Understood as a trinitarian reality this enables us to speak of God's presence in and with the other in such a way that God never becomes identified with the world. In this sense, God as Spirit is God in his otherness; he is not simply a principle of immanence.[113]

Yet to attribute to the being of God the transcending of ontic boundaries has to be balanced by the particularising activity of the Spirit. Jüngel's language of becoming suggests a way of moving beyond the polarities of transcendence and immanence by describing God's being in coming to the world. To speak of God's being in becoming is to express the way in which God may be present in the particular without being dissolved into it. The significance of this will become apparent from our later exposition of Jüngel's theology of the cross and the doctrine of justification.

Before turning to these and investigating the pneumatological implications, a number of points may be addressed by way of criticism.

Critical Discussion

Before considering the significant issues raised by Jüngel's doctrine of God a question mark must be raised over Jüngel's methodology, most notably his engagement with atheism.

By orienting his discussion of the being of God towards a theology of the death of Christ, Jüngel attempts to counter a form of metaphysical atheism by reinterpreting the 'death of God' in christological terms. In his early treatise on the nature of death, the event of the cross is interpreted in terms of the passion of God. 'Every attempt...to hold God aloof and apart from the wretchedness of this death fails to penetrate to the central core of

[113] Contrast, for example, the theology of G. Lampe, *God is Spirit*, London, 1977.

the Christian faith.'[114] This grounds the subsequent understanding of the life of faith as one which is lived in the light of 'the death of death' secured through the death of God in Christ.

This approach, which undergirds the whole diverse structure of *God as the Mystery of the World*, shows the extent to which Jüngel's own doctrine of God is conceived as a response to, and is in some way dependent upon, the arguments of atheism. This is the substance of a group of criticisms.

Mazur identifies four ways in which Jüngel has reinterpreted the philosophy of Nietzsche, notably as the context for Jüngel's doctrine of God. He traces the influence of Nietzsche on Heidegger's anthropological conception of 'being-towards-death' which, in turn, is foundational in Jüngel's interpretation of the life and death of Jesus.[115] Mazur assesses this appropriation of Nietzsche as essentially positive and constructive in its attempt to build a bridge between the original atheistic concern to be set free from restrictive ideologies and the true significance of the atoning death of Jesus Christ. Yet there are surely less helpful aspects to this methodological approach.

Webster has pointed to Jüngel's limited definition of atheism as 'antitheism.' Hence atheism becomes identified with a particular strand of thought which offers a critique of certain metaphysical, theistic ideas, which Jüngel himself finds unhelpful and worthy of severe criticism on different grounds. By limiting the discussion of atheism in this way he is able to work on familiar territory; he works with a form of atheism which 'contains within itself the theology which it combats.'[116]

One result of this is Jüngel's preference for concepts rather than praxis; it is the concept of God, proposed by theism and criticised by this form of atheism, which contextualises the reinterpretation of the cross in terms of the concept of the being of God. As Webster correctly observes, this renders Jüngel's theology largely immune to the critique of other strands of atheism, such as Marxism, which emphasise action over against concept. Jüngel's preference for proper speech about God and his passion in the death of Christ, though valuable within their self-imposed limits,

---

[114] E. Jüngel, *Death: The Riddle and the Mystery*, (Originally '*Tod*,') English translation by I. and U. Nicol), Edinburgh, 1975, p.113.

[115] G. O. Mazur, 'On Jüngel's Four-Fold Appropriation of Friedrich Nietzsche,' in J. Webster (ed.) *The Possibilities of Theology*, Edinburgh, 1994, pp.60-69.

[116] Webster, *Eberhard Jüngel*, p.82, quoting M. Merleau- Ponty, *In Praise of Philosophy*, 1963.

'may in the end merely reinforce contentions that interpreting reality is a very sorry substitute for changing it.'[117]

A similar concern lies behind Newland's observation that 'the greatest problem facing Christianity in many parts of the world is not atheism but the inhuman.'[118] This raises the question of the ethical and political implications of a theology which is so heavily consumed by conceptualising the being of God in engagement with a narrow spectrum of atheistic thought. To what extent can a theology of God's passion truly be worked out in a practical expression of Christian love and justice?

It is of note that Pannenberg begins his *Systematic Theology* by contextualising the concept of revelation within the plurality of world religions. Jüngel's preoccupation with theism and atheism might also be made more pertinent to the contemporary situation if it were to be balanced by a consideration of the fact, and underlying philosophy of, religious pluralism. This must be considered one of the greatest tasks facing the Christian church today. Jüngel's failure to engage with this might signal the extent of his pre-occupation with combating the theistic conception of God from which a certain form of atheism draws its life. Newland's criticism of Jüngel is apposite; 'How is the concept of God in Christianity to be related to the concepts of God in other religious and philosophical frameworks?'[119]

Beyond this methodological issue, significant systematic issues arise from Jüngel's doctrine of God. There are particular difficulties with his use of the term 'event,' and a perceived problem when speaking of the person of the Holy Spirit.

It has been seen that the category of event is central for Jüngel's doctrine of God. Following Barth in understanding God's being as 'being-in-act' the event structure of revelation is read back into the being of God. Watson has questioned the adequacy of the term 'event' as a description of revelation. He argues that the main problem with this is that it is essentially non-relational; 'it does not in itself signify an occurrence of a kind that can only take place between two personal agents, an I and a

---

117 Webster, *Eberhard Jüngel,* p.83.

118 G. Newlands, 'The Love of God and the Future of Theology: A Personal Engagement with Jüngel's Work,' in Webster (ed.) *The Possibilitites of Theology*, p.203.

119 G. Newlands, *God in Christian Perspective*, 1994, p.26 Newlands sees here the consequence of a theology which he regards as essentially an 'insider's view...If we who live in a pluriform society wish to enter into genuine dialogue with those 'outside'....something more needs to be done.'

Thou.'[120] While it is admitted that Barth tried to counter this by seeing revelation as personal in the sense of the divine-human relation, it is argued that there remain three problematic aspects to the general employment of the term to a doctrine of revelation.

Firstly, the event model inevitably emphasises the existential aspect of encounter but plays down the significance of any cognitive information which is a normal part of inter-personal interaction. At the human level, we come to know someone as we learn more about them. It may be countered that while this may be true of an abstract existential event, when contextualised in the form of the Gospel and understood as a 'speech event,' then this criticism loses some of its import. A Gospel based encounter is not lacking content.

Secondly, the term event suggests an interruption; it is disruptive in nature. Yet when viewed in relation to other occurrences, the event has to be integrated into the linear flow of a train of events. The implications of this may be seen in Jüngel's and Barth's understanding of the being of God in the act of revelation in terms of 'repetition.' Since a disruptive event cannot be readily integrated into the linear experience of processes, 'it is said that it must occur again and again.'[121] Yet the concept of repetition seems to give to the category of event a static quality, which is at odds with the essence of an event as a disruption. We will later argue that if this event of encounter is understood eschatologically in terms of our being made new, then this cannot readily be described as 'static.'

Thirdly, an emphasis upon revelation as an event carries a connotation of immediacy. Those in receipt of the revelation are isolated in their experience; there is a heightening of the individual aspect of revelation over against the corporate. Followed through consistently this would lead to a greater emphasis upon the individual divine-human encounter at the expense of the communal, ecclesiological dimension.

With regard to Jüngel's doctrine of God the last two points are of related interest. Since Jüngel interprets Barth in seeing God's self-revelation as an unfolding of his triune being, there follows a tendency to describe the trinitarian distinctions as repetitions of the one divine subject. This is the thrust of Ford's comment that Jüngel's use of event language tends to 'subsume persons within a dynamic of "the same."'[122] It also lies behind Pannenberg's rather polemical point that preference for the

---

[120] F. Watson, 'Is Revelation an Event?' in *Modern Theology*, 10.4, 1994, p.384.

121 Watson, 'Is Revelation an Event?' p.389.

[122] D. Ford, 'Hosting a Dialogue: Jüngel and Levinas on God, Self and Language,' in Webster (ed.) *The Possibilities of Theology*, p.43.

language of 'modes of being' in Barth's thought tends to strengthen the conviction that 'the divine persons become... moments of the *Deus Dixit*, moments of the self-unfolding of this Ego.'[123] In terms of Watson's general critique of the use of 'event' language, this reflects the incipient danger of failing to adequately account for linearity and process without recourse to the concept of repetition.

A similar problem arises from Watson's third critique when applied to Jüngel's doctrine of God. In emphasising the individualistic aspects of encounter at the expense of the communal, when projected back into the being of God it is possible, paradoxically, to detect a tendency to emphasise the trinitarian being of God as an expression of the one, unitary divine essence of the being of God. For example, to expound the doctrine of the triune God as a movement from God to God in which God comes as God leads with some inevitability to speech of God the Father, God the Son and God the Holy Spirit, rather than God, who is Father, Son and Holy Spirit. In pneumatological terms this tends to conflate the biblical distinction between the statement 'God is Spirit' and the third person of the Trinity.

This links with Jüngel's often noted difficulty in speaking of the personhood of the Holy Spirit. Criticism of this may be made from several angles, although all make similar points. If the origin of Jüngel's particular difficulty here lies in his embracing a Barthian 'event' terminology, its formal expression is found in his description of the Spirit as 'mystery' and 'love.'

Gunton sees that Jüngel uses the concept of mystery to hold together the way in which God is and is not identical with his presence in Jesus. The Spirit is the link between the Father and the Son. Yet, as Gunton argues, the 'Achilles heel of Western theology' is an under-determination of the person of the Holy Spirit.[124] This in turn gives inadequate scope for the doctrine of the humanity of Christ. The result of this may be seen in Jüngel's characteristically Lutheran emphasis on the cross and the crucified God; this tends to downplay the systematic significance of the particularity of the man Jesus. In a recent article Webster has highlighted s similar problem with Jüngel's Christology. The use of 'correspondence' (*Entsprechung*) suggests that the man Jesus expresses God; yet Jüngel also heavily employs the language of concealment and hiddenness, as though the man Jesus is a mask for the being of God. This language of

[123] Webster, *Eberhard Jüngel*, p.74, quoting W. Pannenberg.

[124] C. Gunton, 'The Being and Attributes of God. Eberhard Jüngel's Dispute with the Classical Philosophical Tradition,' in Webster, *The Possibilities of Theology*, p.21.

concealment is uncomfortably close to a form of docetism and the doctrine of correspondence may not be quite adequate to remove this tendency.[125]

The related reluctance to speak of the person of the Holy Spirit is reflected in Jüngel's use of the term 'mystery,' which can be regarded as representing an ambivalence in Jüngel's manner of conceiving divine immanence. This reservation is compounded by Jüngel's description of the Spirit as the love which unites the Father and the Son. Gunton argues that to be personal the Spirit must be more than one who holds the Father and the Son together. Webster notes the weakness of Jüngel on this point in his reluctance to articulate clearly the personal agency of the Spirit.[126] Jüngel clearly wishes to say that the Spirit is, in some way, more than the relationship between the Father and the Son. Yet in describing the Spirit as 'the relation between the relations of the Father and the Son' it is not clear that he is doing any more than describing a certain quality of relationship.[127] Similarly, the description of God as love as 'the one who always heightens and expands his own being in such great self-relatedness, still more selfless and thus overflowing,' while seeking to ascribe ontological status to the being of God as Spirit, falls well short of the language of personhood.[128] It also raises the question as to how far one can speak of a self-expansion of God's being which overflows to the world without implying some form of 'increase of change in God.'[129] The question which Jüngel fails to answer convincingly is that posed by Gunton; 'is the Spirit a relation or a person?'[130]

There are other questions which arise from Jüngel's use of the category of 'event.' To what extent does his theology of the death of Christ impose serious limitations on the way in which other areas of doctrine are expressed? How far can an existential theology of encounter and address account for the on-going providential activity of God in creation? These

---

[125] This specific criticism was raised by John Webster in personal conversation.

[126] 'The problem remains unresolved by Jüngel: his account of the Spirit is not so much an account of a personal agent as a description of a state of affairs, of the fact, that is, that God's being remains in coming.' Webster, *Eberhard Jüngel*, p.77.

[127] *GMW*, p.375.

[128] *GMW*, p.369.

[129] J. Thompson, 'Jüngel on Barth,' in Webster, *The Possibilities of Theology*, p.175. Here Thompson notes a similar problem in the theology of Hans Urs von Balthasar.

[130] C. Gunton, 'The Being and Attributes of God:' p.22.

questions are significant for a doctrine of the Spirit and will be addressed in the following chapter, which will examine in greater depth the ontological parameters of Jüngel's thought and follow through the pneumatological implications.

Chapter 2

Presence and Possibility: Eberhard Jüngel's Theology of the Spirit

Introduction

Jüngel has not published a systematic theology or a sustained thesis on pneumatology. Consequently his theology of the Spirit has to be constructed by inference. Jüngel's doctrine of God's being in becoming, that is, the possibility of God's ontologically localised presence in that which is 'other than' God, gives impetus for an inferred doctrine of the Spirit. We have examined the use of the terms 'mystery' and 'love' as pneumatological expressions and noted the reluctance to speak in personal terms of the Holy Spirit. The purpose of this chapter is to examine the underlying ontological structure of Jüngel's theology with reference to two key themes which will guide our discussion of pneumatological implications: the presence of God and the concept of the possible. It will be demonstrated that these ground Jüngel's doctrine of God and hence systematically set the parameters for his implied doctrine of the Spirit.

Jüngel's understanding of the manner of God's presence is an extension of his description of God's being in becoming. Dogmatically this is expounded in a theology of the cross and in a distinctive approach to language as performative. The first two sections of this chapter will therefore examine the presence of God in the death of Christ and how this event becomes an event for us in a word of address.

This will lead to a discussion of Jüngel's doctrine of justification, which he expounds in terms of the ontological priority of the possible. The pneumatological implications of this underlying ontology will then be discussed and this will structure a number of critical comments.

The Presence of God and the Death of Christ

The Death of God as the Theological Response to Atheism

Jüngel draws from Luther, Bonhoeffer and Hegel in his sustained attempt to give theological content to the concept of the 'death of God.' In this regard he is to be clearly distinguished from the more naïve 'death of God' school of thought which, Jüngel correctly argues, misunderstood and misapplied Bonhoeffer's valuable insights.[1] By contrast his interpretation of the phrase 'the death of God' remains within the Lutheran tradition; God is revealed in the cross of Christ as the crucified and hidden God.[2]

Following Bonhoeffer, Jüngel strives to expound the manner of God's presence in a place of apparent absence. In his *Letters and Papers from Prison*, Bonhoeffer argued that the 'God' of religion had become displaced, 'edged out' of the world; 'before God and with God we live without God.'[3] Bonhoeffer asked how we might know God's presence in this situation. How can the presence of God be conceived in his apparent absence. Bonhoeffer approaches this christologically through an examination of the presence of God in the event of the cross. At the cross God 'allows himself to be pushed out of the world; 'the suffering of God in the event of the cross is seen as a way in which God 'wins power and space in the world by his weakness.'[4] Bonhoeffer thus interprets the apparently godless state of the world in the light of an understanding of the being of God in the person of Christ crucified.

Jüngel embraces this as 'a fundamental concept for the Christian faith in God,' seeing that it contains 'a profound insight into the ontological

---

[1] For example, see T. Altizer and W. Hamilton, *Radical Theology and the Death of God*, London, 1968.

[2] The Lutheran influence will be discussed later. The current discussion will reflect the way in which Jüngel is indebted to Luther's theology of the cross as the place of revelation where the revealed God is also hidden behind his revelation; the language of *Deus Revelatus* and *Deus Absconditus* belongs to Luther.

[3] D. Bonhoeffer, *Letters and Papers from Prison*, ed. E. Bethge, (translation by R.H. Fuller), New York, 1972, p.360.

[4] *Letters and Papers from Prison*, p.311.

character of the divine being.'[5] If God's being is understood in the light of the cross as one who allowed himself to be 'pushed out' from the world, then the being of God cannot be expressed in the simple polarities of presence and absence; in some way God must be understood as being 'present as the one who is absent in the world.'[6]

Hegel was perhaps the first to appropriate the phrase 'the death of God' into a philosophical system of thought.[7] His philosophy of the Absolute was, at one level, an attempt to interpret the incipient atheism of the age in the context of the godforsakenness of Good Friday. For Hegel this entailed the interpretation of this godforsakenness in terms of a general philosophical notion of being.

Once again, for Hegel, Luther's theology of the cross was instrumental in his development of the idea of death as constitutive for being. The cross of Jesus becomes foundational for Christology and is also regarded as constitutive for the being of humanity. Since God has entered death in Christ, in the cross the 'death of death' takes place. God has taken death into his own history; 'it is a proof of infinite love that God identified himself with what was foreign to his nature in order to slay it.'[8]

Here the death of Christ becomes the foundation for a more general ontology. Jüngel appreciates the christological orientation of the talk of the death of God and the way in which Hegel appropriates the language in the face of the defining atheism of the period. It is the 'systematic connection of the christological source of the idea of the death of God with the epistemological-metaphysical problematic of modern atheism' which signifies 'Hegel's most significant achievement for theology.'[9]

---

[5] *GMW*, p.62.

[6] *GMW*, p.62. By this Jüngel means that absence is not an alternative to presence, but that their relationship is characteristic of the being of God in his relation to the world. This facilitates a critique of the metaphysical theistic view of God's omnipresence and reorients it to the particular manner of God's presence in the event of the cross. 'The concept of the omnipresence of God must pass through the eye of the needle of the properly understood concept of the death of God.' (p.63)

[7] 'God sacrifices himself, gives himself up to destruction. God himself is dead: the highest despair of complete forsakenness by God.' From Hegel's 'Jena Diary,' recorded in F. Nicolin, *Unbekannte Aphorismen Hegels aus der Jenaer Periode*, Bonn, 1967, p.16.

[8] G.W.F. Hegel, *Philosophy of Religion*, p.91

[9] *GMW*, p.97

Yet Hegel's philosophical appropriation of Luther's terminology subsequently gave way to a severing of the 'death of God' concept from its christological roots, paving the way for the more strident atheism of Feuerbach.

In tracing the christological origins of the 'death of God' understanding of the cross from Luther, through its philosophical appropriation by Hegel and its theological re- emergence in the work of Bonhoeffer, Jüngel maintains that an important question is raised concerning the nature of the divine essence. Metaphysical atheism's questioning of the existence of God is brought into light by the problematic nature of the divine essence. How can the god of the metaphysical theist suffer on a cross? At the time of the Reformation, the question was formulated in terms of how we might understand the deity of Christ in the event of the cross. Barth approached the issue differently, interpreting the deity of Christ as that which is revealed in his lowliness, his humanity being revealed in his majesty; thus 'lowliness and inner-worldliness cannot be excluded from the concept of the essence of God...rather...God is thought of...only when he can be believed to have suffered even death, without ceasing to be God.'[10] For Jüngel this involves an ontological re-negotiation of the concept of the divine essence; this consequently results in a redefinition of key theological categories such as omnipotence and omnipresence in the light of thinking of God's being in the death of Christ.

The Presence of God in the Event of the Cross

The manner of God's presence in the event of the cross is a profound christological problem. Jüngel has not produced a systematic treatise on the person of Christ but certain ideas are consistently apparent from his various essays.

One of the key themes of Jüngel's Christology is the concept of 'identification.' As suggested previously in our discussion of the triune being of God, this involves a two-way movement as God comes *from* God and returns *to* God. 'God is the one who has identified himself

---

[10] *GMW*, pp.101-2. Thus responsible theology must ask about the aporia in the concept of the divine essence; 'both theism and atheism are afflicted by this aporia.' Theism because it operates with a view of the divine essence which separates God from death and suffering; atheism because it is a response to an increasingly untenable, theistic model of God.

with the crucified Jesus; Jesus Christ is the man with whom God has identified himself.'[11]

Clear similarities may be found with Barth's Christology, as expounded in the first three parts of volume four of the *Church_Dogmatics*. Here Barth outlines his doctrine of reconciliation in terms of the threefold confession of Jesus Christ as very God, very man, and the God-man. As the Lord, Christ humbles himself as a servant and moves out to the far country to secure the work of salvation. As the Royal Man he is adopted by God and exalted to fellowship with God. As the God-Man he is the mediator and guarantor of reconciliation. For Barth these three confessions, or 'movements,' correspond to Christ's priestly, royal and prophetic offices.[12]

In following Barth, Jüngel employs the term 'identification' to stress that God's relationship to the crucified Christ cannot be understood apart from God's reconciling work:

> To speak to man of the reconciliation which God has brought about means...God is also involved with man in his godlessness and guilt. It is by taking this godlessness and guilt upon himself that he opposes and contradicts them. Whenever we speak of God's identification with the dead Jesus, this is what we mean.[13]

To articulate this further, Jüngel employs the ancient patristic terminology of 'anhypostasia' and 'enhypostasia.' While these terms have been used in different ways, 'anhypostasia' asserts that there is no independent subsistence of the human Jesus outside that of the eternal Word with which it was united at the incarnation. 'Enhypostasia' stresses that the humanity of Jesus is grounded solely in the person of the eternal Logos. Both terms have been widely criticised on the basis of their relative failure to give due significance to the humanity of Christ; they can tend towards docetism. In particular, 'anhypostasia' can lead to a form of monophysitism which denies the Chalcedonian doctrine of the two natures. 'Enhypostasia' can tend to underemphasise the unique event of the incarnation. Jüngel seems alert to these dangers, though it is interesting that Webster has recently offered a critique suggesting that the humanity of Jesus remains understated; despite the

---

[11] Webster, *Eberhard Jüngel*, p.33

[12] See Barth, *CD, IV/1-3*.

[13] Jüngel, *Death: The Riddle and the Mystery*, pp.113- 14.

significance of the term 'identification' there remains the question as to how far Jüngel portrays Jesus as a personal agent.

In Jüngel's usage, the human Jesus is so totally consumed with the proclaiming of the Kingdom of God and in doing the will of the Father that his whole being can be defined by reference to that Kingdom; 'He was what he was because of the Kingdom that he proclaimed.'[14] In this sense Jüngel speaks of the 'anhypostatic humanity' of Christ.'[15]

Yet this remains hidden in the course of Jesus' life. Only in the light of the resurrection is it revealed that the existence of Jesus in his proclamation of the Kingdom of God is ontologically grounded in the relation of Jesus to the eternal Logos, which in turn makes possible the relationship between Jesus and the Father; in other words, the resurrection reveals 'the enhypostatic grounds of Jesus' anhypostatic existence.'[16]

Jüngel's exposition of the identification of God with the man Jesus in terms of an- and enhypostasia demonstrates Jüngel's approach to the relationship between the Jesus of history and the Christ of the kerygma. It also highlights the identification of God with Jesus as an event. This avoids reducing the relationship between God and Jesus to one highest example of a more general relationship between God and man. Rather, from the perspective of the resurrection it can be seen that the existence of the man Jesus in the 'Word of the Kingdom' is made possible by the 'self-abasement of the eternal Word of God.'[17]

In the tradition of the Lutheran *'theologia cruciae,'* Jüngel rarely employs the language of incarnation. By preferring to use the concept of identification the emphasis is much more upon how God may be conceived as present in the man Jesus, and ultimately in the event of his death. It is apparent throughout Jüngel's writing that the motif which

---

[14] Webster, *Eberhard Jüngel*, p.35.

[15] E. Jüngel. 'Jesu Wort und Jesus als Wort Gottes. Ein hermeneutische Beitrag zum christologischen Problem,' in E. BUsch, J. Fangmeir and M. Geiger (ed.) *Parrhesia, Karl Barth zum 80_Geburtstag*, Zurich, 1966, p.140.

[16] Webster, *Eberhard Jüngel*, p.35.

[17] Jüngel. 'Jesu Wort und Jesus als Wort Gottes. Ein hermeneutische Beitrag zum christologischen Problem,' It is of note that Jüngel criticises Hegel precisely at this point, arguing that he dissolved the unique event of identification between God and Jesus into a more general uniting of the divine and the human in the concept of absolute spirit. This leads to the loss of the proper distinction between God and man.

governs his Christology is the event of the cross. 'Jesus' death is the consummation of his entire existence.'[18]

The doctrine of identification consequently offers Jüngel a way of speaking of the presence of God in the death of Christ. God identified fully with the man Jesus, even in his death, such that we are able to speak christologically of the death of God; this is the supreme refutation of metaphysical theism and atheism. 'God suffers! And just in this way he shows that he is God.'[19]

> In dying, God abandons himself to death but does not surrender to death. The Son of God really dies the death of a sinner. But in dying, God plucks out the sting of death. And so in death he overcomes death. And so in death he remains highest God. And so Jesus Christ is the death of death.[20]

Jüngel's exposition of the death of Christ makes little reference to the person and work of the Holy Spirit, although his account is suggestive. Scripture is reticent to speak of the presence of the Spirit in the death of Christ; the overwhelming testimony is to Good Friday as a time of God's absence. Jesus dies, in forsakenness and abandonment. In what sense can we speak of God's being in identity with Jesus in the event of the cross? For Jüngel this is imperative if the use of the language of 'the death of God' can be justified. Jüngel's approach rests on one of two central ontological principles which ground his theology - the absence of God as a mode of his presence.

The Presence of the Absent God

In his exposition of the concept 'the death of God,' Jüngel approaches the concept of God's presence in terms of the following question: 'How can the divine essence be thought of together with the event of death without destroying the concept of God?'[21] This may be tackled from the perspective of the dogmatic concepts of God's omnipotence and omnipresence.

Metaphysical theism conceived of God's omnipotence as his free, transcendent sovereign power; omnipresence was understood as God's

---

[18] Jüngel. *Karl Barth. A Theological Legacy*, p.137.

[19] *Karl Barth. A Theological Legacy*, p.131.

[20] *Karl Barth. A Theological Legacy*, p.131.

[21] *GMW*, p.100.

eternal, universal presence. Taken together, the omnipotent God is omnipresent in creation, and omnipresence is an expression of active omnipotence. On this view 'absence is excluded as a matter of principle.'[22] Consequently, absolute presence is a quality of the omnipotent God's essence; negating God's presence becomes equivalent to negating his existence.

Jüngel argues that, on the basis of God's self-revelation in the cross of Christ, such an understanding of omnipotence and omnipresence is called into question. To think God in identity with the crucified one will entail a re-negotiation of such concepts. In particular, is it possible to think in terms of God's omnipotence as the withdrawal of his omnipresence and his omnipresence as a withdrawal of his omnipotence? If God was present in Christ in the event of the cross, then this presence may be better expressed in terms of a withdrawal and surrendering of power and sovereignty. The doctrine of identification facilitates an understanding of the cross as a kenosis of the being of God in such a way that God's being is not exhausted but rather fulfilled in the process.

This approach similarly suggests a different approach to the concepts of transcendence and immanence. This has been the significance of Jüngel's doctrine of God from the outset; his doctrine of the Trinity is grounded on Barth's principle of the correspondence of God's being *in se* and *extra se*. When applied to a theology of the cross, God's presence is mediated by that which is most far removed from God, death itself. God is present as the absent one.

This seemingly paradoxical statement is really another way of expressing Barth's dictum that 'the *Deus Revelatus* is the *Deus Absconditus*.'[23] The polemical point which Barth makes through this phrase is that the God who is present in his act of revelation as a result of his free decision to make himself present, is none other than the inscrutable God who, according to his nature, cannot be unveiled to man. It serves to emphasise the free, gracious initiative of God in his self- revelation; he is 'the God to whom there is no way and no bridge, of whom we could not say or have to say one single word, had He not of His own initiative met us as the *Deus Revelatus*.'[24]

---

[22] *GMW*, p.103.

[23] *CD I/1*, p.368.

[24] *CD I/1*, p.368. Barth borrows the terminology from Luther's theology of the cross. Here the revelation of God in the cross reveals God's strength in apparent weakness. There is a revelation of God in his hiddenness; yet in the one event of revelation both the Deus Revelatus and the Deus Absconditus are

Jüngel interprets the statement rather differently from Barth. While for Barth this is an affirmation of the freedom and inscrutability of God in his revelation, for Jüngel it becomes a way of speaking of the presence of God in identification with the death of Christ. This is an ontological approach; God's presence as the absent one is a description of the manner in which God's being *is* in this particular event. Taken this way, the relationship between the 'concealed God' and the 'revealed God' is a way of conceptualising the way in which God's being is in becoming. 'The distinction between "the concealed God" and "the revealed God" means...that even in the situation of god-forsakenness we are dealing with God.'[25]

Jüngel's ontological interpretation of the revelation of God in his hiddenness suggests possibilities for a doctrine of the Spirit. There is the recognition in Jüngel that for this language to remain coherent as a doctrine of God, then it must be interpreted within a trinitarian framework. If the question of the presence of God is approached ontologically, then it must equally be affirmed that there is no contradiction within the being of God itself. The distinction between the concealed God and revealed God must be expressed in terms of the self-differentiation of the triune God. As expressed earlier, within this trinitarian framework, God comes as God in the Spirit.

We have seen that the interplay of presence and absence is one key ontological foundation for Jüngel's doctrine of God and indicated that there are implications for pneumatology. These will be drawn out in more detail later. The immediate question concerns how this understanding of God's presence in the event of the cross might be extended to an explanation of how that event might become significant for us; how does the unique historical event become an event for us?

The Word of Address: The Presence of God and the Being of Humanity

Here we return to a more specific application Jüngel's distinctive understanding of the performative and metaphorical nature of language. His overall conceptuality is heavily influenced by Heidegger's existentialism, most particularly as expressed in the seminal work *Being and Time*.[26] Jüngel takes care to distinguish his position from Heidegger, whose approach was oriented towards the concept of the

---

perceived.

[25] *GMW*, p.346.

[26] M. Heidegger, *Being and Time*. New York, 1962.

self- realisation of authentic being. For Heidegger, being is not understood in terms of permanent essence but in relation to historical situatedness; human existence is determined out of the past and projected into the future. In this process authentic being is realised.[27]

Jüngel approaches his existential analysis from the perspective of the performative nature of language, as developed by Fuchs and Ebeling. In Heideggerian fashion the concern is to establish the ground of authentic being, but this is found in an ontological view of language. 'Language makes being into an event;'[28] 'when God speaks, the whole reality of as it concerns us enters language anew.'[29]

When given the theological framework of Barth's doctrine of revelation, it becomes possible to conceive of the fundamental object of theology in terms of a Word which 'prescribes its own manner of reception and which cannot be resolved into anything more primitive.'[30] From this fusion of ideas Jüngel's earliest work understands the Word of God as disruptive; it interrupts reality as humanity is addressed in such a way that the language carries the reality of which it speaks. Hermeneutically this is to regard the on-going proclamation of the Word of God as God coming to speech in the actuality of a revelatory event. Once again it is critical to realise that Jüngel is ascribing ontological status to this 'speech event.'

The Performative Nature of Language

One function of language is to describe and communicate. They provide a vehicle for our making sense of the world; words signify that to which

---

[27] Heidegger's philosophical programme was focused upon the nature of being (*Sein*) approached from the being of the questioner (*Dasein*). *Dasein* was envisaged as being constituted by possibilities which may be grasped or let slip. There are two basic possibilities which *Dasein* stands before. It can be authentic (*eigentlich*) which means being its own self, or it can be inauthentic (*uneigentlich*), which means it becomes a creature of convention, shaped by the fashion of the environment.

[28] E. Fuchs, *Studies of the Historical Jesus*, p.207.

[29] G. Ebeling, *The Nature of Faith*, ET London, 1961, p.190. The appropriation of Heidegger's view of language is illustrated in the expression that 'the being of everything that is dwells in the word...language is the house of Being.' (M. Heidegger, *Unterwegs zur Sprache, Neske*, 1954, p.166: *On the Way to Language*, English translation by P. Hertz, London, 1971).

[30] J. Webster, *Eberhard Jüngel*, p.10.

they refer. When the word 'God' is taken in this signifying sense we are led to enquire exactly what the content of the being so signified really means. The meaning of a word is usually inferred from its syntactical relationship with other words. So we must question what the word 'God' signifies. Jüngel maintains that within the western tradition the word 'god' has come to mean something akin to the unsurpassable; 'God can do everything. God decides everything. God effects everything...yet God is still "more" than "all"...God himself is undefinable.'[31] Thus, in the sense that the word 'God' is understood as a sign, it points to a being who is beyond human thought and comprehension. As Augustine concluded, 'if you understand, it is not God. Let there be a pious confession of ignorance.'[32]

Jüngel sees that this presents a problem for theology; how is it possible to think 'God?' Thus, while the signitive function of language is important as a means of description and reference, it has serious theological limitations. Yet, as referred to in the previous chapter, language can function differently in that it can perform a function which is much more than the imparting of information. Phrases such as 'I love you' actually penetrate personal being, they affect emotions and attitudes. Speech has an effect in carrying the being of the person addressed into a new experience. I am addressed and therefore I am included in the meaning of the word. In a word of address, consciousness and being are affected.

The influence of Heidegger is apparent. For Heidegger, authentic being is characterised by the comprehending of Being. It is characteristic of Being to present itself; Being gives itself in Discourse and challenges what Heidegger describes as the forgetfulness of everyday existence. Language is the means whereby Being presences itself and authentic existence is disclosed; 'it is language alone which enables man to become that kind of living entity which he is as man.'[33] Thus there is a call or summons to authentic existence; this involves a projection beyond everyday existence and in this 'existential distancing' there is a an unveiling of authentic being. In this process there is a 'gain' or 'increase' in being.

---

[31] E. Jüngel, *GMW*, p.7. As expressed by Aquinas, 'God cannot be defined.' (*Summa Contra Gentiles*, Vol.1, London, 1924)

[32] Augustine, 'Sermo 117, iii, 5' in Migne, 'Patrologia Latina' XXXVIII, p.663. For Jüngel's response to this view see *GMW*, p.8.

[33] P. J. Achtemeier, *An Introduction to the New Hermeneutic*, Philadelphia, 1969, quoting Heidegger 'Unterswegs zur Sprache,' p.11.

In Fuch's work the abstract philosophy of Heidegger is applied to the theological proposition that God reveals himself in a speech event. In the act of speaking the entire being of the person addressed is affected. Jüngel expresses the language event as that in which a 'person is drawn together into the word and there "outside of himself (*extra se*)" he comes to himself in the other word.'[34] This means that our being is fundamentally determined by that which addresses it from outside itself. By an encounter with that which is beyond the here and now of our situation, that situation is itself defined. In a word of address the present is opened up and differentiated, we are taken beyond ourselves and consequently come to a new understanding of ourselves in spatial and temporal ways. 'Every addressing word approaches the addressed ego in such a way that it lets this ego come to itself.'[35]

The function of the addressing word is not only spatial in character; there is a temporal dimension. In the event of address, our being in the present is defined in relation to the past and the future. It may be said that the present is opened up to the future and as a result becomes present in a new way; we 'gain' time. 'The better we understand that which is past, and the more intensively we hope for that which is future, or seek to bring it about, the more present we are.'[36] An addressing word consequently has the function of transcending the here and now; 'it gives the Now, so to speak, space beyond the point of Here and it gives the Here time beyond the point of Now.'[37]

The Word of Address and the Presence of God

Characteristically, Jüngel's concern is to establish in what manner God may be present in the word of address as a 'language event.' The word 'God,' in connection with other words in a given concrete situation, can become a language event. In the context of this event God comes to humanity as an ontological reality. Here God can no longer be thought of as supremely other and above us, a transcendent being, but he is present with us. God communicates and discloses himself in the event of this coming to us:

---

[34] *GMW*, p.12.
[35] *GMW*, p.171.
[36] *GMW*, p.174.
[37] *GMW*, p.174.

> Accordingly, we ourselves are to be regarded from a theological point of view as those who have been and are addressed. Defined theologically, we are those who, having always been addressed by God, are, on the basis of this being-addressed, always newly to be addressed.[38]

Underlying this position is a particular understanding of the language of metaphor. The word 'God' can only have meaning in the context of metaphorical speech. In common usage a metaphor operates by mediating between two otherwise unrelated objects. To say 'Achilles is a lion' does not presuppose an identity but explains the manner in which the being of Achilles is. Yet with reference to God, we can only speak metaphorically on the basis that God has given himself to be known and discovered. In the event of revelatory self-disclosure, 'God lets himself be discovered in such a way that...trust in God can arise.'[39] In this event, God addresses us and is present in the word of address, creating the very possibility of faith; the content of that word of address, for it to be authentic, must be grounded in the historical coming of God to the world in Jesus Christ. 'The being of the God who comes to the world is to be brought to speech out of the history of the God who has come to the world. Intrinsic to this history as its decisive moment is the cross.'[40] Thus the proclamation of the cross, the narration of the Gospel, constitutes the vehicle for God's address to humanity in the Spirit. In the experience of this encounter 'man has a qualitatively new experience with his being.'[41]

On this understanding of the presence of God in the word of address, Jüngel moves towards an ontological interpretation of the doctrine of justification which we shall outline in detail in the next major section. In the current context it will be helpful to examine how, in the word of address, Jüngel understands humanity to enter into a new experience of being.

---

[38] E. Jüngel, 'Metaphorical Truth,' in *Theological Essays, Vol.1*, p.64. Jüngel's meaning here is that God comes to speech in a word of address in the same that way that God came to the world in Christ. It is through the word of address that God is discovered to be the one who comes to the world; we discover new things about God and the world in this event. 'God is a discovery which teaches us to see everything with new eyes.' (p.63)

[39] 'Metaphorical Truth,' p.63.

[40] 'Metaphorical Truth,' p.65.

[41] *GMW,* p.32.

The Doctrine of Justification and the Being of Humanity

In the event of God's word of address to humanity, the human being-here-and-now is transcended in a radical way such that there is an experience of 'total distancing' over against the here-and-now; accordingly 'a completely new qualification of the man's state of being present results, which one would call eschatological spiritual presence.'[42] This existential distancing far exceeds the experience resulting from mere human words of address; in this distancing humanity is drawn into the presence of God, and as such God's word of address surpasses any other word. The word of address 'discloses to the ego a new way of being present, it discloses to its worldly presence as defined by God, as eschatological presence.'[43]

This typically abstract formulation expresses a theologically crucial point. In the word of address, as the one addressed gains time in an existential sense, this temporal distancing refers us to the past, and particularly to the cross. In this encounter with God, the word of the cross comes to us, negating self-centredness and any claim to self-righteousness. The human experience is one of negation, or judgment. Yet, the word of the cross is also a word of promise; it is the guarantee of a 'new, ultimate nearness of himself [God}.'[44]

This constitutes the heart of Jüngel's ontological doctrine of justification. In essence it expresses in ontological terms certain aspects of the Protestant understanding of justification by faith. For Luther, justification involved the gift of the righteousness of God, granted through Christ. Through faith, though not as a result of faith since this would make faith a work, the individual partakes in an exchange whereby Christ bears our sin and we are clothed with the 'alien righteousness' of Christ. Whereas Augustine regarded this as a contingent part of our being, this righteousness remains external to us; it is something which God works beyond us. Consequently, for Luther, the justified believer is *'simul iustus et peccator.'*

At the time of the Reformation there was some debate as to the relationship between the incorporation of the believer into Christ and the doctrine of justification. Melancthon developed the forensic concept of justification, using the terminology of the law court. In his Apologia for

---

[42] *GMW*, p.174.
[43] *GMW*, p.174-5.
[44] *GMW*, p.175.

the Augsberg Confession the idea of justification as the pronouncement of righteousness on the basis of Christ's alien righteousness predominates.[45] Calvin retained the concept of incorporation into Christ as part of the doctrine of justification. He distinguished between justification and sanctification but argued that they could not be separated in practice; both are given together as a 'double grace.'[46] Justification is the forensic declaration of righteousness, the imputation of the righteousness of Christ. This is distinguished from but ineluctably related to the regeneration by the Holy Spirit and the commencing of the process of sanctification.

Jüngel's doctrine of justification is clearly indebted to Luther in that it speaks of God's approach to humanity in the word of address as that which is external and independent of any claim to inherent righteousness. Following Luther, Jüngel combines this external location of righteousness with the real presence of Christ within the believer; a real change of being takes place in the event of justification. Yet, as Webster has pointed out, by emphasising the ontology of justification, Jüngel does seem less alert of the forensic and soteriological aspects of justification; 'man is defined rather than forgiven and restored in justification.'[47]

Systematic Implications as Exemplified in Anthropology and the Doctrine of Election

While detailed criticism of Jüngel's position will be put forward in the final section of this chapter, it will be helpful to follow through this approach to the doctrine of justification. As will be shown shortly, the underlying ontology which supports much of Jüngel's theological output is grounded in his ontology of justification. That in itself poses some serious questions; yet before turning to these we can observe the impact of Jüngel's approach systematically by looking at his anthropology. In particular, to what extent is humanity free to refuse the grace of God?

For Jüngel, to be justified is to have our being beyond ourselves and in the being of Christ. This strong linking of the authentic being of humankind *solus Christus* can imply that our humanity is already given

---

[45] Melancthon, *Apologia*, as summarised in A. McGrath, *Iustitia Dei, Vol.2*, Cambridge, 1986.

[46] See the comments in A. McGrath, *Justification by Faith*, Basingstoke, 1988, p.58.

[47] Webster, *Eberhard Jüngel*, p.102-3.

or accomplished on our behalf. It is difficult to see how a human individual might have their being outside of Christ. In other words, Jüngel's view leaves little room for distinction between those in Christ and the unbeliever. It becomes hard for Jüngel to explain in what sense faith can have any part in determining the being of humanity at all, since human passivity threatens to turn belief into a 'merely formal ratification of prior divine decisions and deeds.'[48]

This problem may be seen as an example of the systematic observation that Jüngel's anthropology is derived from his Christology. In the word of address God constitutes the being of humanity; our being is contingent upon the person of Christ. This might be better expressed in a doctrine of the vicarious humanity of Christ. Jüngel builds on Barth's conception of the image of God in his identification with Jesus. The history of Jesus is the locus of God's revelation and thus humankind is in the image of God in so far as it expresses the history of Jesus.

This distinctively ontological approach to the doctrine of justification coheres when explaining the situation of humanity in union with Christ. In the event of justification, God approaches us in the addressing word; in the Spirit God interrupts our existence and redefines it. In this event we are made new, we have a new experience of our being; in Jüngel's view we become authentically human. It is the work of the Spirit to actualise the particular and unique mediation between man and God realised in Jesus Christ. As justified, the human individual is set free in order to act in obedience to God. Human activity no longer seeks to be self-justifying but responds to the grace of God revealed in Christ through the Spirit. Hence Jüngel applauds Barth for grounding ethics in Christology.

The difficulty emerges when consideration is given to the freedom of the human individual to reject God and yet remain human. Webster helpfully summarises Jüngel's existential structure of the concept of freedom.[49] For Jüngel, freedom is inseparable from the event of liberation; as such it is a divine gift through which humanity is freed from the self- centred desire to establish the self through acts. This freedom only results from God's interruption of the world of our actuality in the word of address; 'as a hearer man is set free for the future.'[50] The implication seems to be that outside of Christ there is no true freedom.

---

[48] Webster, *Eberhard Jüngel*, p.103

[49] Webster, *Eberhard Jüngel*, pp.111-13.

[50] Jüngel. *Paulus und Jesus*, p.62.

The fondness for ontological language in anthropology also raises the question of the status of sin in Jüngel's thought. If human acts are only authentic when they 'express God' then those acts in which God is expressly denied not only contradict our humanity but have no definitive ontological status. Sin can only be described in negative ways as the celebration of nothingness. The whole ontological status of humanity as sinful is called into question.

Jüngel explicates his understanding of human freedom by distinguishing between the 'ontic' and 'ontological' aspects of existence. In this regard he articulates in abstract, philosophical terms issues which systematic theology usually deals with in the doctrine of election.

It was Barth's distinctive proposal that the doctrine of election should be located within the person of Christ. Jesus Christ is both the one elect man and electing God. Barth's understanding of election consequently aligned the action of God in actualising salvation to the primal historic event of the cross and resurrection.

Jüngel takes Barth as his master. His doctrine of election is not overtly expressed but the issues raised in our consideration of the freedom of humankind are pertinent. It is Jüngel's strong assertion that humanity is universally defined in the event of justification; 'justification by faith defines man theologically. This theological definition concerns the whole of mankind and therefore all men.'[51] It is further clear that this definition is fully ontological in status; 'man is ontologically derived from justification by God which takes place in Christ.'[52]

Yet it is clear that there are many aspects of humanity where the ontological reality of this event of justification is not evident. Jüngel distinguishes between the ontological status which applies universally and the ontic realisation of that status. For Jüngel a denial of the ontological status is a failure to realise existentially that which is ontologically true. Through faith in Christ we become what we already are in Christ. Those who deny their ontological status in Christ cannot affect that status. The justifying act of God in Christ is inclusive and

---

[51] E. Jüngel, 'Extra Christum nulla salus - als Grundsatz natürlicher Theologie? Evangelische Erwägun zur "Anonymität" des Christenmenschen,' in *Zeitschrift für Theologie und Kirche*, 72, 1975, pp.337-52.

[52] E. Jüngel, 'Das Dilemma der natürlichen Theologie und die Wahrheit ihres Problems,' in A. Schwann (ed.) *Denken im Schatten des Nihilismus. Festschrift für Wilhelm Weischedel zum 70*, Darmstadt 1975, p.168.

universal in that that which is true at the ontological level has priority over that which is asserted at the ontic level of actuality.[53]

By following Barth, Jüngel demonstrates the tendency to locate the ontologically significant event of justification to the once for all historic event of the cross; this event comes into the present in the word of address in the manner of a repetition. The activity of God in the present seems to be restricted to a re-application of that event to the individual in the present. It is on the basis of that primal act that justification is possible; the actualisation of that past moment of God's election of the man Jesus in his reconciling movement from source to goal can only be understood in terms of union with Christ. This is an important insight and consistent with Jüngel's Lutheranism. Yet it might be argued that a greater emphasis upon the resurrection would facilitate a better rendering of the eschatologically oriented work of the Spirit in the event of justification.

Jenson has provided a distinctive, contrasting contribution in this area. His doctrine of the Spirit attempts to keep a balance between reference back to the past event of God's revelation in Christ and forward to the Eschaton.[54] He emphasises the particularising activity of the Spirit seen uniquely in the life, death and resurrection of Jesus Christ. The Holy Spirit is the Spirit of God as revealed in Christ and given by the exalted Lord. It is further argued that the Spirit of Christ comes to us from eternity. Jenson draws his concepts of eternity and infinity from Gregory of Nyssa. To speak of divine infinity is not to speak of any attribute of God, nor to think of a sheer unboundedness in the being of God. Rather, divine infinity represents the infinite possibilities which arise from the relationship of the Father and the Son in the Spirit. On this understanding God's presence in the world mediates the possibilities inherent in the particular death, resurrection of Christ and the Parousia. The Spirit not only actualises the effect of the death and resurrection of Christ to individuals in the present but in so doing aligns them eschatologically to the final consummation. In the coming of the Spirit in the present, temporal events are transformed in the light of the inexhaustible love of God demonstrated in the Christ event. Consequently, 'pneumatology is the attempt to explicate the whole work of God as a communal activity among us.'[55]

---

[53] Underlying this is a particular view of the priority of the possible over the actual which we shall examine shortly.

[54] See R. Jenson, *The Triune Identity* and 'The Holy Spirit' in C. E. Braaton and R. Jenson, (eds) *Christian Dogmatics*, vol.2, Philadelphia, 1984.

[55] R. Jenson, 'The Holy Spirit,' p.177. This is expressed in the context of

The contrast with Jüngel is instructive. Jenson's trinitarian emphasis and eschatological perspective are helpful. In the context of the present discussion, Jenson proposes that a pneumatological understanding of the doctrine of election may be appropriate.

To this point we have summarised Jüngel's understanding of the presence of God in the event of the cross and in the word of address and seen how that is worked out ontologically in his doctrine of justification. Attention will now be paid to the second fundamental ontological principle which grounds Jüngel's thought, the priority of the possible. It will be shown that this is foundational for his doctrine of God and thus for his pneumatology.

The Priority of the Possible

Much of Jüngel's theology is concerned to combat a metaphysical theism grounded in Aristotelian notions of substance and cause and effect. This leads him to reconstruct the traditional philosophical relationship between that which exists in actuality and the notion of possibility. This is structurally crucial in *God as the Mystery of the World* and is formally expounded in the seminal essay *The World as Possibility and Actuality: The Ontology of the Doctrine of Justification.*[56] In this latter paper Jüngel pursues the ontological implications of Luther's doctrine of justification by faith.

---

expounding what Jenson refers to as a 'Cosmic Pneumatology.' Here the Spirit is seen at work in natural processes such that the Spirit is the creator of the 'novel and new' in the process. Without the active presence of the Spirit of God there would be nothing new; all would be predictable. Thus 'the Spirit of Jesus is the spontaneity of natural process.' (p.171) Put rather differently, and in a way which emphasises the eschatological orientation of Jenson's pneumatology, 'the beauty of the world, natural or historic, is the cosmic actuality of Jesus' Spirit, is the world's occurring openness to the final triumph of his love.' (p.175). In the more recent *Systematic Theology, Vols, 1 and 2,* Jenson pursues this in relation to the being of God, arguing that the Spirit is the power of God's own future, bringing all things towards the final goal, which is God himself. 'The Spirit is God as his and our future rushing upon him and us.' (*Systematic Theology, Vol. 1*, p.160)

[56] In Webster, *Theological Essays*, Vol.1, pp.95-123.

The Ontology of Luther's Doctrine of Justification: The Theological Principle Established

In classical metaphysics actuality has been accorded ontological priority over possibility. Being itself is identified with that which is actual; Aristotle expounded this as a first principle of metaphysics. Jüngel asserts that the statement that '"actuality is prior to potentiality" was of incalculable significance for the history of thought.'[57] Aristotle's dictum meant that the possible could only be defined in relation to the actual, which was of ontological priority. The possible is related to the actual as that which is not to that which already is. 'Being cannot properly be attributed to the possible. Only that which is actual can properly be said to be.'[58]

Jüngel argues that this central philosophical axiom has been extensively employed in theological thought. Even given that the number of possibilities in the world must be infinitely greater than the number of actualities, actuality was seen as ontologically prior since it represents a selection, that which has come to be, from the available possibilities. It is argued that Barth's *Church Dogmatics* is cognitively structured by the primacy of the actuality of God's self-revelation.

Yet Jüngel finds the Aristotelian principle called into question in some recent theological writings. Moltmann's theology of hope points to the future possibilities as somehow determinative for the present. Yet Jüngel finds fault with Moltmann's indebtedness to the metaphysics of Bloch. By grounding the priority of the possible future in a concept of the 'not-yet' this simply disguises the priority of the actual: it is the coming actuality which has precedence over the present. As such a 'now but not yet' theology of the Kingdom of God is equivalent to 'pouring new wine into old wineskins.'[59] It is the influence of Fuchs which is

---

[57] '*The World as Possibility and Actualty*,' p.97.

[58] '*The World as Possibility and Actualty*,' p.99.

[59] '*The World as Possibility and Actualty*,' p.104. The convergence of the priority over the actual with the apocalyptic focus in Moltmann's interpretation of Bloch, in effect, surpasses actuality with further actuality. 'Whilst the "ontology of the not yet" theology finds the most ingenious interpretation of its traditional eschatology, at least in its formal aspects this represents only a modification of apocalyptic expectations in the scheme of the "already-not-yet." To say "not yet" is to think "but then..." And, in good apocalyptic fashion, he asserts the primacy of actuality as Aristotle conceived of it.' (p.102)

foremost for Jüngel, especially as he applies the rather abstract nature of the argument.

The proposed dismantling of the priority of the actual is carefully expounded as an expressly theological issue. There is no questioning of the everyday occurrence of cause and effect; the world 'owes itself to the priority of the actual.'[60] The theological necessity for this renegotiation of the relationship between the possible and the actual is grounded in an interpretation of Luther's doctrine of justification which is regarded as 'an indispensable criterion of proper theology...the *articulus stantis at cadentis ecclesiae...*'[61]

Luther asserted that a person cannot become righteous by doing good deeds. Rather, the doctrine of justification speaks of a change in the person from which good deeds follow.

> We are not, as Aristotle believes, made righteous by the doing of just deeds, unless we deceive ourselves; but rather...in becoming and being righteous people we do just deeds. First it is necessary that the person be changed, then the deed will follow.'[62]

For Luther, the justification of the sinner comes through faith in the justifying, creative Word of God. Jüngel acutely perceives that this runs counter to the Aristotelian view of the priority of the actual; 'how can a person become righteous prior to that person's deeds?'[63] Luther's doctrine speaks of a change of being prior to a change of act. The being of an unrighteous person is unable to become righteous through any human act. There is 'the most radical antithesis between the unrighteous and the righteous person.'[64] Thus the righteous, changed person can only be understood *'ex nihilo creata* (created out of nothing).'[65] This new creation is grounded in the creative Word of God. If the life of the

---

[60] '*The World as Possibility and Actualty,*' p.104. 'Although Christians have a task of changing the world, not only in deed but also in concepts, it is first of all important to define the place which theology occupies in the responsibility which it alone is called to assume before its own object.'

[61] '*The World as Possibility and Actualty*,' p.104; 'the article by which the church stands or falls.'

[62] M. Luther, letter to Spalatia, 19 October, 1516, quoted by Jüngel, '*The World as Possibility and Actualty*,' p.105.

[63] '*The World as Possibility and Actualty*,' p.106. Aristotle declared that 'we become just by doing just acts.'

[64] '*The World as Possibility and Actualty*,' p.106-7.

[65] '*The World as Possibility and Actualty*,' p.107.

unrighteous person is understood ontologically as a negation of being, then apart from the life giving Word of God, 'nothingness holds sway between the *homo peccator* (sinner) and the *homo iustus* (justified person).'[66] It is through the event of the cross and the resurrection of Christ that the sin of humanity is revealed; at the cross Jesus became sin for us. He thus manifests the true nature of sin yet also speaks the word of the Gospel to us. Jesus' resurrection from the dead promises a newness of life out of death and nothingness; we are created *ex nihilo* through faith in the Word of God. Thus 'Christian existence is existence out of nothingness, because it is along the line existence out of the creative power of God who justifies.'[67]

Jüngel's rather densely conceptual argument here is not simply an indulgence in some obscure ontology of nothingness, but rather a further attempt to articulate responsible speech about God and his relationship to the world. On the Aristotelian view, possibilities are understood in terms of a not-yet actuality; the fundamental mode of discourse in our everyday world is oriented to the distinction between the actual and the not-yet actual. This corresponds to an 'absolutising of actuality.'[68] Yet the doctrine of justification offers a fundamentally different understanding of the world as creation out of nothingness. It is this which enables us to think of God as Creator and the world as justified. Consequently, the most significant distinction which theology must bear witness to is that between the possible and the impossible:

> The distinction between the possible and the impossible is incomparably more fundamental because it concerns the distinction between God and the world. And in the distinction between God and the world we are not concerned primarily with actuality but with truth.[69]

The distinguishing between the possible and the impossible is solely a matter for God. It does not consist of God's ratification of an already existing state of affairs; neither is it to see God as making the impossible into a possibility as a 'miracle.' Rather, it is to speak of God's being as

---

[66] '*The World as Possibility and Actualty*,' p.107. On this understanding the sinner is one who lives under the illusion of being but actually 'celebrates nothingness.' Sin is understood ontologically as a loss of relation, a 'nothingness which negates.' (p.108)

[67] '*The World as Possibility and Actualty*,' p.108.

[68] '*The World as Possibility and Actualty*,' p.110. This is seen as 'a decisive dimension of the world' in which theology has its part to play.

[69] '*The World as Possibility and Actualty*,' p.110-11.

actualised in the event of distinguishing. Thus God, and God alone, is conceived as the one who 'makes the possible to be possible and the impossible to be impossible.'[70] It is in this process that God distinguishes himself from the world and grants actuality to the world. In the event of justification, God comes to the world in the very act of his self-distinction from the world. This is the manner in which God's being is in becoming.

> God himself is the one who makes the possible to be possible and the impossible to be impossible, and in this distinction between possibility and impossibility lets the world be actual. Beyond the distinction between possibility and impossibility, God himself is equiprimordially both, or, to say the same thing, God **is** and his being is in becoming.[71]

While there are implications here for many areas of theological reflection, not least pneumatological. Jüngel restricts his comments to the doctrine of justification. In the creative event of the Word, by faith, we participate in God's distinction between the possible and the impossible. It is the word of the Gospel, addressed within the actuality of the world, which makes space for the assertion of a new possibility. The possibility of justification is external to its actualisation but addresses that actuality in the event of the Word. It is this possibility which grants freedom from the tyranny of the actual. Thus, in contradiction to Aristotle, in God's creative, justifying word, the possible is not defined out of the actual; rather, possibility and actuality are both factors in being and 'that which God's free love makes possible has ontological prevalence...'[72]

---

[70] '*The World as Possibility and Actualty*,' p.112

[71] '*The World as Possibility and Actualty*,' p.112 Once again the key to understanding Jüngel's rather dense conceptuality is the notion of the being of God as an event in repetition such that there is distinction within the being of God; this is systematically explicated as the doctrine of the Trinity which interprets the being of God in the act of his revelation. It explains in what concrete way God may be present to and in the world, and particularly in the death of Christ, without ceasing to be God. It is thus a way of speaking of God in such a way that the being of God is properly distinguished from the world.

[72] '*The World as Possibility and Actualty*,' p.116. The distinction between the actual/not yet actual and the possible/actual is essentially that between the power of humanity to transform the world and God to create out of nothing. We can make something of the future out of the past and present. Yet 'what can be made does not become, in the strict sense of becoming *ex nihilo*.' We change

The importance of this ontological premise for Jüngel cannot be overemphasised. It is fundamental for his entire doctrine of God and informs his theological writing in all areas of doctrine. If the being of the human person is not constituted by actions but by the justifying act of God then this tells us something about the being of God as righteous. Because God is righteous he acts righteously. On the basis of an ontological interpretation of the doctrine of justification, Jüngel has argued that it is the being of God in the event which brings about the creative act whereby the sinner is made righteous, a *creatio ex nihilo*. Strictly, the righteousness of God is a relational concept. God is righteous in his self-relation as Father, Son and Holy Spirit such that 'the mutually distinct trinitarian persons "give one another their due"...God corresponds with himself in such a way that difference is not excluded but rather affirmed in himself. In this way God is righteous.'[73] On the basis of our own acceptance by God as justified we must affirm the value of other individuals on the basis of the precedence of the person over their works. 'Those who live out of the righteousness of God know of no hopeless cases.'[74] Anthropology and ethics are thus grounded in this ontology of justification. Yet, it is the theology of the cross which locates the most detailed application of the priority of the possible in Jüngel's thought.

The Death and Resurrection of Christ: The Presence of God in the Perishable

The Aristotelian metaphysics which Jüngel attempts to dismantle theologically can only evaluate death and the notion of perishability in negative ways. That which perishes is destroyed; annihilation negates being. 'The negation in perishing is multiplied into annihilation and the shadow of nothingness falls on everything.'[75] Consequently, perishability cannot be part of that which is eternal. Viewed from this perspective, any talk of the death of God becomes paradoxical beyond the slogans of atheistic rhetoric. 'God is dead' expresses the ultimate

---

and transform; God creates.

[73] E. Jüngel, *'Living Out of Righteousness: God's Action - Human Agency,'* in Webster, *Theological Essays,* Vol. 2, Edinburgh, 1995, pp.249-50.

[74] *'Living Out of Righteousness: God's Action - Human Agency,'*p.256.

[75] *GMW,* p.209.

conclusion of a theology of the cross which is grounded in terms of Aristotelian metaphysics.

Yet on the basis of God's identification with the man Jesus it becomes necessary to conceive of the being of God in unity with perishability. The task is to think of 'a God who is in heaven in such a way that he can identify himself with the poverty of the man Jesus.'[76]

Jüngel maintains that while perishing is synonymous with a tendency toward nothingness, it cannot adequately be defined solely in these terms; there is a positive aspect to the concept. This he expresses in terms of the possible: 'that which is ontologically positive about perishability is the possibility.'[77] On the basis of the theological appreciation of the ontological priority of the possible over the actual, there can be an 'ontological plus' in that which perishes: the power of the possible which inheres in the perished past. Jüngel draws upon the philosophy of Kierkegaard to express this further.

> the possibility from which that which became actual once emerged still clings to it and remains with it as past, even after the lapse of centuries. Whenever a successor reasserts its having come into existence, which he does by believing it, he evokes this potentiality anew.[78]

That which has perished in the past does not have to disappear into nothingness. Loss of reality does not lead to loss of possibility; there remains the capacity to become in the future.

This is crucially important for Jüngel's understanding of time and history. If past events simply pass away into nothingness, one event making room for another, then history can only be viewed as a chain of separate events with no real connection. Such a view is essentially ahistorical since the past cannot shape the future. On the contrary, if past events retain the possibility of being effectively brought to bear on the present, then loss of reality cannot be equated with loss of possibility; the past has the potential to be related to the present and to shape the future.

This view of the possibility inherent in past events which have perished is worked through in the essay *The Effectiveness of Christ Withdrawn.*[79] The actual event, which has passed into history, cannot be repeated, it has perished; but the possibility from which it arose still

---

[76] *GMW,* p.209.
[77] *GMW,* p.213.
[78] *GMW,* p.214-5, quoting S. Kierkegaard, *Philosophical Fragments.*
[79] Webster, *Theological Essays,* Vol. 1, Edinburgh, 1989.

remains. That means that the past can be consciously worked through in the present and new possibilities for the future can result.

> Discovering the possibilities of present existence is a matter for conscious, historical working through of the past which, even if it recedes from us further and further, does not take its potential with it but rather leaves it to our safekeeping.[80]

That which is past, in some way, always belongs to our present. If the past is recognised as a potential for our present then historical events become effective.[81] In relation to the history of Jesus, his effectiveness in bringing salvation to humanity consists in the message of his death which evokes faith. The past event of the death of Christ is unrepeatable in actuality but contains unique possibilities which can impact our present existence. Here Jüngel moves towards a doctrine of atonement, fuller discussion of which will be considered shortly. We are here concerned with Jüngel's ontology as applied to the event of the cross.

Following the pattern of Jüngel's thought to this point it may be argued that perishability itself can be defined ontologically in both negative and positive terms. Negatively, that which perishes tends towards nothingness, there is movement towards non-being. Positively, that which perishes tends back towards the possibility from which it first came. It then comes to an end but is not necessarily nothing. 'In the form of having been, it continues to participate in being.'[82] There is thus a tension within perishability which Jüngel characterises as a struggle between the tendency towards nothingness and the capacity of the possible. To think God in unity with perishability in the event of the cross is to think God in the midst of the struggle between possibility and nothingness, being and non-being. To speak of the death of God, in christological terms, is to proclaim that God has his being in the midst of the struggle and that even in the midst of perishing he is the living one.

---

[80] '*The Effectiveness of Christ Withdrawn,*' p.225. This rests on the notion that actuality is more than a 'brute fact.' Every actuality contains within it potentiality, though this may not always become actualised. Thus 'the actual is more than naked facticity. A brute fact would be meaningless for the present if its actuality did not imply certain possibilities which do not pass away.'

[81] Jüngel interacts here with Gadamer's hermeneutic of 'effective history' as proposed in *Truth and Method*, London, 1979.

[82] *GMW*, p.216.

For Jüngel this is the key to theological discourse. It is on the basis of God's presence in the struggle between being and non-being that God is revealed as the Creator. It is in the context of the identification of God with the crucified one that we understand God to be the one who creates *ex nihilo*; a theology of creation therefore arises out of a theology of the cross. For Jüngel, the resurrection, as an unveiling of the truth of God's unity with Christ, reveals that God has drawn nothingness into his own being. In this way God defines the destructiveness of nothingness and contradicts it. Talk of the death of God, as interpreted in the light of the resurrection means that God has involved himself with nothingness and located it in the divine life. In this way God reveals himself to be the victor over sin and death. Further, he has done that for us. In the event of the cross God has defined himself as love. This is not to say that God became love in the event of the cross, but that the cross is a unique event which 'discloses the depths of deity.'[83]

The Priority of the Possible and the Resurrection of Christ

Before offering a sustained critique of Jüngel's theology it is necessary to ask one critical question of his proposed renegotiation of the relationship between the possible and the actual. To what extent does this inform an understanding of the resurrection of Christ?

It has been previously observed that Jüngel's theology is focused and grounded upon his Christology. It is this which 'gives direction to his theology...and...enables Jüngel's to get purchase on particular problems in Christian doctrine.'[84] From this systematic perspective his ontology serves to explicate the formal concept that God corresponds to himself; it elucidates the manner of God's presence in the cross of Christ and the addressing word of God in justification. Jüngel's understanding of resurrection is, in part, one of an unveiling of the truth about the crucified Jesus and his identity with God. 'On Easter Day there takes place nothing less and nothing more than the disclosure of the mystery of the death of Jesus.'[85] The resurrection is not simply an historic event which follows or reverses the events of Good Friday. It is a way of speaking about the death of Christ.

---

[83] *GMW,* p.220.

[84] Webster, *Eberhard Jüngel*, p.131.

[85] E. Jüngel, *'Das dunkle Wort vom "Tode Gottes,"*' in *Evangelische Kommentare*, 2, 1969, p.136. The resurrection of Christ is the basis of a way of understanding the identification of God with Jesus in his death.

In later writing a similar approach is taken to interpret the renewing effect of the death and resurrection of Christ; the 'dialectic of the death and resurrection of Jesus Christ' is a way of speaking about 'the renewing, creative power of God in and through non-being.'[86]

It is pertinent to enquire whether this emphasis on the resurrection as a disclosure of the identity of God with the crucified Jesus is an adequate summary of the variety of biblical testimony to the centrality of the resurrection. Here the event of resurrection is understood as a vindication of Jesus as Messiah and Son of God, it is the prelude to his exaltation and ascension as Lord, and it is the necessary precondition for the dawning of the new age of the Spirit. As Moltmann has stated in his Christology, God's raising of Christ was the foundation for faith in Christ; 'the Christian faith stands or falls with Christ's resurrection. At this point faith in God and the acknowledgement of Christ coincide.'[87] In what sense does Jüngel's distinctive ontology of the possible relate to the resurrection of Christ and how might this inform a doctrine of the Holy Spirit?

Jenson articulates a theology which in many respects utilises similar conceptuality but which places a much greater emphasis upon resurrection and eschatology.[88] For Jenson, the resurrection of Christ is the proleptic revelation of the deity of Christ which can only be interpreted fully in the light of the Eschaton. In a manner which bears some resemblance to Pannenberg, the Lordship of Christ is seen as the final outcome of God's dealings with the world. As God came to the world in Christ, so he continues to come to the world in and through the Spirit. The Spirit comes to transform all temporal events by opening up the future of creation to the unsurpassable future of God. In this way the Spirit is the 'power of the Eschaton' and the 'very power of futurity.'[89] In his coming the Spirit actualises the promise of the gospel; that which is made possible by the unique event of the death and resurrection of Jesus is actualised afresh. Yet this is more than the recovery of a past event. It is rather the actualising of 'the inexhaustibility of the relation between Jesus as the final Lord and all that precedes his coming.'[90]

---

[86] E. Jüngel. *'The Emergence of the New,'* in Webster, *Theological Essays,* Vol. 2, p.55.

[87] J. Moltmann, *The Way of Jesus Christ*, translation by M. Kohl, London, 1990, p.213.

[88] See Jenson, *The Triune Identity*, Philadelphia, 1982.

[89] *The Triune Identity*, pp. 162, 169.

[90] *The Triune Identity*, p.171. This is expanded in Jenson's *Systematic Theology,* Vol.1, where the identity of the church with the body of Christ is

Jenson explicates this by a particular view of God's freedom in which he closely resembles Jüngel's concept of the being of God in becoming. To be God is 'to be freedom from oneself as given...is to be the power of the future to transcend what is...to be God is to possess oneself only as the opportunity of being other than the possessed self.'[91] To be God is to possess that element of being described by Jüngel as the possible; it is to be creatively present in the act of distinguishing between the possible and nothingness. Expressed pneumatologically, God is Spirit in the sense that he is present in the granting of Jesus as the object of faith; God is present in the Spirit as the Spirit of the risen Christ and as such is the one who creates anew.

Jenson's approach indicates the extent to which a greater systematic emphasis on the resurrection of Christ gives greater scope for explicating a doctrine of the Spirit. Jenson employs the abstract, ontological terms of possibility and actuality, but has less reticence in translating this directly into speech concerning the Spirit of God. Yet this is not without difficulty. While his attempt to expound the idea of God's freedom in terms of the Spirit's presence is close to Jüngel's concern to utter responsible speech about God, it is questionable whether it is sufficient to equate the Spirit with the 'power of the possible.' This question is sharpened when Jenson speaks of 'sheer possibility' as being equivalent to 'stark transcendence.' This might seem to suggest that Jenson is working with a concept of Spirit as pure transcendence. This would imply that while Jenson seems to see the importance of ascribing priority to the possible over against actual, he really retains the priority of the actual in the sense that the present actuality of the world is surpassed by a supreme, eschatological actuality. This is similar to the criticism which Jüngel makes of Moltmann; a theology of the Kingdom which makes much of the category of the 'not-yet' is still referring forward to the greater actuality to come. If Jüngel seems to emphasise the death of Christ at the expense of the resurrection, then Jenson may tend towards the opposite. Jüngel's God defines himself in the death of Christ; for Jenson, God's being is defined by resurrection from the dead and the eschatological consummation.

By contrast, the biblical witness expresses a mutuality between the cross and resurrection. Easter Sunday is certainly a disclosure of the relationship of God to the man Jesus, yet Jüngel's restriction of the meaning of the resurrection to the status of a message proclaimed fails

---

emphasized.

[91] *The Triune Identity*, p.167.

to reckon with the full content of the apostolic message of the New Testament as formalised in the creeds of the Christian church. Jüngel's reticence in this area leads to a restrictive account of the person and work of the Holy Spirit. The typically Lutheran concentration on the death of Christ focuses Jüngel's theology on an event which, in scriptural terms, is relatively silent with regard to the activity of the Spirit. The role of the Spirit in the resurrection of Christ is much more clearly attested. Jüngel maintains the identity of God with the historical Jesus as well as with the Christ of faith as proclaimed by the church, but he risks restricting the work of the Spirit to the actualising of the possibilities of a past event. While this may well be one aspect of the work of the Spirit, this perspective misses the essentially eschatological dimension captured by Jenson. While Jüngel's ontology is more carefully worked out than Jenson's, the locus of his thought is such that it is resistant to the important eschatological thrust of Jenson.

With this general criticism made, we shall now critically examine Jüngel's ontological grounding of his doctrine of God and enquire whether this sets the boundaries for an implicitly restrictive pneumatology.

Jüngel's Ontology and its Implications for a Doctrine of the Spirit: A Critical Assessment

The following critique will focus on five areas which arise directly from the aspects of Jüngel's theology outlined in this chapter. Some of the themes raised will be revisited in the later comparative chapter, which will be structured by a closer look at certain doctrinal loci as they relate to pneumatology. Consequently the critique offered here will to some degree point forward to the later comparison with Pannenberg and raise issues dealt with in greater depth in that context. The current purpose is to expose some weaknesses in Jüngel's theology with special reference to the way in which these impinge on his understanding of the person and work of the Spirit.

Methodology: Christology and the Construction of a Theology

The christological framework of Jüngel's theology is clearly seen even on a most cursory reading of his work. In this respect he follows Barth is seeing the person of Christ as the only possible starting point for proper theology. The metaphor of 'starting point' is made explicit in Jüngel's appreciation of Barth's theology; 'Barth had in mind a specific, concrete starting point...and he called it concrete because the starting point has a name: Jesus Christ.'[92] By this Jüngel means that theology is concerned with the history of Jesus Christ.

The centrality of Christology for Jüngel is the way in which it serves to give structural consistency to his theology; it is the way in which he negotiates an interpretation of other doctrinal loci. Christology provides 'a basic interpretative structure for the other areas of doctrinal material.'[93]

The positive consequence of this is that it provides a certain theological consistency; by analysing other areas of doctrine in the light of christological assertions, Jüngel is able to maintain a logical coherence to much of his thought. Yet this is at considerable cost in other ways. Jüngel is not always alert to the mutuality of different areas of Christian doctrine; Christology must inform and, in turn, be interpreted and informed by other doctrinal foci. There is thus a tendency to oversimplify complex theological arguments by utilising Christology as an over-arching interpretative device.

One example of this is the rather unclear relationship between Christology and the doctrine of God. Following Barth, on the one hand, Jüngel is anxious to deny any grounding of the doctrine of God in anything other than Christology; all true knowledge of God is grounded in the self-revelation of God in Christ. Yet there are times when Jüngel appears to move beyond this by suggesting that Christology serves to 'purify' speech about God; 'in faith in Jesus as the Christ, faith in God is brought to truth and purity.'[94] This suggests the possibility of some degree of knowledge of God as a precursor to the definitive revelation in Christ. This in turn would imply a more nuanced relationship between Christology and the doctrine of God than Jüngel's general approach tends to suggest.

One further result of the christological focus is the way in which Jüngel appears to understate the hermeneutical difficulties in narrating the story of Jesus today. His prime concern is to establish the ontological effectiveness of Jesus, and specifically his death on the cross, for the being of humanity today. His emphasis upon the 'effective history' of Jesus is made in such a way that it appears that once this has been established 'the hermeneutical task is well on its way to

---

[92] E. Jüngel, *'Karl Barth,'* in *Evangelische Theologie*, 29, 1969, p.18.

[93] Webster, *Eberhard Jüngel*, p.131. In this regard Webster gives examples whereby Jüngel's christological emphasis is seen in areas such as the character of the Word of God, the relationship between science and theology,

[94] Jüngel, *Death: The Riddle and the Mystery*, p.108.

completion.'[95] However this is to minimise the hermeneutical task. Ascertaining how we might responsibly speak about the being God in the light of the cross only goes part of the way towards establishing how we might articulate that meaningfully in the contemporary context.

The Theology of the Cross

Jüngel's distinctive exposition of the presence of God in the event of the cross has led to some differing interpretations and understandings, especially in the context of the debate concerning the relationship between the immanent and economic Trinity. By paying such close attention to the reality of God's presence in the event of the cross, Jüngel appears to court the charge that this event is in some way necessary for the being of God. This is the thrust of Thompson's critique.[96]

By comparing Jüngel with Barth it is suggested that both theologians affirm that outside of God's relationship to Jesus Christ, we could not know God and God would not be God. Yet, by way of contrast, Barth is clear that this does not require God to need the world to express his immanent triune being of love. Jüngel goes beyond this in stating that God's selflessness in his movement towards the world is greater than his self-relatedness. This is expressed particularly in his notion of God's love as that which 'heightens and expands his own being in such great self-relatedness, still more selflessness and thus overflowing.'[97] Yet, as Thompson asks, 'how far can one speak in this way of a self-expansion of God manifest as a self-relatedness that overflows to us without implying...some form of increase in change in God?'[98] Thompson goes on to add that Jüngel's talk of God's presence in the event of the cross, in the same context, suggests, contrary to Jüngel's purpose, that God's being is in some way dependent upon the event of the cross. This

---

[95] Webster, *Eberhard Jüngel*, p.135.

[96] J. Thompson, 'Jüngel on Barth,' in Webster, *The Possibilities of Theology*, pp. 143-189. The context of this discussion is a supposed difference between Barth and Jüngel on the relationship between the immanent and economic trinity. Whereas Barth sought to affirm an identity in distinction between the two, it is argued that Jüngel more readily consents to Rahner's thesis of their identity.

[97] *GMW*, p.369.

[98] Thompson, p.175.

suspicion is compounded by the argument that the history of the death of Jesus is the key to the Trinity.[99]

Thompson is alert to the greater nuances of Jüngel who affirms a particular unity of the immanent and economic Trinity in terms which retain the freedom of God's act out of his unmerited grace. Yet Thompson believes that Jüngel has difficulty in distinguishing between God's eternal triunity and his being in becoming. In the eternal Son of God, who came 'eternally from God, God comes as the man who temporally comes from God.'[100] Thompson asks whether it is possible to identify the 'coming eternally from God' and 'coming temporally' without also seeing a genuine distinction between them.

Yet this criticism fails to take full account of Jüngel's dialectic of God's identity with the man Jesus and the mode of his presence in the event of the cross. As Gunton observes, with rather greater insight, Jüngel does maintain the distinction between God and the world by expounding the 'mystery' in which God is and is not identical with his presence in Jesus. There is therefore a real sense in which God and the world are properly distinguished. Yet, as already observed, Gunton questions whether the term 'mystery' is sufficiently strong to carry this particular weight of theological importance. Even given the exposition of this mystery of the dialectic of presence and absence in pneumatological terms, the implied under-determination of the person and work of the Spirit leads to an inadequate formulation of the immanent Trinity.[101]

Molnar similarly finds a problematic exposition of the immanent Trinity in Jüngel, as compared to Barth.[102] Jüngel's theology of the cross, his whole approach to the doctrine of justification and its resultant anthropology, works with a dialectic of being and non-being which 'belongs to the essence of love.'[103] Yet Barth rejected the idea that non-being belonged to the essence of God.[104] As a consequence, Jüngel sees

---

[99] Thus Thompson writes, 'Jüngel comes dangerously close to making incarnation and cross a necessity for God.' (p.175.)

[100] *GMW*, p.384.

[101] C. Gunton, '*The Being and Attributes of God. Eberhard Jüngel's Dispute with the Classical Philosophical Tradition*,' in Webster, *The Possibilities of Theology*.

[102] P. D. Molnar, 'The Function of the Immanent Trinity in the Theology of Karl Barth,' in *Scottish Journal of Theology*, 42, 1989, pp.367-399.

[103] *GMW*, p.325.

[104] See especially Barth, *CD* IV/IV: *The Christian Life Lecture Fragments*, Grand Rapids, 1981, pp.146-7.

a certain mutuality between human love and divine love, something which Barth also completely rejected. As a further consequence, Jüngel's discussion of the deity of God is grounded on the question of God's identity with the human Jesus and, Molnar insists, this easily slips into an example of a presupposed general anthropology and ontology. The root of the problem for Molnar is an inadequate distinction between the action of God in his economy with the immanent being of God. 'Such Christology results whenever the identity of the immanent and economic Trinity is presupposed.'[105]

Presence and Absence: The Paraclete and Christ

Jüngel's understanding of the mode of God's presence in the event of the cross is rooted in the dialectic of presence and absence. The foundation of this in Lutheran thought has been noted, but the exposition of the cross as a place of God's presence in his absence is ontologically important for Jüngel. Yet it must be questioned whether the cross is the appropriate place for such a dialectic to be expounded. In one sense the cross is the place of godforsakenness and divine absence; yet in Christ, God is present. In this sense the event of the cross is the most profound place to offer a dialectical account of the relationship between presence and absence.

Yet, biblically, the relationship between presence and absence, which has far greater pneumatological significance, is found in the farewell discourse of John's Gospel. Jesus promises that after he has gone away he will send the Paraclete, by which he referred to the Holy Spirit. The Paraclete will bring Jesus to his disciples, remind them of his teaching, and lead them into the way of truth. Thus the coming of the Spirit was linked to the overall activity of God in the death, resurrection and ascension of Christ. In the absence of the incarnate Word, the Spirit would bring the presence of God to indwell the followers of Jesus.

It follows that the language of presence and absence used by Jüngel is much more closely allied to the Lutheran revelatory language of the *Deus Absconditus* and the *Deus Revelatus*, as used by Barth. It is determined by the revelatory model of divine action expounded by Jüngel. As such, its theological grounding in the event of the cross makes it difficult for Jüngel to explore the pneumatological implications of this. If greater weight were given to the events of incarnation, resurrection and ascension, then a greater scope for a pneumatological explanation of the dialectic of presence and absence might be easier to

---

[105] P. D. Molnar, p.369.

pursue. This might also result in a clearer exposition of the concepts of presence and absence; it remains uncertain in what way we can conceive of God's presence *as* the absent one apart from a much more carefully constructed doctrine of the Spirit.

Justification and Atonement

Jüngel's utilisation of Luther's doctrine of justification as the basis for asserting the priority of the possible over the actual and its exposition as a justifying act of God *creatio ex nihilo* clearly carries pneumatological significance. To speak of humanity as a new creation is to affirm the biblical account of the work of the Spirit in regeneration and reconciliation. Yet questions have been raised concerning Jüngel's articulation of the relationship between the possible and the actual.

As we have seen, Jüngel is quite clear that the renegotiation of this relationship is a theological task; it has no direct bearing on the cause and effect relationships in creation. Yet, as Thompson argues, Jüngel does understand that the self- revelation of God in Christ is fundamental in making available 'a new range of possibilities not as such inherent in the world of nature...in revelation, by overcoming in reconciliation the negativity of sin and non-being, creates new possibilities for all creaturely being.'[106] Yet Thompson asks whether this is quite as radical as it sounds; 'is Jüngel not to some extent stating that what God in the first place is doing in overcoming the negativity, the sin, the disobedience, the non-being which exists in the world in order to enable these possibilities to take place?'[107] In other words, Jüngel's rather tortuous attempts to ascribe ontological priority to the possible over the actual on the basis of the doctrine of justification results in a securing of the freedom of God to become the God of another. It is in danger of becoming a complex expression of the ontological priority of God over his creation; he is the God of the possible.

A similar, but rather more elaborate, critique of Jüngel's attempt to theologically dismantle the Aristotelian primacy of actuality is offered by Welker. He argues that the interpretation of Spirit in Aristotelian terms as 'the power that thinks itself insofar as it takes part in and receives a part of what is thought' crucially divorced the statement 'God

---

[106] Thompson, *'Jüngel on Barth,'* p.186.

[107] *'Jüngel on Barth,'* p.187. Thompson's point is that this was exactly Barth's concern, to establish the priority of God as a being in the act of his revelation, going out from himself as a result of his free determination to reconcile the world to himself.

is Spirit' from its biblical roots.[108] For Aristotle, Spirit becomes equated with the activity of thinking.

Welker maintains that Jüngel's critique of the primacy of the actual understates the significance of Aristotle's understanding of Spirit. Jüngel views Aristotelian metaphysics as conceiving of actuality as simply a process of 'self- actualisation.' We become what we are as a result of our acts. This is the view which is most amenable to criticism in the light of Luther's doctrine of justification. Yet, Welker suggests, Aristotle's conception of Spirit as intellectual self-actualisation is not contradicted by the concept of possibility, but can unite with it; Spirit is a 'living power that can definitely claim to stand in union with perishability and with possibility.'[109] Consequently, Jüngel's own frame of reference does not effectively break free from Aristotelian thought, but rather expresses it in a different form. 'Jüngel's critique offers no objection strong enough to prevent the continued use of Aristotelian conceptions of actuality, spirit and God.'[110]

Developing out of the account of the priority of the possible, and its foundation in the doctrine of justification, it has been questioned whether Jüngel has any well worked out doctrine of atonement.[111] While this would be a sweeping generalisation, there are serious questions raised by Jüngel's account of justification as the basis of humanity's restoration to God. In the event of justification humanity is defined ontologically as distinct from God; to be justified is to have authentic being. 'Salvation for Jüngel is not so much the imputation of righteousness as the attainment of being.'[112] The emphasis falls upon humanity as '*wortbestimmt*;' defined through the word.

---

[108] M. Welker, *God the Spirit*, English translation by J. F. Hoffmeyer, 1994, Minneapolis, p.284. Aristotle understood the concept of Spirit in self-referential terms, something beyond the world and yet related to it in such a way that it comprehended everything.

[109] Welker, *God the Spirit*, p.299.

[110] Welker, *God the Spirit*, p.300. Welker's own approach operates with the notion that it is the selflessness of God as Spirit which alone can offer the necessary theological approach to divorcing the primacy of the actual when considering the powerful acts of God in and through the Spirit. Through this selfless activity the Spirit of God effects liberation from self-determination and open us for selflessness towards others.

[111] For example Thompson argues that, as with Moltmann, in Jüngel 'the atonement has never been developed to any great extent.' J. Thompson, 'Jüngel on Barth,' p.189.

[112] J. Webster, *Eberhard Jüngel*, p.91.

This might be taken to imply a soteriology which is lacking any traditional notion of judgement and forgiveness. We are not pardoned through the death of Christ, the past is not something for which atonement needs to be made; sin is not hostility towards God but an absence of relationship. Consequently, if is possible to see an insufficient emphasis on the moral aspect of salvation. 'Jüngel shifts out of a moral understanding of the relationship between God and man.'[113] In place of a soteriological theology of the cross, Jüngel prefers to speak of the being of humanity as it resides in Jesus Christ as the true man. Even when deploying the notion of Christ as our substitute, Jüngel understands this in terms of the relationship between God and man in Christ; 'the concept [of substitution] is only meaningful' in so far as 'in the person of Jesus Christ God took our human place.'[114] Consequently, the category of divine justice becomes less central in Jüngel's understanding of salvation and this must be viewed as a significant difficulty, not least on the grounds that it weakens the link between salvation and ethics as moral action lived out of the new life in Christ, lived in the power of the Spirit.[115]

A similar problem can be seen with Jüngel's articulation of the concept 'eternal life.' To have eternal life is to achieve meaning with

[113] J. Webster, *Eberhard Jüngel*, p.102.

[114] E. Jüngel, *'The Mystery of Substitution,'* in J. Webster (ed.) *Theological Essays, Vol. 2*, p.155. This essay constitutes an appreciation of the German theologian Heinrich Vogel. It is true that in this essay Jüngel speaks of the sacrifice of Christ as his 'act of substitution.' This might go some way to responding to the criticism of an inadequate theology of atonement. Yet Jüngel approvingly writes of Vogel's conceiving of 'Jesus Christ's whole being as a substitutionary existence' and the importance of the incarnation as an exposition of the substitutionary existence of Christ (pp.156-7). In his essay *'The Sacrifice of Jesus Christ as Sacrament and Example,'* in the same volume. pages 163-190, Jüngel speaks of the cross as sacrifice, but in terms of the history of the man Jesus 'which effectively changes the being of humanity' (p.169). Once again the emphasis is upon a change of being as opposed to forgiveness for sin.

[115] The development of a Christian ethic is pursued in the essay *'The Sacrifice of Jesus Christ as Sacrament and Example,'* where Jüngel distinguishes between the atoning significance of the life and death of Jesus and the concept of Jesus as our moral example. 'Only when Jesus Christ is affirmed and believed to be our saviour...is it then also really permissible, indeed really required, to emphasise that Jesus Christ is our example, the one who offers a model for our own action.', p.181.

respect to the life we have lived. This means that what is of supreme significance is not the human experience of eternal life but the eternality of God. The heart of the problem here is the essential passivity of humankind. Jüngel's theology of death is strongly theocentric which means that it is hard to see how death can constitute a mutual relationship between God and man. In the event of justification we are defined but humanity seems unable to enter into a relationship with God with any degree of recipricocity.

Speaking of God and the Truth of Christian Theology

Jüngel's predisposition to debate the proper language for theological speech about God involves him in developing his view of language as performative. In doing this he makes strong use of the notion of metaphor, analogy and parable. We have mentioned the use of metaphor previously; for Jüngel, 'the language of faith is metaphorical through and through.'[116] In Jüngel's distinctive manner, metaphor, in disclosing a new use of a word, discloses a new context of being. Metaphors are the vehicle for bringing to speech new ways of being. As such they convey truth, which is understood not as the correspondence of a conscious mental judgement to the actuality, but rather as an interruption of actuality. Theological metaphor 'enters the actuality of the world...in such a way that the world is confronted with the possibility of its own non-being, from which new being can arise.' Jüngel goes on, 'this is the essence of all religious language,' it is the language which proclaims the 'existence of a new creation.'[117]

In this sense, Jüngel rejects the correspondence theory of truth on the basis of its indebtedness to literalism and the consequent orientation towards actuality. Rather. Jüngel operates with a notion of truth as that which interrupts actuality; 'Truth...is the interruption of the continuity of being which makes us human.'[118] In biblical terms, 'interrupted by God, one comes to a disclosive confrontation with oneself...One is made true and one is now (in Johannine terms) of the truth.'[119]

---

[116] Jüngel, 'Metaphorical Truth,' p.58.

[117] Jüngel, *'Metaphorical Truth,'* pp. 66,67.

[118] E. Jüngel, *'Value-Free Truth,'* in J. Webster (ed.) *Theological Essays, Vol.2,* p.207. Here Jüngel takes Heidegger and Hegel as his guides.

[119] *'Value-Free Truth,'*, p.210. Once again the emphasis for Jüngel is ontological; it is 'the experience of possible non-being' which has 'become an experience of enhanced being.'

This concept of metaphorical truth as interruptive is oriented towards Jüngel's ontological approach to anthropology. Our being is enhanced as our being is interrupted by God; this is to participate in the truth. Clearly there are pneumatological implications here; biblically it is the Spirit who leads us into all truth, who actualises our participation in Christ who is the truth. Understood thus, metaphorical truth understands truth as relational in structure.

This accords with Jüngel's particular use of the analogy of advent in which God and the world are not directly compared, but in God's coming to the world he enables the human and worldly to speak of God. God comes to speech in parable and the proclaiming of the Kingdom of God, not because of any intrinsic power within human language but as God comes to speech within human language.

There is certainly much value in this as far as it repudiates a simple, literalistic approach to theological language. Yet Jüngel's use of metaphor and analogy can prove to be a limitation. There are many other ways in which language might be used to speak of the Christian faith; indeed, the very emphasis on language, while important, tends to exclude other ways in which the Christian faith can be explicated, through sign and act. This is the substance of Newland's observation that 'theology is illuminated by many different sorts of discourse, some of which are compatible with Jüngel's mode....but very many of which are not.'[120] Webster makes a similar point; 'language needs to be placed within the context of a whole range of human symbolic and cultural activity.'[121]

If one over-arching criticism could be made of Jüngel which runs throughout these specific points it would be to point to his preference for the language of ontology at the expense of following through the considerable pneumatological promise in his conceptualisation of the being of God in relation to the world. As has been noted before, this pneumatological reticence is partly a result of his insistence on focusing on a theology of the cross where the activity of the Spirit is most difficult to expound. To speak of God encountering death and coming to the world as a disruptive event of justification from which we are made new is to speak of God defining our being; the essential outworking of this with regard to the Spirit is left largely unexplored.

By conceiving the theological task in such limited terms, Jüngel fails to offer a constructive means of engagement with major contemporary ethical and moral issues. As one example, this sort of theology of a

---

[120] Newlands, *God in Christian Perspective*, 1994, p.28.
[121] Webster, *Eberhard Jüngel*, p.51.

suffering God, conceived in the aftermath of so much human misery in the twentieth century, raises as many questions as it answers. To see God's being somehow defined in suffering and perishabilility still fails to offer any significant contribution to theodicy. It may be that we have to conceive of the triune being of God as both engaged with and beyond the suffering of creation, and yet still admit that a proper theodicy is ultimately unattainable. It remains disappointing to find a theologian so deeply engaged philosophically in notions of death and pain while still failing to engage in any meaningful way with the issues of the world.

PART 2

The Presence of the Infinite God:

The Theology of Wolfhart Pannenberg

Chapter 3

The Revelation of the Triune God: The Doctrine of God in the Theology of Wolfhart Pannenberg

Introduction

It has been argued that Pannenberg is a 'breaker of moulds.'[1] While this assessment is broadly correct and indicates the considerable conceptual originality of his thought, Pannenberg's theological approach owes much to his personal background as well as the formative influence of his teachers.

Born in 1928 in what was then part of Germany, Pannenberg was actively engaged towards the end of the Nazi era in defence of his country. He grew up with little church connection and it was only during a period of studying philosophy under Hartmann that he turned towards Christianity. This seems to have been an intellectual decision, seeking a response to atheism, which he had come to regard as devoid of use to humanity, yet also questioning the viability of traditional claims to truth, which he saw as prohibitively authoritarian. The die was cast with regard to the direction of this theological method.

Among his theological mentors most notable was Edmund Schlink, a Lutheran heavily influenced by Barth, who supervised Pannenberg's doctoral thesis 'Die Pradestinationslehre des Duns Scotus.'[2] The significance of the Lutheran tradition is apparent in many aspects of Pannenberg's theology and, as we shall see, is central to his understanding of the Spirit. With regard to Barth, while Pannenberg distances himself from what he regards as epistemological authoritarianism, he shares the foundational principle that God is 'the

---

[1] T. Bradshaw, 'God's Relationship to History in Pannenberg,' p.48, *Issues in Faith and History*, ed. N. M. de S. Cameron, Edinburgh, 1989.

[2] Published as *Die Pradestinationslehre des Duns Scotus im Zusammenhang der scholastischen Lehrentwicklung*, Göttingen, 1954.

power that determines everything.'[3] Of further significance were Pannenberg's encounters with Gerhard von Rad's theological reconstruction of the Old Testament as the history of the transmission of traditions; God is revealed in his acts in history.[4] This contrasted with what Pannenberg saw as a retreat from history in the theology of Barth and Bultmann; von Rad emphasised that the faith of Israel was essentially historical in character. This move towards a greater theological significance for history was further prompted by engagement with Bornkamm who emphasised the importance of the historical Jesus for New Testament theology and Hans von Campenhausen's enthusiasm for patristic theology which Pannenberg identifies as fuelling his own desire for a theology which 'did not bifurcate faith and reason.'[5]

The Doctrine of Revelation: Historical Process and the Person of Christ

Pannenberg's early, distinctive doctrine of revelation, as initially expounded in *Revelation as History*, marks a decisive shift from the work of Karl Barth.[6] While concurring with the basic insight of Barth that 'revelation is not God making known a set of arcane truths, but....the self-disclosure of God,' it is argued that this self-revelation is not a direct manifestation, located primarily in a word of encounter, but is indirect and observed in the historical acts of God.[7] Pannenberg traces the concept of self-revelation back to Hegel's understanding of the Christian Faith in terms of the full self-disclosure of the nature of the

---

[3] S. Grenz, *Reason for Hope*, Oxford, 1990, p.8.

[4] The implications of this for a doctrine of revelation were followed through by Rolf Rendtorff's exposition of God's self-revelation in history as indirect. *'The Concept of Revelation in Ancient Israel,'* in W. Pannenberg (ed.), *Revelation as History*, London, 1968.

[5] W. Pannenberg, 'An Autobiographical Sketch,' in Braaton and Clayton (eds) *The Theology of Wolfhart Pannenberg*, Augsberg, Minneapolis, 1988. For an extended account of the formative influences on Pannenberg's early theology see E.F. Tupper, *The Theology of Wolfhart Pannenberg*, Westminster, Philadelphia, 1973.

[6] Pannenberg, *'Dogmatic Theses in the Doctrine of Revelation,' Revelation as History*, 1968, pp.123-158.

[7] Pannenberg, *Revelation as History*, p.4.

Absolute as Spirit (*Geist*).[8] Pannenberg argues that if strictly applied to a doctrine of revelation this tends to give emphasis to the uniqueness of this act of self-disclosure. To identify this self-revelation of God with the person of Jesus Christ in such a strict form runs the risk of denying revelatory significance to any other event in history. 'If God is already totally revealed in the special decisiveness of the Christ event, then he cannot in consistency be "also" revealed in other events, situations and persons.'[9] This is the essence of Pannenberg's early critique of Barth's doctrine of revelation.[10]

Pannenberg suggests that revelation is better understood as the indirect manifestation of God through his acts in history. It is the 'totality of his (God's) speech and activity, the history brought about by God, which shows who he is in an indirect way.'[11]

In order to expound this approach to the idea of revelation Pannenberg develops an understanding of history as the totality of reality. In his early writings Pannenberg states that 'history is the most comprehensive horizon of Christian theology.'[12] Behind this statement lies a view of the totality of reality which is encompassed and disclosed in the course of history. It has been frequently observed that universal history provides the central structural concept of Pannenberg's early theology.[13]

The fuller development of this early thought is detailed in the *Systematic Theology* where the doctrine of revelation is expounded in a more mature form from the perspective of the history of religions. Within the context of the world religions Pannenberg traces the development of the faith of Israel and the subsequent development of apocalyptic literature. It is within this historical framework that the self-revelation of God in the person of Jesus is understood. Following Pannenberg's own pattern of tracing the historical development of the

---

[8] Hegel, *The Phenomenology of Mind*, vol.2, 1962, pp.695- 6.

[9] *Revelation as History*, p.6. Put another way, a multiplicity of revelations implies a 'discrediting of any particular revelation.'

[10] Pannenberg argues that Barth's conception of self-revelation was partly a development of the Hegelian thought of Marheineke. See *Revelation as History*, p.5 and *Jesus - God and Man*, p.127, London, 1968.

[11] *Revelation as History*, p.13.

[12] 12 *'Redemptive Event and History'* in *Basic Questions in Theology*, Vol.1, p.15, ET London, 1967.

[13] K. Gnanaken, *God and Man in Universal History*, unpub. PhD Thesis, King's College, London, 1981. For early critical assessments see G. Stroup, *The Promise of Narrative Theology*, Atlanta, 1981.

doctrine, we shall summarise the progressive unfolding of his own thought over recent decades of writing.

Revelation as History

Pannenberg's view of history is first set out in contrast to Bultmann who is criticised for dissolving history into 'the historicity of existence.'[14] Bultmann distinguished historical fact from the interpretation of fact in such a way that it becomes significant for us existentially; '*Historie*' is differentiated from '*Geschichte*.' For Pannenberg this constitutes an unacceptable epistemological dualism.

Pannenberg also contrasts his own proposals with Kahler's thesis that the content of faith is 'suprahistorical,' grounded in a form of 'redemptive history' (*Heilgeschichte*) over against historical realism (*Historie*).[15]

Pannenberg argues that both positions are a negative response to the rise of historical criticism in that they ground faith in personal experience which can only be expressed in a theology which effectively exempts itself from public debate or scientific enquiry.[16] He prefers to engage positively with historical criticism by interpreting history theologically.[17] It is argued that 'only the concept of God makes it possible to conceive the unity of history in a way that maintains the peculiar characteristics of the historical' thus theology should be 'indispensable to the historian.'[18]

The conviction that the Christian Faith is open to historical investigation lies at the heart of the much criticised thesis in *Revelation as History* that the self-revelation of God is open for all who 'have eyes to see.'[19] The point of this proposed epistemic openness is that the

---

[14] *Basic Questions,* Vol 1, p.15.

[15] *Basic Questions,* Vol 1, p.15.

[16] Pannenberg describes this in scathing terms as a retreat into a 'harbour supposedly safe from the historical flood tide.' *Basic Questions,* Vol.1, p.16.

[17] Pannenberg is critical of the enlightenment view of history which sees the human agent as the creator of history. One main problem of this from the Christian perspective is that it denies the possibility of anything creative or new; there is little scope for the work of a creative and active God. If the end of history is understood to have arrived in anticipation in the resurrection of Jesus then it becomes possible on historical grounds to speak of the unity of history. This is the crux of the argument in *'Redemptive Event and History,'* pp.66-80.

[18] *Basic Questions,* Vol.1, p.76.

[19] *Revelation as History*, p.135.

revelation of God in his acts is 'no secret' and does not stand in contrast to natural knowledge as some sort of 'gnostic knowledge of secrets.'[20] This provocatively expression indicates the extent to which Pannenberg, in his early writing, differs from Barth whose own comment in correspondence at that time suggests the profundity of the shift; 'we are theologically...very different if not separated people.'[21]

The central axiom of Pannenberg's doctrine of revelation is a holding together of historical events and their interpretations within given historical contexts; 'the natural events that are involved in the history of a people have no meaning apart from the connection with the traditions and expectations in which men live.'[22] What is most apparent from the structure of the three volume *Systematic Theology* is that the interpretation of the Christian concept of God has to be understood within the wider context of the history of religions; it is here that the truth claims of the Christian Faith must be openly debated.

Revelation and the History of Religions

For Pannenberg, religious subjectivism signifies a 'retreat to commitment' which is based upon an individual conviction concerning the truth of experience.[23] Rather than asserting the truth of the Christian Faith on such a subjective basis, Pannenberg argues that the contestability of the truth about God must become the theme of systematic theology. This is to take seriously what he terms an 'innate, unthematic' human knowledge of God as interpreted and expressed in the variety of world religions; 'in some form or other religion is a constitutive part of human nature.'[24] His discussion here is grounded upon the important distinction between an innate or natural awareness of the infinite and the explicit working out of that awareness within the various religious traditions. The natural intuition of the infinite does not by itself comprise knowledge of God; it is the mediation of particular

---

[20] *Revelation as History*, p.135.

[21] Barth writing to Pannenberg on the publication of *Grundzüge der Christologie*, in a letter dated 7.12.64. K. Barth, *Letters 1961-68*, English translation by G.W. Bromiley, Edinburgh, 1981, p.177.

[22] *Revelation as History*, p.152.

[23] *ST 1*, p.47. 'To claim unconditional certainty is to make...the believing I the locus of absolute truth.'

[24] *ST 1*, p.155. Pannenberg identifies the anthropological side of this in terms of 'eccentricity' and 'self- transcendence.' There is a 'religious disposition' which is inseparable from humanity.' (p.156)

knowledge by the religions which enables reflection upon the earlier unthematic experience.[25] It is therefore the history of religions that provides the context for the theological quest for truth.

For Pannenberg, the concept of revelation arose and developed in particular historical situations; as Grenz has pointed out, Pannenberg insists that the biblical idea of revelation had its genesis in experiences found in other religions. The concept of revelation is thus 'not foisted on the historical material but arises out of the religious history itself.'[26]

Pannenberg is anxious to avoid the suggestion that there exists some sort of common essence in all religions, such as Troeltsch's thesis of an awareness of the absolute or Otto's concept of the holy.[27] Neither does Pannenberg wish to rest his case on the subjectivity of individual faith and the consequent claim for subjective truth which cannot easily avoid religious relativism. For Pannenberg the task of Christian theology is the quest for truth which can only be undertaken in response to the self-revealing of God in history.[28] He seeks to show that the biblical concept of revelation, in that it grew out of a more general religious history, is fundamentally historical in character.

This account of the history of religions contextualises the discussion of the way in which events in the history of Israel were determinative for changing understandings of the concept of revelation. It is critical for Pannenberg that the developing understanding of the acts of God in his dealings in history with the nation of Israel facilitates the conceptualisation of revelation as the criterion for expounding human knowledge of God. The story of Israel is the exposition of the awareness of the divine in the religions in thematic terms.

---

[25] The innate unthematic experience yet carries implications as to its meaning; these 'become thematically explicit on the plane of religious statements...' *ST 1*, p.164.

[26] S. Grenz, *Reason for Hope*, 1990, p.26

[27] See E. Troeltsch, *The Absoluteness of Christianity and the History of the Religions*, English translation, Richmond, 1971 and R. Otto, *The Idea of the Holy*, New York, 1958. Troeltsch argued that the basis of religion lies in the psychological creation of ideals as they relate to an ideal, infinite power. Otto argued for the concept of the holy as the common feature in the history of religions.

[28] 'The manifestation of divine reality even within the unresolved conflicts of religious and ideological truth claims is called revelation...Christian talk about the revelation of God does not add anything alien to the history of the manifestation of God in the history of the religions.' *ST 1*, p.171.

In the Old Testament, the God of Israel is portrayed within the context of competing claims to deity as the unique, sovereign, universal God; the prophetic witness constitutes a present disclosure of this truth, an unveiling of the end-time events while, at the same time recognising that the demonstrability of the universal truth of the message would only be revealed at the end of history.[29] Present experience and knowledge of God is therefore provisional in character.

In the New Testament this emphasis is taken up in the person of Jesus Christ. The final revelation of God still looks to the future eschatological fulfilment; the revelation of God in Christ is interpreted as a disclosure of that which will be universally manifest in the future.

It is clear that Pannenberg affirms an inherent relation between the revelatory acts of God in the history of religions and yet recognises in so doing the conflicting ability of these religions to explain human reality. In this context of competing claims to truth the unfolding of biblical ideas of revelation leads to the distinctively Christian assessment that the God of Jesus Christ is the one, unique God of all people. That truth will be openly manifested at the Eschaton but has already been revealed in the person and work of Jesus Christ, in anticipation. It is not a matter of asserting the uniqueness of Christianity in the present on the basis of a subjective faith commitment that claims to be authoritative. It is the very debatability of the Christian claim to universal truth which is upheld as consistent with the historical revelation of God. For Pannenberg religion becomes idolatrous when it claims to possess absolute knowledge of the truth. Debatability as evidence of a real openness to the future is consequently viewed as the quintessential characteristic of authentic religion; 'by bringing the debatability of all religious truth claims into their understanding of truth, [the religions] test themselves by the reality of the world so far as we can experience it.'[30]

---

[29] 'The universal recognition of the sole deity of Yahweh by the nations...was always open to challenge, was seen as something that would happen only in a distant, eschatological future.' *ST 1*, p.193.

[30] *ST 1,* p.214. Of particular interest is Pannenberg's linking this concept of the debatability of truth claims to the cross of Christ as the place where the truth claim of Jesus and his message was uniquely brought into question. Behind this lies a form of Luther's concept of the hiddenness of God in the event of the cross. See later discussion in chapter five.

Revelation and the Resurrection of Christ

Pannenberg's quest for the locus of divine revelation in history and in the context of the religions leads him to the development of a distinctive understanding of resurrection of Christ. This is interpreted historically by way of a substantial dependence on Jewish apocalyptic and metaphorically in terms of resurrection to new life by the Spirit.

It is argued that apocalyptic texts employ two related ways of describing the character of revelation. First, the eschatological future, which was largely understood in terms of the end of the world, is disclosed and communicated; second, there remains the future actuality of what has been disclosed in advance, the final manifestation of the glory of God, often accompanied by reference to the general resurrection of the dead. It is this combination of the provisional and the eschatological actuality which is determinative for Pannenberg's own thought. This was notably expressed in thesis four in the 'Dogmatic Theses on the Doctrine of Revelation' in *Revelation as History*, where apocalyptic is set out as the most important way of interpreting the life, death and resurrection of Jesus of Nazareth.[31] 'The universal revelation of the deity of God is not yet fully realised in the history of Israel, but first in the fate of Jesus of Nazareth, insofar as the end of all events is anticipated in his fate.'[32] The tension between the 'universal revelation of the deity of God' in Jesus and the anticipatory nature of that revelation remains unresolved in a manner which characterises Pannenberg's early theology. It is the reality of this tension which Pannenberg asserts to be the unique characteristic of the historically developing concept of revelation as found in Jewish apocalyptic at the time of Jesus and as echoed in the message and fate of Jesus.

The centrality of apocalyptic for Pannenberg's interpretation of New Testament concepts of revelation remains in the *Systematic Theology*, and is argued more thoroughly. It is clear that Pannenberg does not understand a simple, unmodified apocalyptic style of thought to be typical of the New Testament; there is reference to the diverse elements of New Testament ideas of revelation. Yet, he maintains that in the New Testament, 'the total conception does not differ from that of apocalyptic....Christian statements win their distinctive profile as a modification of apocalyptic ideas.'[33]

---

[31] For Pannenberg's early summary of this argument see *Revelation as History*, pp.139-148.

[32] Revelation as History, p.139.

[33] *ST 1*, p.208.

While it is argued that the New Testament concept of revelation remains within an apocalyptic framework, it is suggested in the content of the event of present disclosure a significant change is forged in the New Testament. This shift is due to the christological focus of the present disclosure. 'This one thing, the identity of the Messiah and world Judge, is the content of the revelation.'[34] The content of the revelation is the person of Christ and the message of the Kingdom which he preached. Accepting these modifications with regard to content, the parallel strands of eschatological actuality and provisionality are seen to run through both apocalyptic literature and the New Testament.

Given this context, Pannenberg's Christology develops from consideration of the history of Jesus of Nazareth. In *Grundzüge der Christologie* criticism is levelled at all attempts to derive a coherent Christology 'from above' since this assumes the eternal deity of Jesus as the Word.[35] By taking this approach the central question for Christology becomes one relating to incarnation; how can the Divine take human flesh? Pannenberg believes that it is impossible for us to construct a meaningful Christology from this starting point since it requires us to attempt to view things from the divine perspective when, in reality, we can only work from the perspective of human history.[36] This is not to deny the important insights of earlier theological expositions of the incarnation; it is rather to affirm the importance of taking seriously the history of the man Jesus. The central question then concerns his divinity; how can we understand this man in union with God?

Pannenberg's Christology is thus grounded on the historical particularity of Jesus of Nazareth. His position is to be contrasted with

---

[34] *ST 1*, p.209.

[35] This title is rather inaccurately translated *Jesus - God and Man*, English translation by L. Wilkins and D. Priebe, London, 1968.

[36] The same argument underpins Pannenberg's Christology in the *Systematic Theology*; 'a total presentation of Christian doctrine must try to integrate Christology from below into the context of...the doctrine of God and the economy of his work in the world.' *ST* 2, p.289. The point Pannenberg makes here is that to work methodologically from below does not necessarily challenge the material primacy of the eternal Son and his incarnation. In one sense the Dogmatics is an attempt to derive Christology by seeing 'from above' and 'from below' as complementary lines of argument. Yet Pannenberg maintains that 'the task of interpreting the appearance and history of Jesus in relation to God' must be 'to the fore' when constructing Christology.

any 'quest for the historical Jesus' which focuses on the continuity between the message of Jesus and the proclamation of the church.

Pannenberg's position, drawing upon the apocalyptic tradition noted, sees in the resurrection the proleptic disclosure of the end-times. In the resurrection of Jesus the end of history has already happened in anticipation, though the final actuality remains in the future. It is on the basis of the historical resurrection of Jesus that his earthly message and actions are vindicated; if the resurrection is seen as a prolepsis of the Eschaton, so also the resurrection has retroactive significance for the person of the man Jesus and his relationship to God.[37]

The logical progress of the argument in *Grundzüge der Christologie* lies at the heart of the more mature reflection in the Dogmatics. If Jesus has been raised then the end of the world has begun. If Jesus has been raised then God has unambiguously confirmed and vindicated the earthly ministry of Jesus of Nazareth. If Jesus has been raised then God is revealed in unique relationship to Jesus and is uniquely revealed in Jesus.

> Only because in Jesus' resurrection the end of all thing which for us has not yet happened, has already occurred can it be said of Jesus that the ultimate already is present in him, and so also that God himself, his glory, has made appearance in Jesus in a way that cannot be surpassed. Only because the end of the world is already present in Jesus' resurrection is God himself revealed in him.[38]

It is of comparative interest here that Moltmann has utilised apocalyptic thought rather differently to interpret the significance of the death and resurrection of Christ.[39]

---

[37] 'Only the Easter event determines what the meaning was of the pre-Easter history of Jesus and who he was in his relation to God.' *ST* 2, p.345.

[38] *ST* 1, p.69. A general point of criticism is pertinent here. By pursuing Christology on the basis of the resurrection Pannenberg runs the risk of minimising the significance of the cross. The death of Christ is understood primarily in terms of the post-resurrection vindication of the work of Christ by God; the atoning significance of the cross therefore rests on a post-resurrection understanding of the death of the man Jesus in his relation to God. In the disruption of that relationship Jesus has stood as the universal substitute for humanity so that 'the Godforsakenness of death is overcome for all men.' It is questionable whether this constitutes an adequate doctrine of the cross.

[39] Moltmann, *The Way of Jesus Christ*, English translation by M. Kohl, London, 1990, pp.151-59.

For Moltmann, the cross is as much an apocalyptic event as the resurrection; in the sufferings of Christ the end-time tribulation is anticipated and vicariously experienced. His death is 'the anticipation of the death which is universal and absolute' and is an act of divine judgment out of which comes the eternal kingdom of righteousness; 'Golgotha is the anticipation of the end of this world and the beginning of a world that is new.'[40] This interpretation of apocalyptic in terms of judgment and new creation might be seen to facilitate a fuller exposition of the death of Christ than a Christology founded upon the doctrine of resurrection as history expressed by Pannenberg.

It is in keeping with Pannenberg's whole approach and crucial to his theology that the resurrection of Jesus is understood primarily as an historical event. This he supports from exegetical and theoretical consideration of the post-Easter appearances combined with the stream of tradition which centres on the empty tomb. 'Decisive for confidence in the facticity of the resurrection of Jesus...are the primitive Christian testimonies to the appearances of the risen Lord to his disciples.'[41] In the *Systematic Theology*, it is the appearances that form the primary historical data. Arguing from the report of Paul in 1 Cor.15.1-11, Pannenberg maintains vigorously the veracity of this early account of the resurrection appearances. The historical case was first clearly set out in *Grundzüge der Christologie* and is developed further in *Systematic Theology, Volume Two*.[42]

Pannenberg is clear that even if the historicity of the resurrection is accepted, this tells us little about the content of the appearances. For that he turns to the second strand of tradition, the empty tomb. Here we are more concerned with the type of reality that appeared; it is at this point that he links with his conception of the Spirit in what is essentially a Spirit Christology of the risen Christ. The empty tomb functions so as to confirm 'the reality of Jesus encountered in the appearances with his resurrection from the dead.'[43] It is in discussion of the kind of event that

---

[40] *The Way of Jesus Christ*, p.155, It should be noted that Moltmann works with a dialectical understanding of the cross and the resurrection which is not so dependent on historicity as Pannenberg.

[41] *ST* 2, p.352-53. Pannenberg is at pains to point out that these testimonies cannot simply be accepted as authoritative without submission to 'the kind of testing by which we prove other reported facts.'

[42] *Jesus - God and Man*, pp.88-105; *ST 2*, pp.353-363.

[43] *ST* 2, p.359. The pneumatological significance of this rests upon Pannenberg's view that the meaning of the event inheres within that event; hence the empty tomb functions so as to confirm that it is the man Jesus who is

the language of resurrection signifies that Pannenberg utilises the concept of metaphor. This is not to deny the reality of the event; it is rather to point beyond the language to the new life which it describes, a life born of the Spirit. 'The language of the resurrection of Jesus is that of metaphor...yet a real event was in view.' It points to 'the new eschatological life' which is 'life in the full sense.' It is because the 'transition' from death to life is beyond 'everyday experience' that this must be stated metaphorically.[44] The implications of this will be detailed in the later discussion of Pannenberg's pneumatology.

The significant issue here is the need for Pannenberg to maintain the historical veracity of the resurrection if his theology is to remain coherent. Yet it is precisely here that, as Grenz points out, Pannenberg's conception of provisionality and debatability is brought to bear, in that however detailed the supporting argument offered, Pannenberg will not affirm that the historical question is closed. All truth remains open to question; we may argue from the basis of what has been provisionally revealed, in anticipation, but there can be no full and final claim to authoritative truth before the eschatological consummation. 'Assertion of the historicity of an event does not mean that its facticity is so sure that there can no longer be any dispute regarding it.'[45]

It is clear that the whole structure of the *Systematic Theology* and the centrality of the resurrection of Christ arise from Pannenberg's conviction that revelation is not simply a religious concept born out of historical experience, but that it is constituted by the totality of Gods acts in history.

.the risen Christ, and that event, together with its later apostolic interpretation, is a product of the work of the Spirit.

[44] *ST* 2, pp.346-47.

[45] *ST* 2, p.361. Put from the perspective of Christian faith the facticity of the resurrection will inevitably remain open to debate until the Eschaton due to the uniqueness of the event which 'transcends an understanding of reality that is oriented only to this passing world.'

The Doctrine of the Trinity: The Threeness of the One God

Early criticisms of Pannenberg's theology of revelation identified a lack of emphasis on the structural importance of the Trinity. As Olson has argued, *Systematic Theology, Volume One*, shows that, for Pannenberg, the doctrine of the Trinity is not only structurally central but distinctive in its emphasis.[46] Through a sustained engagement with historical theology, Pannenberg seeks to construct his doctrine of the Trinity from the trinitarian revelation of God as Father, Son and Holy Spirit. In other words the doctrine of the Trinity is 'grounded on revelation...on the economy of salvation - on the way that the Father, Son and Spirit come to appearance in the event of revelation and relate to each other.'[47] This constitutes a reversal of the traditional approach which has tended to begin with the unity of God and then seek an understanding of the three persons. In establishing the problematic nature of this method Pannenberg engages at length with historical theology from the early Fathers to Barth.[48]

The attempts of the early church to formulate the doctrine of the Trinity within the historical framework of Judaistic monotheism resulted in the deity of the Son being derived from that of the Father. Apologists such as Philo and Justin articulated this through the development of the Logos concept; the Logos was united with the Father by virtue of derivation from him. This 'seemed to guarantee the validity of Christology from a monotheistic standpoint.'[49] By contrast, Athanasias approached the unity of the Father and the Son from the idea of distinct persons in relation. The Father cannot be thought of as 'Father' without the Son; Pannenberg appropriates the significant point that the deity of the Son does not rest on a notion of origin, but on his relationship to the Father. Yet it is suggested that Athanasias not fully develop this thought and that the same argument was not pursued with respect to the Spirit.[50]

---

[46] R. Olson, 'Wolfhart Pannenberg's Doctrine of the Trinity' in *Scottish Journal of Theology*, 43, 1990, pp.175- 206. Schwöbel makes the same point in stating that in Pannenberg's earlier writing trinitarian reflection either plays a minor role or is confined to 'specific loci of Christian dogmatics.' 'Wolfhart Pannenberg' in D. Ford (ed.) *The Modern Theologians,* Vol.1, Oxford, 1989.

[47] S. Grenz summarising Pannenberg's distinctive reversal of traditional method, *Reason for Hope*, Oxford, 1990, p.48.

[48] See especially *ST* 1, pp.259-299.

[49] *ST,* 1, p.277.

[50] 'Only from the fact that the Father is God can it be urged with any cogency that he cannot be thought of without the Spirit.' *ST* 1, p.279. The point

Pannenberg is equally critical of the Cappadocians; while clearly seeing that the trinitarian personal distinctions are relationally defined, it is argued that they still asserted that the Son and Spirit received their deity from the Father such that 'the Father is the source of all deity and principle of unity.'[51] For Pannenberg this led to a view of the divine essence as originally unique to the Father, and consequently a collapse into subordinationism;

> the idea of the mutual defining of the distinctiveness of the persons does not lead to the thought of an equal mutual ontological constitution of their personhood but is interpreted in terms of relations of origin, of which it can be said that strictly they are constitutive only for the personhood of the Son and Spirit if the Father is the source and origin of deity.[52]

From the Middle Ages onward trinitarian theology tended to start with the question of the existence of God and the divine attributes prior to the idea of the Trinity. Reformation dogmatics asserted that the Trinity could only be known by revelation and consequently on the basis of Scripture, yet arguments concerning God's essence still utilised Scholastic conceptuality. As a result, the conceptual link between the unity of God and the doctrine of the Trinity became less obvious. It is in this context that Pannenberg sees the emergence of the distinction between a Trinity of revelation and an eternal, essential Trinity; here may be discerned the starting point of the relative decay of the doctrine of the Trinity in subsequent centuries of Protestant theology.

Hegel is credited with raising the doctrine to a new level of importance, deriving the Trinity from the idea of God as Spirit and expressing the plurality of persons in terms of love. Yet Pannenberg is critical of Hegel, since he asserts that any attempt to ground the doctrine of the Trinity in the concept of God as one being, whether the essence of that being is described as Spirit or love, inevitably leads to a form of modalism or subordinationism; plurality of persons cannot be derived from the essence of the one God 'without relapse into a pre-trinitarian monotheism, that of the subjectivity of the one God as one who generates the other persons.'[53]

---

for Pannenberg is that this once again implies the monarchy of the Father.

[51] *ST* 1, p.279. Consequently the Father was seen as being without origin.

[52] *ST* 1, p.280. For Pannenberg this means that later theology had to grapple with the question of the relation between unity of persons and unity of the divine substance.

[53] *ST* 1, p.298. Pannenberg sees the inconsistency in Hegel arising from his

Karl Barth's renewed emphasis upon the doctrine of the Trinity as an expression of God's self-revelation in Jesus Christ is regarded as vital. Yet Pannenberg criticises Barth for failing to develop the doctrine from the historical revelation of God as Father, Son and Holy Spirit. Rather, Barth is viewed as building his doctrine from a formal concept of revelation as self-revelation. This involves a subject of revelation, an object and revelation itself, all of which are viewed as a unity. Here Pannenberg detects a form of trinitarian distinction which is markedly less than personal; 'there is no room for a plurality of persons in the one God but only for different modes of being in the one divine subjectivity.'[54]

For Pannenberg the doctrine of the Trinity cannot be satisfactorily derived from a prior concept of the unity of God's essence. On the contrary, 'we must begin with the way in which Father, Son and Spirit come on the scene and relate to one another in the event of revelation.'[55] It is important not to misunderstand Pannenberg at this point. He does not dispute that talk of God as Trinity must in some way pre-suppose a prior understanding of God. His distinctive suggestion is that this knowledge does not come from philosophical reasoning but from the human experience of the history of religions, and most notably from the historical acts of the God of Israel.[56]

Consequently, for Pannenberg, the doctrine of the Trinity must be grounded on the revelation of God in Jesus Christ. Most particularly it must begin with an examination of the relation between the man Jesus and the one he addressed as Father and whose Kingdom he announced; 'we must begin with the relation of Jesus to the Father as it came to expression in the message of the divine rule.'[57]

---

inability to reconcile the idea of God as Spirit with the expression of that in terms of plurality of persons. Hegel actually posits the subsuming of personality within the divine unity (see Hegel, '*Vorlesungen*,' 1824, pp.71,72).

[54] *ST* 1, p.296. Pannenberg argues that there is a clear indebtedness to Hegel in Barth's thought; 'this model of the trinity of revelation is easily seen to be structurally identical with that of the self-conscious Absolute...'

[55] *ST* 1, p.299. Consequently an understanding of the essence and attributes of the one God will flow out of the doctrine of the Trinity.

[56] In this respect Pannenberg is being consistent with his overall understanding of revelation as history as detailed in the earlier chapters of the *Systematic Theology*.

[57] *ST* 1, p.304. Here we meet with Pannenberg's distinctive view of the intimate relationship between the message and work of Jesus to the Father's deity and rule. This will be expounded later.

The Self-Differentiation of the Father and Son

The key term Pannenberg employs in his conceptualisation of the Father-Son relationship is that of reciprocal self- distinction. Pannenberg notes that the idea of self-distinction is not new, having been traditionally used to describe the sending forth of the Son and the Spirit by the Father. This again serves to highlight the priority of the Father. Yet Pannenberg offers a 'radical reinterpretation of self-differentiation' drawing upon Hegel's understanding of personhood.[58] The essence of person is understood in the giving of self to another such that in this self-giving personal identity is achieved; in other words self-differentiation is bound up with dependency on another.

Pannenberg explicates this with regard to the message of Jesus whose central concern was that God's lordship would be honoured. 'To establish the lordship of God is the chief content and primary goal of the mission of Jesus.'[59]

It is in the complete abandonment of Jesus to the will of the Father, in his bearing witness to God as his Father, that Jesus distinguishes himself from the Father as the Son. It is in this self-distinction from God, and his determination to do the will of his Father, that Jesus shows himself to be the Son; through this self-distinction Jesus seeks not to glorify himself but the Father. In living in subjection to his Father and proclaiming the lordship of God, Jesus gave place to the Father's claim to deity. In this way Jesus shows himself to be the Son.[60] Indeed, for Pannenberg this voluntary subordination in the earthly ministry of Jesus is the essential qualification for the ascription of sonship to Jesus; this is a central part of Pannenberg's argument concerning the deity of Christ in the Christology section of the *Systematic Theology*.[61] It is in this

---

[58] S. Grenz, *Reason for Hope*, p.49. Pannenberg defines his understanding of self-differentiation as 'the one who distinguishes himself from another defines himself as also dependent on the other.' *ST,* 1, p.313 (footnote 167).

[59] *ST* 1, p.309.

[60] 'By giving place to the Father's claim to deity as he asked others to do in his proclamation of the divine lordship, he showed himself to be the Son of God and one with the Father who sent him (John 10.30).' *ST,* 1, p.310.

[61] 'Only in this subordination to the rule of the one God is he the Son.' *ST* 2, p.373. Behind this emphasis lies a particular view of the relation between the humanity and deity of Christ whereby his deity is revealed in his humanity. Precisely in his self-differentiation from the Father do we come to understand his relation to the Father. For further discussion of this see later in this chapter.

complete correspondence of will with the Father that Jesus is understood to be one with the eternal Father; 'in corresponding to the claim of the Father (Jesus) is so at one with the Father that God in eternity is Father only in relation to him.'[62] Here Pannenberg asserts that the self-distinction of the Son, is not simply something which relates to the earthly Jesus; it is the eternal God whom Jesus reveals as Father and consequently the relationship of Jesus to the Father is eternal. This is understood as an aspect of the humanity of Jesus which is 'the eternal correlate of the deity of the Father and which precedes his human birth...hence self-distinction from the Father is constitutive for the eternal Son in his relation to the Father.'[63]

Having asserted the self-distinction of the Son from the Father, Pannenberg then asks whether the same can be argued for the self-differentiation of the Father from the Son? In raising this question Pannenberg challenges the view of the Father as '*anarchos*', without origin and fount of all deity. For Pannenberg this view seems to 'rule out genuine mutuality in the relations of the trinitarian persons.'[64] Pannenberg wishes to assert complete mutuality and argues that the Father would not be the Father without the Son, a position he finds akin to that of Athanasias.

To explicate the self-distinction of the Father Pannenberg utilises the biblical testimony to the handing over of lordship from the Father to the Son. (Matt.28.18) The Son not only proclaims the lordship of the Father 'he executes it.'[65] The Son reigns in his exaltation and will reign until the eschatological consummation of the Kingdom of God. (1 Cor.15.24-25) When this occurs the Son will subject himself to the Father that God may be all in all. (1 Cor.15.28) For Pannenberg this mutual exchanging of lordship is characterised by mutual interpenetration; 'the lordship of the Son is simply to proclaim the lordship of the Father...His own lordship is consummated when he subjects all things to the lordship of the Father and all creation honours the Father as the one God.'[66]

---

[62] *ST* 2, p.373.

[63] *ST* 2, p.373 It may be asked whether this makes the incarnation a necessity for the being of God. This question will be examined later. A related issue concerns the idea of the two natures of Christ. Pannenberg is clear that the eternal God cannot be thought of directly as related to a temporal, creaturely reality unless this is itself in some way eternal; this is the root of the distinction between the two natures.

[64] *ST* 2, pp. 311,312.

[65] *ST* 2, p.312.

[66] *ST* 2, p.313. Of particular note in this quote is the mention of the Father as

In this mutual exchange of lordship Pannenberg identifies a mutuality of relationship between Father and Son.

> By handing over lordship to the Son the Father makes his kingship dependent on whether the Son glorifies him and fulfils his lordship by fulfilling his mission...his kingdom and his own deity are now dependent upon the Son.The rule or kingdom of the Father is not so external to his deity that he might be God without his kingdom.[67]

It is in this context that Pannenberg understands the significance of the cross of Christ. 'In the death of Jesus the deity of his God and Father was at issue.'[68] It was truly the Son who suffered and died and so to speak of the death of God is theologically incorrect. Yet it is necessary to speak of the death of Jesus as the Son of God; in his acceptance of death Jesus chose the path of ultimate obedience and humiliation. For Pannenberg this constitutes the 'ultimate consequence of his self-distinction from the Father and precisely in so doing showed himself to be the Son of the Father.'[69] The Father must also have suffered 'sympathetically' in the passion of the Son if God is to be understood as love. In this sense at least the cross leaves its impression in the eternal being of God.

It is at this point that Pannenberg moves towards a consideration of the role of the Spirit, constructing this from the perspective of the resurrection of Christ.

---

the one God. Behind this statement lies Pannenberg's belief that the deity of God is expressed in his rule. In this sense he maintains a view of the monarchy of the Father, but sees this as the eschatological fulfilment of all things; it is a fulfilment of the trinitarian relations and thus dependent upon them. See the later critical discussion.

[67] *ST* 2, p.313 As Grenz points out this rests upon Pannenberg's often repeated conviction that God's deity is inextricably tied to his rule over creation.

[68] *ST* 2, p.314. Here Pannenberg finds some common ground with the view of Moltmann in *The Crucified God*, New York, 1972..

[69] *ST* 2, p.314. In this context it may be asked whether the purpose of the cross was primarily revelatory. Later Pannenberg does establish a doctrine of reconciliation and argues a distinctive view of the substitutionary death of Jesus, though this remains closely linked with the person of Christ here outlined. See *ST 2,* pp.297-323.

The Resurrection of Christ and the Self-Distinction of the Spirit

For Pannenberg, the resurrection of Christ is the work of the Spirit who is the Creator of all life. All three persons of the Trinity are at work in this event but there is a sense in which the resurrection demonstrates the dependence of the Father and the Son on the Spirit as their 'medium of communication.'[70]

This working of the Father and the Son through the Spirit is most clearly articulated in the Johannine statements concerning the glorification of the Son. (eg. John 17.4, 16.14). It is by the Spirit that the revelation of the Father by the Son is completed; 'glorifying the Son, the Spirit also glorifies the Father and their indissoluble fellowship.'[71]

This is seen to be a self-distinction of the Spirit from the Father and the Son but in such a way as to remain related to them both. In the same way that Jesus obeyed the Father and sought to glorify him, so the Spirit does not speak of himself but glorifies Jesus and, in him, the Father. In this sense the Spirit is more than the communion of love (*caritas*) between Father and Son; the Spirit must be understood as truly personal in self-distinction from the Father and the Son. Pannenberg argues that it is this personhood of the Spirit which is the 'necessary premise' of the same Spirit being the medium of fellowship between Father and Son.[72] Whether this constitutes an adequate description of the person of the Spirit will be discussed in detail in a later chapter.

In the light of this Pannenberg has great difficulty with the filioque clause. His main criticism of this is its dependence upon the definition of the trinitarian relations in terms of origin. It is this which Pannenberg has consistently sought to deny since it fails to do justice to the true recipricocity of relations, the mutual self-distinction of Father, Son and Spirit. For Pannenberg it is better to say that the Spirit 'proceeds from

---

[70] C. Schwöbel, *Wolfhart Pannenberg*, p.276.

[71] *ST* 1, p.315.

[72] *ST* 1, p.316. Important here is the concept of mutual dependence. Pannenberg makes reference to Luke's infancy narrative as well as Romans 1.4 to establish a dependency of the Son on the Spirit; equally Christians are adopted as children of God by receiving the Spirit. Again an interesting comparison is Moltmann's differing 'forms of the Trinity' in his exposition of the history of the Son where a similar mutuality is envisaged. However, Pannenberg would dispute the concept of changing forms of the Trinity. J. Moltmann, *The Trinity and the Kingdom of God*, English translation by M. Kohl, London, 1981, pp.61-96.

the Father and is received by the Son.'[73] This does not preclude the Son giving the Spirit to his people or believers receiving adoption through the 'Spirit of Christ.' At heart, what matters for Pannenberg is the mutual recipricocity of the trinitarian relations.

Grenz points out that this rejection of the filioque leads to a fuller pneumatology than is common in the Western theological tradition.[74] Further this serves to illustrate Pannenberg's ecumenical concern to engender debate between the various Christian traditions in the East and West.

The Unity of the Three Persons: The Monarchy of the Father

Pannenberg clearly states that the trinitarian persons, having the form of mutual self-distinction, must be understood in terms of three distinct 'centres of action.'[75] In preparing the way for a full discussion of the unity of God, certain historical solutions to the problem are discussed and rejected in turn.

Firstly, if the persons of the Trinity are genuinely understood as three distinct centres of activity then this rules out the idealist approach which posits God as one divine subject. The divine persons are not simply three modes of being of the one God.

Secondly, as argued previously in the formulation of the trinitarian relations, their unity cannot rest on a relation of origins whereby the Son and Spirit receive their deity from the Father. Pannenberg rejects the traditional language of generation and procession on the basis that it derives from such a view of the unity of God; he finds no exegetical ground or theological necessity for these terms without their being expanded in meaning to include relational concepts such as obedience and glorification.[76]

---

[73] *ST* 1, p.317. Cf. Moltmann's reinterpretation of the filioque as procession 'from the Father of the Son,' the Spirit receiving 'his form from the Father and the Son.' *The Trinity and the Kingdom of God*, p.187.

[74] Grenz, *Reason for Hope*, p.51. This can be seen in a number of doctrinal areas, including Christology and ecclesiology. It also facilitates an ecumenical doctrine of the church set out in *ST* 3.

[75] *ST* 1, p.319. Here Pannenberg distinguishes his position from Moltmann and Jenson on the grounds that they fail to give weight to the idea of self-distinction. See footnote 183.

[76] See especially the discussion in pp.305-6 in *ST* 1 in which the biblical texts normally employed to defend the traditional use of the language of begetting and breathing are examined.

It is clear that the trinitarian relational nexus is understood to be more complex than a simple relation of origins suggests. Drawing upon Athanasias, it is argued that the self-distinction of the Father and the Son involves the mutual handing over of lordship; the Father 'hands over his lordship to the Son so as to have it anew in him.'[77] By extension of this argument the actual deity of the Father is thus seen to be dependent on the Son. 'As the Father is not the Father without the Son, he does not have his Godhead without him.'[78]
Pannenberg seeks to re-assert a doctrine of the monarchy of the Father, but not in any sense that the Father is the origin of deity. Rather it is through the message and work of Jesus that the kingdom of the Father is consummated in creation. 'By their work the Son and the Spirit serve the monarchy of the Father.'[79] The Father does not have his monarchy without the Son and the Spirit. Equally what is true of the historical relation of the work of the Son and Spirit to the Father is also true of the eternal relations. The Son subjects himself to the Father; 'in this regard he is himself in eternity the locus of the monarchy of the Father.'[80] Hence, the monarchy of the Father is not understood as a presupposition but as a result of the trinitarian relations;

> only because the communion of the persons finds its content in the monarchy of the Father as the result of their common working may we say that the trinitarian God is none other than the God whom Jesus proclaimed, the heavenly Father whose reign is near, dawning already in the work of Jesus.[81]

---

[77] *ST* 1, p.322. Pannenberg quotes from Athanasius; 'Since the Father has given all things to the Son, he possesses all things afresh in the Son.'

[78] *ST* 1, p.322. Consequently the common view of a relation of origins which accepts the deity of the Father as unconditional and unconditioned is seen to deny the true recipricocity of the self-distinction of the trinitarian persons; 'their equal deity is not upheld.' Pannenberg faults the Cappadocians for failing to see this and suggests that the genuine insight of Athanasias was not pursued. In agreement with Jenson's analysis in *The Triune Identity*, Gregory of Nazianus is credited with pursuing genuine mutuality of personal relationships in the Trinity, but only to the extent of describing the outward actions of God. By contrast Pannenberg detects a 'subordinationist imprint' on Gregory's account of the inner life of the Trinity.

[79] *ST* 1, p.324.

[80] *ST* 1, p.325.

[81] *ST* 1, p.327. This discussion is set in contrast to Moltmann who certainly states that the persons constitute their distinction and their unity, but who

Here questions arise relating to the eschatological focus of the monarchy and the deity of the Father. These will be addressed later as will the underlying ontological question.

The issue with which Pannenberg prepares his full discussion of the unity of God is the relationship between the immanent Trinity and the economic Trinity.

Here Pannenberg interacts with recent German theology, tracing the developing arguments concerning the relationship between the immanent Trinity and economic Trinity. Karl Rahner developed the thesis, already inherent in Barth's doctrine of revelation, that there is an identity between the immanent and economic Trinity.[82] For Rahner this identity rests on the sending of the Son and the Spirit through whom the Father acts in the world. In this sense all three persons of the Trinity stand in a particular relation to the economy of salvation.

Jüngel and Moltmann see in the event of the cross a sense in which the deity of the Father is not just questioned but affected, suggesting that the mutual trinitarian relations involve the Father in the central events of salvation history; 'in an advance on Rahner the person of the Father is implicated...in such a way that the progress of events decides concerning his deity as well as the deity of the Son.'[83] Moltmann subsequently developed his thesis of the eschatological identity of the economic and immanent Trinity. Through the glorifying work of the Son and the Spirit in the world the union of the Father and Son is effected as well as our union with God; hence the consummation of the history of salvation would coincide eschatologically with the consummation of the trinitarian life of God. When God is 'all in all' then the economic Trinity is subsumed in the immanent Trinity. 'The economic Trinity completes and perfects itself to immanent Trinity when the history and experience of salvation are completed and perfected.'[84]

---

distinguishes between the constitution of the Trinity from the Father and the perichoretic relations of the three persons. Pannenberg finds these two models impossible to reconcile.

[82] See discussion in Rahner, *Theological Investigations*, IV, pp.94ff. In a brief excursus on Barth, Pannenberg maintains that while the structure of *CD* I/1 constantly links the Trinity in the eternal essence of God with historical revelation, the result is a doctrine of revelation which implies the identity of the economic and immanent Trinity, rather than a doctrine of the Trinity.

[83] *ST* 1, p.329. Here Pannenberg draws upon Jüngel's *God as the Mystery of the World* and Moltmann's *The Crucified God*.

[84] Moltmann, *The Trinity and the Kingdom of God*, p.161.

Yet Pannenberg questions whether this simply amounts to the 'absorption' of the immanent Trinity in the economic Trinity; if so this 'steals from the Trinity of salvation history all sense and significance' since this significance is only gained if God is the same in his acts of salvation as he is in eternity.[85] Pannenberg also wishes to affirm an eschatological identity of the economic and immanent Trinity but not in any way that is divorced from the unity of the three persons of the Trinity.

> The question of the unity of Father, Son and Spirit in the unity of the divine essence and the question of the unity of the so-called immanent Trinity with the economic Trinity are closely related questions. The unity of God in the Trinity of persons must also be the basis of the distinction and unity of the immanent Trinity and the economic Trinity.[86]

In other words, the unity of God in the relations of the three persons 'must serve as the ground of the difference and the unity of the immanent and economic Trinity.'[87]

The consequent discussion of the unity of God therefore ranges beyond the unity of the three persons to include a discussion of the essence of God but in such a way that this concept is not understood to be separate from the trinitarian relations. 'Discussion of the unity is a task for a doctrine of God's nature and attributes.'[88]

The Doctrine of the Trinity: The Unity of the Divine Essence

Following the discussion of the doctrine of the Trinity, Pannenberg goes on to consider the unity of the divine essence. Since he uses the Trinity as the organising focus of his whole doctrine of God, Pannenberg connects the unity of God's essence with the divine attributes. It is critical for him to address the problem of how the three persons within the Trinity can be understood in terms of one divine essence in such a way that does not imply that essence is a fourth subject behind the Trinity.

---

[85] *ST* 1, p.331, drawing upon criticism of Moltmann made by Kasper.

[86] *ST* 1, p.333. This is a critical move in Pannenberg's argument and means that his discussion of the unity of God is also an explication of the identity of the economic and immanent Trinity

[87] S. Grenz, *Reason for Hope*, p.53.

[88] *ST* 1, p.335.

In establishing his account of the divine essence, Pannenberg rejects the view that this may be known through rational reflection on creation whereas the doctrine of the Trinity is only known by special revelation.[89] By contrast it is argued that once the expression of the doctrine of the Trinity came to fulfilment in the fourth century creeds, 'the central problem of the doctrine of the Trinity was not the Trinity but the unity of the trinitarian God.'[90]

God's Essence and Existence

Pannenberg contrasts two models which express the divine essence. The first is exemplified by Aquinas and utilises the concept of God as the first cause. We come to a knowledge of God's essence by analogy with creation; 'perfections that pre- exist in God in unity and simplicity are divided and multiple in creatures.'[91] The second model, and the one preferred by Pannenberg, is the conception of God as infinite, as first outlined by Gregory of Nyssa.[92]

Pannenberg traces the theological and philosophical pedigree of this through Scotus, Descartes, Hegel and Cremer. Scotus emphasised the central importance of infinity for the whole concept of God, regarding it as the defining attribute of God, not simply one attribute among many.[93] Interestingly, Pannenberg sees this thought being developed by Descartes who is credited with reversing the traditional philosophical approach of working from the concept of existence to essence. Here the concept of the infinite is understood as 'the first intuition of the intellect' on which all other knowledge rests.[94] This intuition of the

---

[89] Pannenberg interacts in this part of the discussion with older German Protestant dogmatics as well as Neo- Scholastic Roman Catholic theology. *ST* 1, p.341.

[90] *ST* 1 p.342.

[91] Footnote 13, *ST 1*, p.344. Thus only by analogy can we trace back from creation to God on the basis of God's causal relationship to creation.

[92] Gregory was reacting against the Arian conception of God as a being without origin. In utilising the concept of infinity he reasserted the incomprehensibility of the divine essence.

[93] Pannenberg is critical of Scotus for not utilising the concept of the infinite in place of the idea of a first cause. Rather he resorted to the traditional causal argument to prove the importance of the infinite.

[94] *ST* 1, p.350. According to Descartes everything finite is limited by the infinite; even the concept of perfection is contained in the idea of the infinite. In this way thinking about God as infinite does not rest upon an argument from

infinite is closely related to the idea of God. Yet here Pannenberg faults Descartes for failing to distinguish between the intuition of the infinite and consequent reflection upon that intuition; 'an explicit idea of the infinite arises only later from the standpoint of reflection on experience of the world as a whole.'[95]

Of importance here is the way in which the concept of a non-thematic intuition of the infinite, as outlined by Descartes, meshes with Pannenberg's understanding of the religious nature of the human person and the non-thematic awareness of God in the religions. In this non-thematic human experience of God the perception of the existence of God precedes an understanding of the divine essence.

> God is always present already in all human life. He is there for us and our world even though he is not known as God. He is there as the undefined infinite which is formed by the primal intuition of our awareness of reality...an indefinite awareness of something which with an increasing consciousness of finite objects is known to transcend them all.[96]

This epistemic awareness becomes thematised as we discover more about the essence of God through revelation and consequent reflection. Thus, God exists as an active presence within the world, understood in his essence only in the context of specific acts of revelation.

Now this argument seems to hold together at the epistemological level; the question remains as to how we can understand the relationship

---

first cause. 'From the intuition of the infinite as the condition of all ideas of finite things he moved on to the thought of God by way of the idea of perfection that is contained in this intuition.' (p.351) This interpretation of Descartes runs counter to what Pannenberg describes as a 'persistent misunderstanding' that the thought of God originates within the human mind. While materially beginning with the cogito, this simply introduces the fundamental thesis that the infinite is the defining condition of all finite things. Hence it is mistaken to describe Descartes as the founder of epistemological subjectivism. If this view of Descartes is accepted then Jüngel's critique of Descartes loses its force. See *GMW*, pp.123-126.

[95] *ST* 1, *p.353.* See also Pannenberg, *Metaphysics and the Idea of God*, 1990, pp.26-29 where the critique of Descartes is more fully expressed in terms of the unthematic nature of our intuition of the infinite as well as a fundamental questioning of the notion of perfection for the idea of God; 'reflection on perfection...is not sufficient to derive the concept of God, unless the idea has been derived from another source, namely, from the religious tradition.'

[96] *ST* 1, p.356.

between God's eternal essence and his existence in his acts of revelation at an ontological level. Here Pannenberg argues that God's existence can only be understood in terms of specific acts, 'moments' of God's activity in the world. In these moments the essence of God comes to a specific manifestation; 'the individual moments of his active presence in the world...to the extent that they are known to be moments of the existence of God, are moments in which the essence of God comes to manifestation.'[97] Yet such individual manifestations do not exhaust the essence of God, since this can only be defined in terms of 'the sum total of its manifestations and existence.'[98] The critical point that Pannenberg wishes to make is that while we can speak of particular moments of manifestation of God's essence, we can only fully define that essence by reference to the totality of those manifestations.

Here Pannenberg interprets this perspective within a trinitarian framework. The essence of God is revealed as Father, Son and Spirit in that they constitute three forms of the existence of God in the world and in eternity. In the three persons the divine essence has a specific form of existence; the non-thematic awareness of the infinite is not sufficient to define God, but 'the specific form of the existence of God as Father, Son and Spirit is identical with the unlimited field of God's non-thematic presence in creation.'[99] The full meaning of this statement will only become apparent in the context of a discussion of the concept of the divine field of God's presence which is detailed later, but the methodological significance of this is clear. While the unity of the divine essence, as with the unity of the immanent and economic Trinity, is posited at the Eschaton, that same essence is manifested in specific moments, in anticipation of the final totality of such moments. The non-thematic awareness of God's presence in human religious experience both anticipates and is interpreted by the revelation of the one God as Father, Son and Holy Spirit.[100] In this sense the divine essence cannot be

---

[97] *ST* 1, p.358.

[98] *ST* 1, p.358. Underpinning this view is an ontology which is expounded in terms of appearance and anticipation; the unity of God's essence is posited at the Eschaton yet manifested in particular moments of existence in time and space. For a critical discussion see the following chapter.

[99] *ST* 1, p.359.

[100] The difficult question which arises is whether this makes the religious experience in different faith traditions a necessary part of the revelation of God in Jesus or whether this ultimately reduces the significance of other faiths as religions in their own right. These issues arise acutely at this point and will be pursued in the critical discussion later in this chapter.

understood in terms of the 'substance' of classical metaphysics, but rather as being constituted relationally both within the Godhead and with regard to the world. Consequently the category of divine action is important for Pannenberg in his discussion of the divine attributes.

Divine Action and the Presence of God

Pannenberg rejects any account of the divine attributes which rests on a metaphysical concept of substance. Rather, he approaches it from the concept of divine action, a suggestion first put forward by Cremer.[101] Whereas previous doctrines of the divine attributes had been grounded on the idea of God as the first cause, Cremer maintained that we can only know the nature of God from his activity towards us; 'the God who acts, who sets and achieves goals, can no more be without qualities than his action can.'[102]

Yet Pannenberg sees that such an emphasis on action as the basis of the divine attributes is fraught with difficulty, not least since this can imply the notion of God as a self- conscious being who wills and determines certain objectives. This can very easily lead to an 'anthropomorphic' view of God who acts purposefully in such a way that presupposes a divine 'intellect and will.'[103] This model appears problematic when applied to the infinite God.

For Pannenberg, the underlying problem consists in an understanding of God as '*nous*,' by which is meant a self-conscious mind , a sort of 'supreme reason.'[104] This view arose in the context of the patristic exposition of the otherness of God. This contrasted with what was seen at that time as the only alternative view which understood God as a corporeal being. Consequently theology came to interpret the biblical language of Spirit in Platonic, transcendental terms.[105] The way around

---

[101] H. Cremer, *Die christliche Lehre von den Eigenschaften Gottes,* Gutersloh, 1897.

[102] *ST* 1, p.368, making reference to the argument used by Cremer.

[103] *ST* 1, p.370. Despite his initial reliance on Cremer, Pannenberg observes that he slips into this trap.

[104] see especially the discussion, *ST* 1, pp.370-374, where Pannenberg traces the historical fusing of the Platonic idea of *nous* with the biblical language of pneuma.

[105] 'The strength of the understanding of the divine pneuma as reason in the context of late antiquity lay especially in the fact that the only alternative seemed to be to think of God as a corporeal reality.' *ST* 1, p.372. Pannenberg traces this influential understanding of Spirit to Origen.

this errant view is to recapture the idea of Spirit in terms of life-giving, creative energy and Pannenberg expresses this by utilising the language of field theory as developed in modern science. He argues that the biblical understanding of Spirit has parallels with the scientific concept of a universal field of force. 'The Spirit is the force field of God's mighty presence.'[106] The attraction of this for Pannenberg is that it avoids any conceptualisation of God as a self-conscious subject but enables him to retain the ideas of life and energy. The essence of God as Spirit is thus understood as a creative field that is manifested particularly in the persons of Father, Son and Spirit. 'The deity as field can find equal manifestation in all three persons.'[107]

This point needs further elucidation however, since, as Schwöbel has pointed out, this model seems to challenge the theological conception of divine agency that Pannenberg set out to establish.[108] Is the divine essence alone to be understood as acting subject, or should that action be ascribed to the persons of the Trinity? If the latter, how can a coherent understanding of the divine attributes of the one God be constructed? Pannenberg is clear that the divine essence cannot be the subject of the divine action since this would imply that the persons are mere 'aspects of the divine subjectivity.'[109] Rather, the three persons are understood to be the direct subjects of the divine action, whether that action be directed towards one another or towards creation. Yet in their relations and co-operation their action can only be that of the one God. It is through the work of the Son and the Spirit in the world that the monarchy of the Father is eschatologically established; it is only through the actions of the trinitarian persons that we can understand the one God to be the active, living God. Hence we can ascribe attributes to God on the basis of his trinitarian action in the world.

> The action of Father, Son and Spirit in the world is thus ascribed not merely to the three persons of the Trinity but also to the one divine essence...the one God is thus the acting God. But this being as subject is

---

[106] *ST* 1, p.382.

[107] *ST* 1, p.383. Pannenberg here makes the important distinction between the 'impersonal' nature of the field as opposed to the 'person' of the Spirit who can be thought of only as 'a concrete form of the one deity like the Father and the Son.' The implications of this distinction will be followed through in the next chapter.

[108] C. Schwöbel, *Wolfhart Pannenberg*, p.279.

[109] *ST* 1, p.384.

> not a fourth in God alongside the three persons of Father Son and Spirit. It expresses their living fellowship in action towards the world.[110]

The Attributes of God: The Infinity of God

Having grounded the discussion of God's essence and existence in the idea of the Infinite, Pannenberg explores this more fully as the foundation of the first of his two part exposition of the divine attributes.

Following Hegel, Pannenberg argues that the concept of infinity cannot simply be understood as that which stands over against the finite.[111] If this view is taken, as Hegel argued, the concept of the Infinite comes to be defined in terms of that which is finite and thus is limited by that finitude. Neither can the idea of the infinite be simply a mathematical one in any quantitative sense, for similar reasons.[112] Rather, the concept of the Infinite must include within it all that is finite without destroying the difference between the finite and the Infinite. 'We have to think of the Infinite as negation, as the opposite of the finite, but also that it comprehends this antithesis in itself.'[113]

In order to explain this further Pannenberg points to the biblical concept of God's holiness. The basic meaning of holiness is separation from that which is profane, but this is not simply to protect the deity from the profane; it also protects the world from the holy, since God's holiness is primarily seen in his judgement over against the profane.[114] Yet God enters the world in such a way that his holiness incorporates the profane while not collapsing the separation between the holy and the profane; 'the power of the holy, which is a threat to life in its destructive

---

[110] *ST* 1, p.389. Pannenberg explicates this still further by asserting t.he 'repetition' or 'reiteration' of the deity of God in relation to the world in the achievement of his goal, which is understood to be the consummation of creation and the revelation of God's deity as Creator. This reiteration, in contrast to Barth and Jüngel, only applies to God's relation to the world and not to the inner trinitarian life. Behind this concept lies a distinctive view of God's eternity as present to the world at all times and a view of the priority of the future of God which 'breaks into the present of creatures' (p.391).

[111] Cf. Hegel, *Science of Logic*, I.1.

[112] This form of the infinite Hegel referred to as the 'bad infinite' (*das schlecht Unendliche).* See Pannenberg's detailed engagement with Hegel in *Metaphysics and the Idea of God*, pp.35-36.

[113] *ST* 1, p.400.

[114] Here Pannenberg draws heavily upon the concept of holiness elaborated by von Rad. See von Rad *Old Testament Theology,* I, pp.204ff.

force, invades the human world in order to incorporate it into its own sphere.'[115] Here Pannenberg sees a structural parallel to the concept of the Infinite. In terms of the New Testament message this holiness, which comes to the world, is mediated through Jesus Christ and is part of the work of the Holy Spirit. Consequently we can see this structure of the Infinite in the work of the Spirit. The Spirit in his creative and life-giving movement is the form of the coming of the transcendent God to the world to both create and renew that which is finite in such a way that the distinction between God's transcendence and immanence is not removed. 'The biblical view of the divine Spirit in his creative and life-giving work also contains the thought that God gives existence to the finite as that which is different from himself and to give it a share in his own life.'[116]

This structure of opposition and incorporation is determinative for Pannenberg's exposition of eternity, omnipresence and omnipotence. Eternity cannot be viewed simply in antithesis to time as unending time; following Plotinus, eternity is better understood as the presence of the totality of life. Consequently, eternity is the presupposition that facilitates an understanding of time as separate but related moments within the totality of eternity. 'Time is seen as the dissolution of the unity of life into a sequence of separate moments, and yet it is constituted a sequence by reference to the eternal totality.'[117] Pannenberg traces the development of this thought through Boethius to Barth, identifying the significance of Barth's attempt to give a trinitarian interpretation of Plotinus's doctrine of time.[118] Yet Pannenberg focuses on the implied priority of the future in this understanding of time. 'Eternity as the complete totality of life is thus seen from the standpoint of time only in terms of fullness which is sought in the future...the future thus becomes constitutive of the nature of time.'[119] The decisive step for

---

[115] *ST* 1, p.398. 'the holiness of God both opposes the profane world and embraces it, bringing it into fellowship with the holy God' (p.399).

[116] *ST* 1, p.400.

[117] *ST* 1, p.404. See also Pannenberg's discussion of Plotinus and the relation of his thought to Heidegger in *Metaphysics and the Idea of God*, pp.76-82.

[118] Pannenberg observes that Barth's thesis that eternity is the condition of the possibility of time is the basis of his thought, drawn from Boethius, that God's possession of life is central to an understanding of eternity. See *CD* II/1, p.611; see also J. Colwell, *Provisionality and Actuality: a study of the relationship between Karl Barth's Doctrine of Election and Eternity*, PhD Thesis, King's College London, 1985.

[119] *ST* 1, p.408.

Pannenberg is to link this abstract insight with the eschatological fulfilment of the lordship of God. 'Is not the coming of God's lordship the force field which permeates the message and work of Jesus? And is not its future the dawning of the eternity of God in time?'[120] Here Pannenberg's distinctive understanding of the relation between eschatology and time and eternity is outlined; yet the overall structure of this relationship reflects and gives further content to his concept of the Infinite. Eternity is not that which opposes time, but that which embraces it and is positively related to it.

In this model of eternity, all things are present to God, whether they are past, present or future. Consequently this implies a particular view of God's omnipresence in which God is present 'to all things at their place of existence.'[121] Pannenberg is clear that this cannot mean any simplistic extension of the divine essence throughout creation.[122] Rather, after the pattern of the Infinite, God's omnipresence is regarded as combining the concepts of transcendence and immanence.[123] For Pannenberg, the only way in which the union and tension between transcendence and immanence can be clarified is through the doctrine of the Trinity. The transcendence of the Father is mediated in this world by the Son and the Spirit; through the perichoresis of the three persons the Father can be present to humanity through the Son and the Spirit; 'the trinitarian life of God in his economy of salvation proves to be the true infinity of his omnipresence.'[124]

The omnipotence of God is closely related to his omnipresence. God is present to all things as the power and dynamic of the Spirit; 'no power, however great, can be efficacious unless present to its object. Omnipresence is thus a condition of omnipotence.'[125] Yet it is omnipotence that gives content to the meaning of omnipresence. God's omnipotence does not imply unlimited power in any abstract sense;

---

[120] *ST* 1, p.408 This important point, together with its ontological and pneumatological implications, will be examined in the following chapter.

[121] *ST* 1, p.410.

[122] This would imply some corporeal nature to God and inevitably leads to some form of spatial limitation to God; equally this would imply that extension is a divine attribute (as in Spinoza).

[123] Here Pannenberg is critical of Barth who related the omnipotence of God to his love while linking the concept of eternity to his freedom. For Pannenberg this introduces an unacceptable polarisation between the divine attributes.

[124] *ST* 1, p.415.

[125] *ST* 1, p.415 Here Pannenberg follows Barth more readily in agreeing with the statement that 'God's presence includes his lordship.' *CD* II/1, p.461.

rather it is the power of the Creator who wills the existence of his creatures. Further, God exercises his omnipotence in overcoming the alienation between himself and his creation. In this sense his saving acts and especially the incarnation of the Son, have to be understood as 'the supreme expression of the omnipotence of God.'[126] Not that this must be seen as an encounter with the fallen world in power; it is only in the life of the creature, as the incarnate Son, that God overcomes alienation 'in the position of the creature itself.'[127] In this sense the structure of omnipotence again mirrors that of the Infinite as that which embraces that which opposes it and includes the antithesis. Yet, in the case of omnipotence, this is not the mere exercise of raw power; it is the 'power of divine love.'[128]

The Attributes of God: The Love of God

The group of attributes outlined above derive from and expound the idea of God as Infinite; the second group of attributes are expounded under the overall concept of love. These attributes are regarded as those that are predicated on the trinitarian action of God.

From the biblical evidence, Pannenberg asserts that the love of God for the world is the essential content of the history of Jesus; further the love of God is said to come to all who believe (Rom.5.5). Hence Pannenberg argues we must see here the Spirit of God as the subject of this love at work in us and through us.[129] With regard to the statement 'God is love' we must understand this as a statement concerning the essence of God; 'the Johannine saying is not describing a quality of God but his essence or nature as love.'[130] This love is manifested in the

---

[126] *ST* 1, p.421. At the heart of this assertion is Pannenberg's understanding of the Son's relation to the Father as self-distinction; in the incarnation of the Son, God's power enters creation in order to overcome the alienation of the creature but in such a way that the independence of the creature is not violated. This anticipates both the later doctrines of creation and reconciliation.

[127] *ST* 1, p.421.

[128] *ST* 1, p.422.

[129] *ST* 1, p.424.

[130] *ST* 1, p.424. Pannenberg enters into dialogue here with Jüngel's critique of Feuerbach. If the love of God is regarded simply as a quality and not an essence then there remains the possibility that God might be a subject that might exist without love. Pannenberg agrees with Jüngel that theology has to learn from this and seek to equate the concept of God and love at an ontological level. Yet Pannenberg parts company with Jüngel in that he sees the only

mutual relations of the three persons of the Trinity in their actions towards the world. At heart Pannenberg seeks to link the statements 'God is Spirit' and 'God is love' in terms of the unity of the divine essence which is established in the fellowship and mutual working of Father, Son and Holy Spirit. 'Love is no more a separate subject than the Spirit apart from the three persons...(they) constitute the common essence of deity.'[131] Here Pannenberg wishes to expound the Spirit as a dynamic field actively manifesting the love of God, uniting the divine persons and flowing out to the world; in this sense 'The Spirit is the power of love that lets the other be. This power can thus give existence to creaturely life...'[132]

It remains for Pannenberg to explain how the personal presence of the love of God in the hearts of believers relates to the Holy Spirit as third person of the Trinity. He asserts that the Spirit must be understood as a separate hypostasis in that he stands over against the Father and Son; yet the Spirit is never biblically described as the object of the love of Father or Son. Thus the Spirit must be seen as the love which mutually relates Father and Son while standing over against them as a distinct hypostasis; 'the Spirit is the love by which the Father and Son are mutually related...as a hypostasis, however, the Spirit...can be at work in creation.'[133] Hence Pannenberg sees the Spirit as love constituting the essence of God while coming forth as a separate hypostasis as the Holy Spirit.

---

possible explication of this in terms of the fellowship of the persons of the Trinity. Jüngel is criticised for making God the subject of his self- giving love; 'if...the one loves self in the other instead of loving the other as other , then love falls short of the full self-giving which is the condition that the one who loves be given self afresh in the responsive love of the one who is loved.' (p.426) For Pannenberg, the trinitarian God is the subject of his love only in the outward activity of the three persons.

[131] *ST* 1, p.428-9.

[132] *ST* 1, p.427. This outward creative act is predicated on the eternal reciprіcocity of the trinitarian relations. Here Pannenberg is at pains to distinguish his explicitly trinitarian concept from an existentialist theory of being (cf. J. Macquarrie, *Principles of Christian Theology*, 1966, pp.311-12 which Pannenberg criticises in some detail).

[133] *ST* 1, p.429.

> Thus divine love constitutes the concrete unity of the divine life in the distinction of its personal manifestations and relations...but...unity in the divine essence makes sense as the concrete reality of the divine love which pulses through all things and which consummates the monarchy of the Father through the Son in the Holy Spirit.[134]

Pannenberg goes on to present the remaining attributes, goodness, grace, mercy, righteousness, faithfulness, patience and wisdom as 'concrete aspects' of the divine love.[135] These are seen as descriptive of the aspects of the divine love in the sense that love unites them. Of particular note is Pannenberg's repeated appeal to the Eschaton as the point of resolution for tensions in some of these concepts. For example, in the discussion of God's faithfulness, it is argued that historicity and the contingency of world events do not contradict ideas of God's eternity. Contrary to traditional views of divine immutability, God is at work in the world bringing history to a consummation at the Eschaton. Viewed from the perspective of history there is thus room for a 'becoming' in God understood strictly in terms of the relation of the immanent and economic Trinity. Eternity and time coincide only at the Eschaton; only here is the unity of the immanent and economic Trinity conceived.[136]

With the enumeration of these attributes Pannenberg concludes the formal presentation of his doctrine of God. The central notion of God as Infinite is given dogmatic expression in the doctrine of God as Spirit; here the implications of Pannenberg's use of the image of a field of force will require detailed investigation. The Spirit is revealed in trinitarian form as the divine love in which God exists as Father, Son and Holy Spirit. Love 'gives concrete form to the divine unity in its

---

[134] *ST* 1, p.432. A full discussion of this formulation will follow in the next chapter. In particular it may be questioned whether this understanding of the relationship between the essence of God as Spirit and the third person of the Trinity is adequate, and to what extent this is dependent on Pannenberg's concept of the Infinite.

[135] *ST* 1, p.432.

[136] *ST* 1., p.438 It is most important here to see that Pannenberg is not advocating the 'divine becoming' of Process thought, neither does he understand this term in the same way as Jüngel. Rather it is the involvement of the eternal God in time, in anticipation of the eschatological consummation, which means Pannenberg can speak of God 'becoming something he previously was not when he became man in his Son.'

relation to the world; it also represents the taking up of the plurality of the divine attributes into the unity of the divine life.'[137] Hence it is through the concept of love in its trinitarian structure that Pannenberg conceptually links the unity of the divine essence with existence, and consequently the immanent and economic Trinity. It is thus the trinitarian conception of love which is the 'coping stone' of Pannenberg's doctrine of God.[138]

Critical Discussion

The following critical discussion will focus on three areas that are most pertinent to our theme.

Methodology

Pannenberg's desire to find a mediating position between a dogmatic theology which fails to give adequate reason for belief and the alternative rationalist perspective has drawn varied criticism. For some, Pannenberg fails to take seriously the human problem of sin and spiritual blindness which brings into question his view of the epistemic openness of revelation.[139] He is consequently accused of failing to adequately conceive of the consequences of the fallen state of humankind. Such criticisms tend to regard Pannenberg as a rationalist, refusing to ground theology on presuppositions accepted in faith.

Yet there are those who find in Pannenberg the opposite tendency, accusing him of his own form of subjectivity. Reacting to Pannenberg's earlier writing, Obitts argued that a particular understanding of faith is presupposed in the contention that historical events contain within themselves their own meaning.[140] In response to the approach in the *Systematic Theology*, it has been argued that Pannenberg himself does not avoid a form of subjectivism. By grounding our knowledge of God in the human religious experience of the infinite, whether unthematic or given content in the resurrection of Christ, there is an inevitable sense in

---

[137] *ST* 1, p.447.

[138] Schwöbel, *Wolfhart Pannenberg*, p.287.

[139] J.R. Ross, 'Historical Knowledge as a Basis for Faith,' *Zygon*, 13, 1978, 209-224.

[140] S. Obitts, 'Apostolic Eyewitnesses and Proleptically Historical Revelation,' in Inch and Youngblood *The Living and Active Word of God*, Eisenbrauns, 1983, pp.137-149.

which the noetic becomes essential to our concept of God; what gives final validity to the concept of God? Is it the ontological reality of God or the reality of God defined by our experience of God? It is suggested that Pannenberg affirms the former, but his methodology assumes the latter.[141]

A related point may be made with regard to Pannenberg's understanding of the historical content of revelation. If historical events are viewed as bearing revelatory significance, does this simply imply a prior faith commitment which facilitates that understanding? This is the thrust of Newland's observation; 'To see the events themselves as constitutive of revelation, as disclosures of the character of God, is itself an act of faith.'[142]

Yet it is hard to portray Pannenberg as a theologian for whom the task is an explanation of reality from the perspective of faith. Schwöbel has identified a significant problem in Pannenberg's methodological use of the universal religious awareness as the foundation for expounding the universal truth claims of the Christian Faith.[143] When anthropological and epistemological reflection are used as the ground for systematic exposition of the contents of faith, the risk then is not simply a confusion between the epistemic and the ontic, but that theological foundations are built on non-theological, rationalist concepts.[144]

The fundamental question remains; is it necessary to find a basis for the universality of the Christian Faith before expounding the contents of faith as revealed, or can that universality be regarded as an outcome of the view of reality argued from the perspective of faith which is grounded in revelation?

If this constitutes the primary question concerning Pannenberg's methodology, then certain more specific questions concerning particular loci of doctrine emerge.

One group of criticisms centres around the uniqueness of Christianity and Pannenberg's assessment of other religions. Cobb has argued that Pannenberg undervalues the role of world religions; regarding them as

---

[141] P. Molnar 'Some Problems with Pannenberg's Solution to Barth's "Faith Subjectivism,"' *Scottish Journal of Theology*, 48.3, 1995, pp.315-339. This argument rests on a critique of Pannenberg's use of Heidegger's concept of anticipation as the ground of our knowledge of God.

[142] Newlands, *God in Christian Perspective*, 1994, p.236.

[143] Schwöbel, *Wolfhart Pannenberg*, pp.286-7.

[144] Schwöbel, *Wolfhart Pannenberg*.. 'The central role of the concept of the Infinite would seem to provide evidence for this danger.' p.287.

contributions or provisional forms fails to do justice to them as complex, self-enclosed entities.[145] Others have questioned Pannenberg's understanding of the soteriological significance of the religions; in what sense might the history of religions be 'oriented to salvation, as the history of the unending human quest for wholeness,' yet not be 'ways of salvation.'[146] Grenz points out that Pannenberg's approach in the *Systematic Theology* does not deny that different religions may have differing conceptions of the ultimate; rather the history of religions is seen as the struggle between rival truth claims as to which conception best illuminates the human experience of reality.[147] It remains questionable whether Pannenberg's use of the history of religions simply serves to ground his understanding of the foundational importance of the doctrine of revelation for the doctrine of God. In this respect it may be observed that the underlying philosophical presupposition in his view of the history of religions is the unthematic awareness of the presence of the Infinite; it is open to question whether Pannenberg's exposition of the attributes of God in terms of the Infinite is required by this presupposition.[148]

Pannenberg's doctrine of revelation has been much debated since his earliest writing, and early criticism of a certain narrowness of view has been redressed to a degree in the *Systematic Theology*. 'Categories such as word, sign, divine wisdom and hidden mysteries now revealed all find their place in Pannenberg's understanding of revelation.'[149] Yet Pannenberg continues to deny any conceptualisation of a direct revelation in 'the word of God,' whether that is understood in a conservative sense of inspired Scripture or the existential sense of an event which conveys its own revelatory significance.[150] Rather, he

---

[145] J. Cobb, 'The Meaning of Pluralism for Christian Self- understanding,' in L. Rouner (ed.) *Religious Pluralism*, Notre Dame, 1984.

[146] C. Braaton, 'Christianity among the World Religions,' in Braaton and Clayton (eds) *The Theology of Wolfhart Pannenberg*, p.311.

[147] Grenz, *Reason for Hope*, pp.35-36. In this sense 'the point of congruence between the religions' is the provision of 'a unified understanding of experienced reality.'

[148] Cf. the critique of Schwöbel, *Wolfhart Pannenberg*, p.286. It is this emphasis on the non-thematic awareness of the Infinite which, in turn, is central to Pannenberg's religious epistemology.

[149] Grenz, *Reason for Hope*, p.37.

[150] At the heart of this lies Pannenberg's conviction that revelation is indirect and seen in the acts of God; 'the various biblical ideas of the Word of God do not treat God himself as the content of the Word...when we think of God's self-

emphasises the divergent use of the phrase 'word of God' in Scripture and understands that in terms of the historical development of the biblical tradition.

This has led some to accuse Pannenberg of elevating the historical at the expense of the existential encounter, seeing the historian as greater than the prophet.[151] While this may overstate the case, it is central for Pannenberg to maintain the historical foundation of the Christian Faith; what he argues for is an understanding of the decision of faith as grounded on historical events.

For some this leaves no room for the traditional view of the Spirit as 'inspirer;' in particular there seems to be little room for an understanding of the work of the Holy Spirit as an 'external agency' in the human grasp of revelation. Fuller's early critique pointed to biblical examples of the lack of response to apostolic preaching and interpreted this in terms of the 'missing work' of the Spirit.[152] McDermott argues that the Spirit is necessary not only to overcome the barrier of human sinfulness but to interpret the mystery of God and attune the finite human mind to the things of God.[153] Pannenberg's view is that the Spirit is present in the process but not in any sense that the Spirit is external, acting by way of supernatural inspiration. Events carry their own meaning within them. Grenz correctly locates Pannenberg's understanding within the context of Luther's view of the Spirit which inheres within the word and is actively present within it; 'event and word are for Pannenberg a unity in which the Spirit is already present, similar to the Lutheran concept of the sacramental power of the word.'[154]

Detailed discussion of the person and work of the Spirit will form the main substance of the following chapter.

---

revelation we have to think of it as mediated by his action.' *ST* 1, p.243.

[151] See A. Dulles, *Models of Revelation*, Doubleday, New York, 1983, pp.64-66. See also the extended response of Pannenberg to criticisms of James Barr in chapter four of *ST* 1.

[152] D. Fuller, *Easter Faith and History*, Eerdmans, Grand Rapids, 1965.

[153] B. McDermott, *'The Personal Unity of Jesus and God according to W. Pannenberg*,' PhD, Nijmegan, 1973.

[154] Grenz, *Reason for Hope*, p.41.

The Resurrection of Jesus

In perceiving the central importance of the resurrection of Jesus for Pannenberg's whole dogmatic structure, many have focused their criticisms at this point. For the purposes of this thesis two general areas will be outlined since these have implications for Pannenberg's pneumatology.

First, Pannenberg staunchly maintains the historicity of the resurrection, basing his argument on the convergence of the two streams of tradition, the resurrection appearances and the empty tomb. Some criticism has been levelled at the exegetical level; Placher argues that Paul never refers to the empty tomb and maintains that early Judaism would not have regarded an empty tomb as a necessary evidence of resurrection.[155] Grenz makes the point that, since many of these criticisms come from differing theological perspectives, they tend to contradict one another, thus losing much of their force. In the *Systematic Theology* there is greater emphasis on the resurrection appearances as the primary historical evidence, the empty tomb tradition telling us more about the kind of reality that the risen Christ presents us with.[156]

More generally, it has been questioned whether the resurrection as a unique event is susceptible to the normal methods of historical enquiry. Jenson remarks that 'without the historical verifiability of Jesus' resurrection, the structure of Pannenberg's doctrines of Christ and God would have to be altered drastically;' yet Jenson is not convinced that '"Jesus is risen" is an assertion which a historian can confirm.'[157] In the light of such criticism does this make Pannenberg's own commitment to the public nature of theology difficult to pursue, since resurrection is not part of 'the commonsense body of knowledge of contemporary society?'[158]

Here Pannenberg's appeal to the provisionality of all knowledge prior to the Eschaton means that, for him, the question of the historicity of the resurrection remains open. Yet given the importance of the

---

155 W. Placher, 'The Present Absence of Christ,' in *Encounter*, 40, 1979.

156 Grenz, *Reason for Hope*, p.143.

157 R. Jenson, 'Jesus in the Trinity: Wolfhart Pannenberg's Christology and Doctrine of the Trinity,' in Braaten and Clayton (eds) *The Theology of Wolfhart Pannenberg*, pp.190-91. Jenson further notes that the historical method demanded by Pannenberg here leaves him isolated from most historians.

158 Y.S. Kim, '*Jesus and the Triune God: a Study of the Relationship between Christology and the Doctrine of the Trinity in Wolfhart Pannenberg's Theology*,' PhD, King's College London, 1992, p.223.

verifiability of the resurrection in Pannenberg's thought, the underlying philosophical concepts of provisionality and anticipation are asked to carry a great burden in retaining some semblance of coherence to this theological edifice.[159]

Equally strongly criticised is Pannenberg's attempt to contextualise the resurrection within Jewish apocalyptic thought. This is important since it illustrates how the interpretation of an event can arise out of the event itself within its historical context. Polk has argued that Pannenberg makes uncritical use of a view of apocalyptic put forward by Rossler.[160] This work argued that the main theme in Jewish apocalyptic was the unity of all history. Polk identifies the affinity between this interpretation and Pannenberg but questions whether this is an accurate portrait of apocalyptic thought; he suggests that there is far greater diversity within the apocalyptic literature and, generally, a much less positive view of history is found.[161] Although Pannenberg maintains that the resurrection of Christ gave new meaning to apocalyptic thought, it is open to question whether the idea of resurrection played such an important role in this as Pannenberg maintains. The significance of this critique for the purposes of this thesis is that it questions the way in which Pannenberg sees events as containing within them their own interpretation, and this in turn relates to Pannenberg's pneumatology.

The second major focus of criticism of Pannenberg's doctrine of the resurrection which impinges upon his pneumatology is the nature of the reality of the risen Christ. For Pannenberg the language of the resurrection is metaphorical.[162] Some have found the recourse to metaphor surprising, variously suggesting that Pannenberg has proposed that the resurrection be understood as 'metahistory,' or give some form

---

[159] These concepts will be analysed fully in the following chapter.

[160] D. Polk, *On the Way to God. An Exploration into the Theology of Wolfhart Pannenberg*, Lanham, 1989, making reference to D. Rossler, *Gesetz und Geschichte: Untersuchangen zur Theologie der Judischen Apokalyptik und der Pharisaischen Orthodoxie,* Neukirchen, 1960.

[161] Polk's critique must be weighed in the light of his own preference for process thought and also in contrast to widely varying understandings of apocalyptic. See D.S. Russell, *The Method and Message of Jewish Apocalyptic*, London, 1964.

[162] *ST* 2, pp.346-47. Pannenberg is anxious to maintain that his use of the term metaphor does not bring into question the historical reality of the resurrection. It is a 'real event' yet since it is a unique event, not in everyday experience, it is 'stated metaphorically' (p.346).

of special historicity.[163] Yet in the *Systematic Theology*, Pannenberg expands the concept of metaphor to include the goal of the process it describes, namely new life.[164] Since this new life is understood to be the gift of the Spirit, when applied to the resurrection of Jesus this leads to a form of 'Spirit-Christology of the risen Lord.'[165] For Pannenberg, the resurrection is not simply a confirmation of the claims of Jesus in his ministry; this event 'determines what the meaning was of the pre-Easter history of Jesus...to do this the event had to be an event with its own weight and content, namely the resurrection of Jesus to a new life with God.'[166] The implications of this for pneumatology and, in particular, the relationship of the Spirit to Christ will be investigated in the next chapter.

The Trinitarian Doctrine of God

As Jenson correctly comments, the goal of Pannenberg's formulation of the Trinity is to expunge any view of the triune life of God in terms of the unfolding of a single divine subject.[167] Consequently Pannenberg rejects any attempt to derive the trinitarian distinctions from the one reality of God on the grounds that any such derivation will inevitably result in a form of subordinationism or modalism. Yet he has been criticised for introducing a new form of subordinationism through his distinctive view of the monarchy of the Father.[168] Given that the Father's monarchy is mediated by the Son and the Spirit and is regarded as the goal of the trinitarian relationships rather than the origin, there are

---

[163] R. North, 'Pannenberg's historicizing exegesis,' *Heythrop Journal*, 12, p.136, 1971.

[164] Pannenberg specifically makes the point that here "life" is not used metaphorically but refers to the new eschatological life, eternal life. *ST* 2, p.347.

[165] Grenz, *Reason for Hope*, p.141.

[166] *ST* 2, p.345. By the Spirit Jesus was raised to new life as the eschatological 'new man' and by the same Spirit humanity is granted fellowship in that new life. The retroactive view of the effect of the resurrection rests upon Pannenberg's problematic ontology, which will be examined in the next chapter.

[167] R. Jenson, *Jesus in the Trinity: Wolfhart Pannenberg's Christology and Doctrine of the Trinity*, p.201. Such a model is regarded as deriving from German Idealism.

[168] R. Olson, 'Wolfhart Pannenberg's Doctrine of the Trinity,' *Scottish Journal of Theology*, 43, pp.175-206, 1990.

still strong hints towards the supremacy of the Father; Pannenberg affirms Harnacks view that 'the Gospel has to do with the Father only.'[169] 'In his monarchy the Father is the one God;'[170] however heavily such statements are qualified, the fact that Pannenberg reverses the orthodox understanding of the monarchy of the Father by positing it as the eschatological goal, does not necessarily leave him free from such accusations. This is even more the case when one considers his view of God as the power of the future. Olson's charge of subordinationism, on closer consideration of the truly reciprocal nature of the trinitarian relationships envisaged by Pannenberg, may be hard to substantiate. Yet an element of confusion is caused by statements such as those cited.

A second area of criticism concerns Pannenberg's use of the term self-differentiation. As Grenz argues this raises the complicated question of Pannenberg's relationship to the thought of Hegel. Certainly Pannenberg credits Hegel with recognising the importance of the Trinity and the need to examine God's being in relation to his historical acts. This intellectual pedigree has caused some to criticise Pannenberg as Hegelian.[171] For example, it has been suggested that the concept of universal history is as important for Pannenberg as it is for Hegel.[172] Yet Pannenberg is critical of Hegel for failing to make an adequate distinction between God and history. It is through the concept of mutual self-distinction and the related reciprocal relationship between the economic Trinity and the immanent Trinity, that Pannenberg develops an understanding of God's activity in history without the being of God being limited by the process. For Grenz this marks an 'important move beyond Hegel.'[173] Pannenberg still wishes to identify the reality of God from his historical immanence, attempting to hold together God and the world in such a way that the world, in some way, shapes the being of God, while God remains the one on whom all things depend. As Gunton has argued, this approach reveals Pannenberg's indebtedness to

---

[169] *ST* 1, p.325. Yet this should be balanced by the qualifying comment that 'there is no justification for applying the term Father to the triune God as a whole.'

[170] *ST* 1, p.326

[171] For example, T. Bradshaw, *Trinity and Ontology*, in which the comparison of Pannenberg with Barth seeks to expose a strong degree of mutual indebtedness of Hegel.

[172] C.P. Venema, 'History, Human Freedom , and the idea of God in the Theology of Wolfhart Pannenberg,' *Calvin Theological Journal*, 17, April 1982, p.75.

[173] Grenz, *Reason for Hope*, p.72.

Hegelian philosophy which locates God's being and action within God's presence in the world.[174]

A third, related area of criticism relates to Pannenberg's exposition of Father, Son and Spirit as persons. Here the lengthy critique of Jenson is significant.[175] While accepting the principle of mutual self-distinction as constitutive for the deity of the trinitarian persons, Jenson questions whether the modern term 'person' can be adequately applied to denote the three in God; neither does he see the necessity for surrendering the concept of the one God as personal. Jenson sees that the language of 'person' in the modern sense of a self-conscious being can be used of Jesus, but finds it hard to relate the concept to the Father and the Spirit. 'Pannenberg's interpretation of the Spirit's glorification of the Son or the Father's giving over of rule to the Son as acts of personal self-distinction seems to me a bit stretched.'[176] Further, the consequence of Pannenberg's position mean that the persons are not persons in the same way, they are inter-related by a multiplicity of relations. The abandonment of the language of the begetting Father, the begotten Son and the breathed Spirit undermines the concept of the trinitarian persons as subsisting relations, a key doctrine which Jenson holds to be a 'major achievement of Western thought.'[177] This critique serves to highlight the profound shift in major areas of doctrine which Pannenberg proposes.

A similar point is made by Gunton. The language of the self-distinction of the Son from the Father underpins Pannenberg's understanding of the distinctiveness of creation from God. Not only does this displace the traditional language of the Father 'begetting' the Son, but this can attribute to great a role for the Son in initiating creation. Biblically, the Son is the agent of creation, the one through whom the Father creates. In other words, the self-distinction of Jesus from the Father tends to override his being sent into the world.[178]

A cluster of critical comments centre around Pannenberg's complex view of the relationship between God and the world. Theologically this is expressed in terms of the relationship between the immanent Trinity

---

[174] C. Gunton, 'The Being and Attributes of God,' in Webster (ed.) *The Possibilities of Theology*, pp.7-22. This point is made in the context of discussion of the influence of Hegel on modern German Christology, specific reference being made to Jüngel and Pannenberg.

[175] R. Jenson, *Jesus in the Trinity*, pp.201-203.

[176] Jenson, *Jesus in the Trinity*, pp.202.

[177] Jenson, *Jesus in the Trinity*, p.203.

[178] C. Gunton, *The Triune Creator*, Edinburgh, 1998, p.159.

and the economic Trinity. Philosophically this involves the concept of the futurity of the being of God.

For Pannenberg, the deity of the Father is dependent upon the work of the Son in history and the eschatological work of the Spirit. In essence, the concept of self-differentiation, understood in a fully reciprocal form, leads to a view of the being of God as not only eternal but eschatological. For Pannenberg, the actual being of God is linked to the consummation of the Kingdom which is future. Olson questions whether, in this scheme, it is possible to understand the unity of God in the present.[179] He suggests that it might be possible to conceive of a future completion of God's glory and power, but argues that the same is doctrinally more difficult with regard to the unity of God. Once again the nuances of Pannenberg's position should not be underestimated; in particular the reciprocal relationship of the immanent and economic Trinity allows Pannenberg to posit the unity of God in terms of the eschatological monarchy of the Father while insisting that the unity of Father, Son and Spirit 'finds expression in the relations of salvation history...their mutual perichoresis must also be seen as an expression of the unity of the divine essence.'[180]

The carefully worked argument relating the immanent Trinity and economic Trinity to some degree dissipates earlier criticisms regarding a perceived dependence of God on history.[181] By contrast, some have perceived a strong element of determinism in Pannenberg's ontology of the future. McKenzie, writing from a position more sympathetic to Process thought, argues that Pannenberg has completely failed to integrate divine causality with human freedom.[182] This type of criticism requires more careful structuring in the light of the proposals in the*Systematic Theology*.

Underlying these critical stances is the difficult concept of the ontological priority of the future. Grenz maintains that the *Systematic*

---

[179] R. Olson, 'Wolfhart Pannenberg's Doctrine of the Trinity,' p.199. Olson actually questions whether Pannenberg's theology requires a way of viewing the unity of God in the present.

[180] *ST* 1, p.334. It should be noted that Pannenberg cannot accept the concept of perichoresis as a basis for the unity of the persons; rather it presupposes a different basis of that unity.

[181] For example, Hill suggested that Pannenberg effectively equated God with history; W.J. Hill, *The Three-Personed God*, Washington, 1982.

[182] D. McKenzie, *Wolfhart Pannenberg and Religious Philosophy*, Washington, 1980.

Theology is, at one level, an explication of this concept.[183] Here Grenz, usually positive in his assessment of Pannenberg, admits that the relationship between epistemology and ontology is a 'ticklish question.'[184] Olson questions whether the newly formulated doctrine of the Trinity sheds light on Pannenberg's ontology or whether it simply deepens the enigma.[185]

Olthus argues that Pannenberg's ontology leads him to his particular view of God as Infinite.[186] It is argued that the result of this is a reworking of the major theological concepts in a way which runs counter to biblical thought and theological tradition. For example, reconciliation becomes a participation in the infinity and unity of God rather than an act of grace and mercy; the fall, sin and evil become part of a cosmic process, they are 'domesticated' and seemingly have no destructive power.[187] These are significant criticisms and show how the underlying philosophical perspectives, when worked out in various doctrinal loci, reveal a substantial reworking of Christian thought.

One particular example of this is seen in Pannenberg's pneumatology. Here many questions relate to those raised above. Is the concept of field the best descriptive model for the essence of God as Spirit? How does this model relate to an understanding of the Holy Spirit as personal? Within the Trinity is the Spirit best described as person or as love?[188]

---

[183] Grenz, *Reason for Hope*, p.74.

[184] Grenz, *Reason for Hope*, p.74 Grenz briefly contrasts Pannenberg with Moltmann. 'Pannenberg's position would be simplified....were he only intending to speak epistemologically' (p.75).

[185] R. Olson, *Wolfhart Pannenberg's Doctrine of the Trinity*, p.199. Olson concludes that the enigma is deepened.

[186] J. Olthus, 'God as True Infinite: Concerns about Wolfhart Pannenberg's Systematic Theology Vol.1,' in *Calvin Theological Journal*, 27.2, Nov.1992, pp.318-25.

[187] J. Olthus, 'God as True Infinite: Concerns about Wolfhart Pannenberg's Systematic Theology Vol.1,' Olthus grounds his argument by seeking to demonstrate how Pannenberg replaces the concept of fallenness with the idea of finitude.

[188] For a preliminary examination of these questions see S. Grenz, 'The Irrelevancy of Theology: Pannenberg and the Quest for Truth,' in *Calvin Theological Journal*, 27.2, Nov. 1992, pp.307-11.

The answers to such questions will illuminate Pannenberg's exposition of the doctrine of the Spirit. To this more detailed enquiry we now turn.

Chapter 4

Pannenberg's Doctrine of the Spirit and the Infinity of God

Introduction

We have seen that, for Pannenberg, it is axiomatic that the divine essence is not understood as 'external to the category of relations.'[1] The particular model which Pannenberg employs to describe the divine essence is the scientific idea of a force field. He sees in this concept possibilities for a 'new understanding of the relations between the trinitarian persons and divine essence that is common to all of them.'[2] The idea of a field of force facilitates a particular interpretation of the biblical concept of God as Spirit; in this sense Pannenberg uses the idea to explain both the divine essence as Spirit and to expound an understanding of the person of the Holy Spirit.

Closely related to Pannenberg's use of the field concept is his appropriation of the idea of God as the true infinite. Part of the purpose of this chapter is to explore the relationship between Pannenberg's use of field theory and his view of the infinity of God. His doctrine of the Spirit will be seen to depend on this relationship.

We will firstly examine Pannenberg's use of field theory as a model for interpreting the statement 'God is Spirit.' This will involve an assessment of the structural importance of Pannenberg's related understanding of the divine essence in terms of infinity. This will give rise to key ontological questions that ground Pannenberg's use of these concepts. The resulting critical analysis will focus on the implications of these ideas for Pannenberg's pneumatology. It will be questioned whether the concept of the Spirit as an infinite field of force is the most appropriate approach to Trinitarian pneumatology and to what extent this restricts description of the Spirit in personal terms.

---

[1] *ST* 1, p.335
[2] *ST* 1, p.335

The Divine Essence as a Dynamic Field of Force

Pannenberg's concept of divine essence as relationally defined contrasts with the Aristotelian view of essence as substance.[3] Pannenberg outlines how this has become problematic in modern thought. In the light of the philosophy of Kant and Hegel, and in keeping with theories in modern physics, we are to think of relations as 'above that of substance.'[4]

This has profound consequences for a theological expression of the essence of God. Pannenberg sees that the concept of essence as relational gives opportunity to expound the trinitarian relations and God's relationship to the world in new ways. As previously noted, in exploring these relationships, the concept of divine action is of central importance

It is here that Pannenberg sees the importance of interpreting the idea of the essence of God as Spirit in terms of modern field theory. This model provides Pannenberg with a way of ascribing to God the dynamic functions of creativity and life, without describing the essence of God in terms of a self-conscious willing subject which is independent of the trinitarian relations. It enables him to speak of the unity of the divine essence in relational terms and to express the three persons of the Trinity as manifestations and 'concretions' of the divine essence as Spirit.

The Divine Presence as Field: The Trinity and Creation

Pannenberg constructs his model of the Spirit as a field of force from three sources. He brings together biblical teaching concerning the Spirit, the philosophical origins of the concept *pneuma*, and modern scientific field theory as originally developed by Clark Maxwell. By looking at these three sources the main characteristics of the proposed field theory will become apparent. Pannenberg develops his theological appropriation of field theory within his doctrine of creation.[5]

---

[3] 'Aristotle thought of the essence of things as substance, as that which remains the same beneath all change.' *ST* 1, p.365.

[4] *ST* 1, p.366.

[5] It might be pointed out here that by developing a pneumatology within the context of the doctrine of creation Pannenberg exhibits the Lutheran

From the Old Testament Pannenberg characterises the Spirit as a creative and life giving dynamic; 'The Spirit is the force field of God's mighty presence.'[6] He is the 'life-giving principle, to which all creatures owe life, movement and activity.'[7] The life-giving activity of the Spirit is the first of two main emphases that Pannenberg finds in the biblical testimony. Central to this exposition is a trinitarian understanding of creation.

The mutual self-distinction of the Father and the Son forms the basis for the distinction between God and creation. 'The Son is the origin of all that differs from the Father;'[8] in other words the differentiation of the eternal Son from the Father is the ontic basis for all other creaturely existence.

Underlying this we can discern Hegel's 'principle of otherness' by which all that is finite is grounded in the person of the Son. Pannenberg re-interprets this by affirming the mutuality of the trinitarian relations. Whereas Hegel made creation a necessary development of the Absolute, Pannenberg regards his formulation of the Trinity as preserving God's freedom; the divine life is 'a self-enclosed circle, which needs no other outside itself.'[9]

While the Son is therefore seen as the principle of created distinction and particularity, the Father is regarded as the 'origin of creatures in their contingency.'[10] It is the Father who grants their existence and makes possible their continued life. The Father loves

---

emphasis most clearly summarised in Prenter's study *'Spiritus Creator,'* Philadelphia, 1953. The significance of the Lutheran tradition for Pannenberg's own pneumatology will be examined in the following chapter.

[6] *ST* 1, p.382. Here Pannenberg relates the Spirit as the immanent presence of God to God's omniscience. Because God is present with his creatures he possesses all-embracing knowledge of them.

[7] *ST* 2, p.76.

[8] *ST* 2, p.22. Pannenberg supports this understanding by appealing to the biblical language of the Son's mediation and the agency of the Logos in creation (Hebs. 1:2, John 1:3).

[9] *ST* 2, pp.28-9. Yet it is the event of the incarnation through which the Son 'gives validity' to the independent existence of other creatures. The self-distinction of the Son is, for Pannenberg, the basis of creaturely existence in distinction from God. It is a matter of debate as to whether this completely avoids the idea of a necessity of creation for the being of God. By focusing on the incarnation as the ground of creaturely existence the problem may simply be seen to arise but in a different form.

[10] *ST* 2, p.21.

his creatures, yet this love is mediated through the Son. 'The creatures are the objects of the Father's love as they are drawn into his eternal turning to the Son.'[11] The self-distinction of the Son from the Father is the ground of created reality.

Pannenberg goes to considerable lengths to maintain the freedom of God in this process. The Father sends the Son but the Son freely acts to fulfil his Sonship; there is complete unity of will between Father and Son who are united in their distinction by what Pannenberg refers to as 'a third thing,' namely the fellowship of the Spirit:

Thus creation is a free act of God as an expression of

> the freedom of the Son in his self-distinction from the Father, and of the freedom of the fatherly goodness that in the Son accepts the possibility and the existence of a creation distinct from himself, and of the freedom of the Spirit who links the two in free agreement.[12]

The distinctive role of the Spirit as the giver of life is thus expressed in two ways. On one side, the Spirit functions as the principle of divine immanence whereby the transcendent God is present in creation. On the other hand he is the means by which creatures participate in the divine life; 'the Spirit is the element of the fellowship of the creatures with God and their participation in his life, notwithstanding their distinction from him.'[13] Continued existence is only possible by participation in God. This is true not only because God is the life-giver, but also because the goal of the creature is to find fulfilment in transcending its own finitude.[14]

---

[11] *ST 2*, p.21 In other words the love of the Father is directed towards his creatures 'because the eternal Son is manifested in them.' Once again, the self-distinction of Jesus from the Father is constitutive.

[12] *ST 2,* p.30. Once again Pannenberg distinguishes his position from Hegel on the basis of creation as a free act of God based upon the principle of self-distinction.

[13] *ST 2,* p.30

[14] Pannenberg describes this as 'the special work of the Spirit in creation,' This is understood in part as an 'inner dynamic' of the life of creation whereby increasing complexity is understood in terms of growing participation in the life of God. Here Pannenberg interacts with the writings of Teilhard de Chardin where the evolution of life forms is interpreted as increasing intensity of participation in the divine life. This is marked by

This leads to the second main way in which Pannenberg describes the work of the Spirit in creation. He is not only the giver of life but he is also the 'creative principle of movement.'[15] This concept is drawn primarily from an exegesis of the Hebrew word 'ruach.' The first account of creation in Genesis refers to the 'wind' of God moving over the 'face of the waters.' (Gen. 1:2) The Spirit of God is here depicted as a violent wind; this is close to the idea of the life-giving breath of God, and is related to the creative speech of God. 'God's breathing is a raging storm and from its dynamic issues the creative speaking. The Spirit of God is the creative principle of movement...'[16] It is movement towards a goal; the Spirit orientates the creature eschatologically.

It is here that Pannenberg finds an affinity between the scriptural account of the Spirit's work in creation and the moving forces which are a main theme of modern physics. Classical dynamics viewed forces in terms of the movement of bodies and the relations between bodies. Newtonian mechanics marked an advance on this view by not limiting the idea of force to the movement of bodies; force came to be regarded as an independent reality that could result in the movement of bodies. Newton's theory of gravity was particularly relevant in marking this shift of emphasis. Subsequent developments by Farady and Clark Maxwell emphasised the idea of force and its manifestations in terms of the relationship between differing degrees of energy at different spatial points within a field.

Pannenberg argues the theological significance of this in three ways.

First, the origins of the field concept can be traced back to pre-Socratic philosophy. Following Max Jammer, Pannenberg argues that the Stoic idea of *pneuma* was the forerunner of the modern field concept. This *pneuma* was the fine substance which held all things together. As mentioned earlier, the equating of the divine Spirit with the Stoic concept of *pneuma* met fierce opposition in the light of the material nature of the *pneuma*. Modern field theories do not require this material nature since the concept of the ether has been dismissed; 'insofar as the field concept corresponds to the older doctrines it...does justice to the history and concept of spirit if we relate the

---

increasing self-distinction from God as the creatures increasingly participate in the life of the Spirit.

15 *ST* 2, p.30.

16 *ST 2*, p.79.

field theories of modern physics to...the dynamic work of the divine Spirit in creation.'[17]

Secondly, Pannenberg finds here a philosophical alternative to Aristotelian metaphysics. Like the pre-Newtonian physics, Aristotelian philosophy focused upon the body as the source of movement. All natural events were grounded in God as the first cause of all movement, the 'unmoved mover.' With the renewed understanding of the primacy of force over against substance it is possible for Christian theology to interpret the function of the Spirit in creation in terms of energy and movement.

Thirdly, Pannenberg is anxious to maintain that theology has its own reasons for using the field concept, such as those worked out in his own doctrine of the Trinity; in this sense theology is 'justified in developing such concepts in a way appropriate to its own themes.'[18]

Following his brief excursus into the history of science Pannenberg makes some significant statements concerning the role of the Spirit in creation and how the concept of field might relate to the third person of the Trinity.

The Holy Spirit and the Divine Essence

Pannenberg uses the concept of field to expound the difference between the divine essence as Spirit and the third person of the Trinity. Understood in terms of a force field of divine presence the idea of Spirit seems impersonal. Yet, in trinitarian terms, the Holy Spirit must be viewed as standing in distinction from the Father and the Son; he has his own 'centre of action.'[19] In a critical move, Pannenberg makes the self-distinction of the Spirit the basis of the unity of the Father and the Son. 'Precisely because the common essence of the deity stands over against both in the form of the Spirit, they are related to one another by the unity of the Spirit.'[20] This statement becomes clearer as Pannenberg explains more precisely the relationship between the divine essence of the Spirit and the person of the Holy Spirit. The third person of the Trinity is understood to be a singularity, or 'unique manifestation' of the field of the divine

---

[17] *ST 2,* p.79.
[18] *ST* 2, p.83.
[19] *ST* 1, p.384.
[20] *ST* 1, p.384.

essence.[21] The immanent presence of God in creation, described as a field of force, has a trinitarian structure; it is relationally constituted. The person of the Holy Spirit is 'one of the personal concretions of the essence of God as Spirit in distinction from the Father and the Son.'[22]

With regard to the Spirit's work in creation, this is distinct from the work of the Son. Through the Son the distinctiveness and particularity of all created beings is mediated. The Spirit relates the creatures to one another and brings them into fellowship with God. 'We thus ascribe to the third person of the Trinity both the positive relation, in the sense of the fellowship of what is distinct, and also the associated dynamic, whether in the trinitarian life of God or in creation.'[23]

Pannenberg's doctrine of the Holy Spirit is therefore grounded within the trinitarian understanding of mutual self- distinction. The Holy Spirit stands over against the persons of the Father and the Son in such a way that his own subject is defined in terms of the unity of the Father and Son. This means that the three persons are differently defined as persons. Each is defined by virtue of their distinctive relation to the other two persons.

The Dynamic of the Spirit in Space and Time

Pannenberg's exposition of the Spirit in terms of field theory leads him to develop a relationship between the eschatological aspect of the work of the Spirit and modern quantum field theory. He approaches this from a consideration of the nature of space and time.

---

[21] *ST* 2, p.83. In other words the person of the Holy Spirit is not himself the field although his work in creation 'has the character of dynamic field operations.' It will be questioned later whether this gives adequate scope for an exposition of the personhood of the Spirit.

[22] *ST* 2, p.83.

[23] *ST* 2, p.84. This constitutes Pannenberg's clearest distinction between the concept of God as Spirit and the third person of the Trinity. It is certainly amplified as other areas of doctrine are expounded, but the foundational concept is expressed in this way. Whether this is an adequate definition of the person and work of the Spirit will be considered later in this chapter. In the light of an alternative construction of the trinitarian doctrine of creation we shall also question whether the functions ascribed to the Son and the Spirit might profitably be reversed so that the Spirit establishes particularity within creation.

In the act of creating, God 'gives creatures space alongside himself' in such a way that his presence still, in some way comprehends them.[24] As has been argued previously, the distinctiveness of each creature is grounded on the distinction of the Son from the Father. Each creature is distinct and related to other creatures spatially; 'space is the epitome of relations between...points of space.'[25] Yet it is time which is constitutive for space since it is the simultaneous existence of distinct and separated creatures which constitutes space.[26] The significance of this for Pannenberg is that it facilitates a theological interpretation of the presence of God in the Spirit as a dynamic field. He achieves this via a particular view of time and eternity.

Time is understood to proceed from eternity; eternity is constitutive for time. Eternity is not endless time but that which is positively related to time and embraces time. Following Plotinus and Boethius, Pannenberg views eternity as 'the simultaneous and perfect presence of unlimited life' and mediates this understanding through a trinitarian perspective.[27]

If eternity is the simultaneous totality of life, from the perspective of time it is the future which becomes constitutive for the present; 'only in terms of the future could the totality be given to time which makes possible the unity and continuity of time's process.'[28]

The dynamic presence of the Spirit in creation is therefore understood in terms of the arrival of the future; it is 'the creaturely power of the future' which is the 'source of what is new.'[29] In this sense the Spirit's presence in creation is the basis of the 'openness of

---

[24] *ST* 2, p.86. This presupposes plurality within the Godhead in the eternal life of the Trinity, although the eternal cotemporaneity of the three persons must not be understood in spatial terms; 'the trinitarian divisions are not fixed divisions.'

[25] *ST*, 2, p.87.

[26] Pannenberg relates this philosophical reflection with the idea of space-time as a multi-dimensional continuum. He is also alert to the problems of simultaneity in the light of relativity theory, which relates time to the speed of light.

[27] *ST* 1, p.404. Pannenberg interacts with Barth who also saw the theological importance of this view of time and eternity and whom he credits with giving a trinitarian basis for the relationship.

[28] *ST* 1, p.408. Heidegger is regarded as seminal in recapturing this idea in philosophical terms.

[29] *ST 2*, p.98.

creation to a higher consummation' and constitutes the 'field of the possible.'[30]

Expressed in pneumatological terms, the presence of the Spirit with Jesus reveals him as the 'eschatological revealer of God;' the Spirit brings believers into the eschatological new life of the resurrection.[31] The dynamic of the Spirit in creation can be viewed as the anticipatory presence of the coming consummation; it is an 'expression of the power of his future.'[32]

At this point Pannenberg argues for the universal validity of this model as a way of describing the natural world. He attempts this by interacting with a particular philosophical interpretation of quantum field theory. By engaging with and developing the thought of Hans-Peter Durr, it is argued that quantum indeterminacy may be seen as a movement which comes from the future; priority is given to the 'field of possibility of future events.'[33] Each event which occurs is regarded as a manifestation of the future; each event which occurs in the present is contingently derived from the possible field of future events. This field of possibility 'may be seen as a field of force with a specific temporal structure.'[34] The dynamic of the Spirit thus establishes the contingency of all individual events while also giving the processes of natural occurrence reliability and predictability.

Underpinning this position is the relationship between eternity, time and space. We have seen that eternity is the constitutive concept which embraces time, which in turn, it is argued, is constitutive for

---

[30] *ST* 2, pp.97-8. This gives theological expression to Pannenberg's much discussed ontological 'priority of the future.' The clear link to Jüngel's priority of the possible and their common heritage in the thought of Heidegger will be analysed in the following chapter.

[31] *ST* 2, pp.97.

[32] *ST* 2, pp.98.

[33] *ST* 2, pp.99. Underlying Pannenberg's argument is an ontology of anticipation which he expounds in some detail in his *Metaphysics and the Idea of God.* We will look at this later in this chapter.

[34] *ST* 2, p.100. This is not to deny that the field concepts of physics describe the mutuality of the relations between material bodies and their movements within the field. There is a certain dialectical relationship between the creative work of the Spirit and the resultant activity of creatures. For the sake of the creatures the working of the Spirit 'can adjust itself to the conditions of (creaturely) existence and activity and thus give them room to affect the field structure of the Spirit's working.' p.101.

space. In the field of the Spirit God's eternity breaks into time; the goal of the Spirit's working is to give creatures a share in eternity.

> We are thus to think of the dynamic of the divine Spirit as a working field linked to time and space - to time by the power of the future that gives creatures their own present and duration, and to space by the simultaneity of creatures in their duration. From the standpoint of the creature, origin from the future of the Spirit has the appearance of the past. But the working of the Spirit constantly encounters the creature as its future, which embraces its origin and its possible fulfilment.[35]

The concept of eternity which facilitates this fusion of the eschatological thrust of the Spirit with a particular interpretation of quantum field theory itself rests upon Pannenberg's distinctive use of the idea of infinity in relation to the divine essence.

Before discussing this more fully, it will be instructive to compare Moltmann's doctrine of the operation of the Spirit in creation. He also sees the Spirit as the principle of creativity; he is the creator of new possibilities, 'the principle of evolution.'[36] The Spirit also directs creation towards the future; here is an affirmation of the eschatological thrust of the Spirit. Where Moltmann differs from Pannenberg is in seeing the Spirit as the 'principle of individuation' which differentiates creatures in their particularity. The Creator Spirit is certainly also the uniting, or 'holistic principle' yet there seems to be greater scope here for the particularising activity of the Spirit. This is paralleled by Moltmann's view of Christ as the ground of the existence of creation where the emphasis falls on the mediating role of the Son for the whole creation rather than the particularising function envisaged by Pannenberg. It is the 'universality of Christ's sovereignty' which leads to the conviction that everything has been created through him.[37]

It is of note that Moltmann also works with an understanding of the Spirit as that which manifests the infinite within creation. He is adamant that 'there is no other way of conceiving the presence of the

---

[35] *ST* 2, p.102.

[36] J. Moltmann, *God in Creation*, London, 1985.

[37] Moltmann, *God in Creation*, p.94. It is the emphasis upon the universal nature of Christ's work in creation which contrasts with Pannenberg

infinite in the finite' than to speak of the indwelling of creation by the Creator Spirit.[38]

The relationship between the Creator Spirit and the Holy Spirit is worked out by reference to the human spirit and the experience of self-transcendence. What believers experience through the Holy Spirit reveals the structure of the Spirit in creation; they are brought into solidarity with other created things.[39]

Ultimately Moltmann attempts to hold these theses together through a concept of the presence of creation in God whereby 'God does not manifest himself to an equal degree in everything.' This Moltmann terms a form of 'panentheism.'[40]

The Structural Significance of the Concept of the Infinite

There appears to be a two-fold purpose behind Pannenberg's use of the concept of the infinite. Firstly, as already observed, he is anxious to demonstrate that it remains possible to integrate philosophical and theological notions of God without contradiction. This accords with his methodological conviction that a *via media* can be found between reason and faith. Secondly, the structure of the infinite in Pannenberg's thought is closely related to that of the notion of Spirit as field. It therefore illuminates the idea of divine essence as the force field of the Spirit. Yet, as Grenz points out, the Spirit goes beyond the infinite since through the Spirit God brings the finite into being; in this way the biblical view of God is seen to 'transcend the philosophical without contradicting it.'[41]

The idea of the infinite is not understood mathematically as a quantitative notion; it is not something without end. Rather it 'stands

---

[38] *God in Creation*, p.101.

[39] We should note two things in relation to this. Firstly Moltmann shares with Pannenberg a tendency to pull back from a full discussion of the personality of the Holy Spirit in favour of the structural relationship of the Spirit to creation. To what extent this is a product of their common Lutheran tradition will be investigated in the following chapter.

Secondly, the goal of the work of the Spirit understood in terms of human solidarity with creation seems to indicate the extent to which Moltmann's own theology is directed towards his ulterior concern to construct an 'ecological doctrine of creation.' *God in Creation*, p.1.

[40] *God in Creation*, p.103.

[41] Grenz, *Reason for Hope*, p.63.

opposed to the finite...is the antithesis to the finite.'[42] Yet this is an incomplete definition. Drawing upon Hegel, the infinite is not simply the opposite of the finite. This would result in the absurd idea of a limited infinity. The infinite must therefore transcend and comprehend everything finite within itself, while maintaining the distinction between the finite and the infinite.

This concept is worked out in some detail in *Metaphysics and the Idea of God*. Here Pannenberg traces the historical pedigree of the infinite in relation to God from Gregory of Nyssa through to Duns Scotus.[43] Gregory's treatment of God as infinite accounted for the transcendent 'otherness' of God, expressed biblically as God's holiness. For Gregory the concept of infinity facilitates a way of understanding God's transcendence and immanence. Pannenberg summarises Gregory thus:

> in his transcendence beyond everything finite, God is holy, and it is precisely because of such transcendence that he is not bound to any place "up there" or "out there" but can also be present within the world of finite realities.[44]

From Hegel's treatment of the Infinite, Pannenberg derives a similar philosophical understanding of the relationship between transcendence and immanence. The Infinite 'must be conceived both as transcendent in relation to the finite and as immanent to it.'[45] Yet, as Hegel argued, the concept of the Infinite cannot be simply equated with the Absolute, or with God, since it cannot by itself give rise to that which is finite. This is one reason why Hegel explicated the concept of Spirit as the mediating concept between the opposition of infinity and the finite. While Pannenberg wishes to distinguish himself from Hegel, speaking of the 'inadequacy' of his view of Spirit, he is clearly indebted to him for his own understanding of the infinite as the most important philosophical notion which must

---

[42] *Reason for Hope*, p.63. While this is not the mathematical notion it underlies it since the opposing and negation of the finite is the basis of the idea of freedom from limitation.

[43] Pannenberg, *Metaphysics and the Idea of God*, Edinburgh, 1990. Scotus employed the concept primarily to expound the unity of God.

[44] W. Pannenberg, *An Introduction to Systematic Theology*, Edinburgh, 1991, p.30.

[45] Pannenberg, *An Introduction to Systematic Theology*, p.36

regulate discussion of the attributes of God. It represents the minimum condition through which we might speak of God.

We have already noted that Pannenberg explicates the notion of God as infinite by reference to the holiness of God, which is viewed as having the same structure. Holiness stands over against that which is profane; the holiness of God is thus seen in his judgment. Yet God enters the world and brings the hope of salvation; 'the sending of the Son to save the world aims at the bringing of the world into the sphere of the divine holiness.'[46] Thus the holiness of God both stands against all that opposes it yet embraces it and moves to bring it into fellowship with God. The dialectic of unity in distinction is once again central.

Consideration of the holiness of God gives further content to Pannenberg's doctrine of the Holy Spirit. The holiness of God is mediated to the world through the Son, yet it is also the work of the Holy Spirit, whose name reflects that he is the Spirit of the holy God.[47] Here we see one of the most illuminating and structurally significant aspects of Pannenberg's method. Rather than developing this thought in terms of the third person of the Trinity he proceeds to show that the dialectical structure of his understanding of the essence of God as Spirit both parallels and transcends that of the idea of the infinite. The dynamic of the Spirit, understood in the light of God's holiness and infinity, expresses the fact that 'the transcendent God himself is characterised by a vital movement which causes him to invade what is different from himself and to give it a share in his own life.'[48] It is apparent that, for Pannenberg, the concept of the infinity of God both grounds his discussion of the philosophical attributes of God and underpins his notion of the divine essence in terms of the dynamic force field of the Spirit. Whether or not this is required by his particular understanding of revelation in terms of the historical

---

[46] *ST* 1, p.399. This thought is developed in the context of the concept of God's electing of a people to be holy and separate from the world.

[47] See *ST* 1, p.400. Yet even here the course of the argument switches back into discussion of the dialectical movement of the Spirit as it parallels the idea of the infinite.

[48] *ST* 1, p.400. In fact the idea of the Spirit in transcending the concept of the infinite enables Pannenberg to express the creative life-giving function of the Spirit as giving life to that which is finite 'as that which is different from himself.' Yet at the end of this exposition he is still forced to admit that the way in which this dialectical structure works is simply grounded in the work of God's Spirit and remains 'a mystery' (p.401).

acts of God and the proleptic arrival of the future consummation is open to question.

The Ontology of the Future: Anticipation and the Temporal Structure of Being

We have noted that Pannenberg's systematic approach may be read as an attempt to demonstrate the compatibility of the Christian doctrine of God derived from revelation with a renewed, philosophical metaphysics. The ontological foundations for this were first outlined in *Theology and the Kingdom of God.*[49] These ideas were expressed in more detail in the later *Metaphysics and the Idea of God.*[50]

In this work Pannenberg attempts to reformulate a notion of the Absolute which will facilitate a way of speaking metaphysically about God and his relationship to the world. This constitutes an attempt to 'find a new foundation for the metaphysics of the Absolute.'[51]

Our concern in this section is to summarise Pannenberg's argument as it relates specifically to his conceptualisation of the relations between time and eternity, the Infinite and the finite. We limit ourselves to these since, as will be shown, they are foundational to Pannenberg's theological method.

Being and the Primacy of the Future

A renegotiated metaphysics of the Absolute must take seriously the notion of the self-conscious. In the same way in which Jüngel recognises and responds to the powerful atheistic critique which arose out of philosophical theistic ideas of God, Pannenberg is aware of the need to avoid postulating any idea of the Absolute solely on the basis of human subjectivity. Feuerbach's notion of God as a projection of human self-consciousness is seen as the natural

---

[49] Pannenberg, *Theology and the Kingdom of God*, Philadelphia, 1969. Of special significance is chapter four, 'Appearance as the arrival of the future' which gave an initial outline of Pannenberg's understanding of the relationship between time and eternity.

[50] Pannenberg, *Metaphysics and the Idea of God.*

[51] *Metaphysics and the Idea of God*, p.62

outcome of regarding the idea of the Absolute in terms of human subjectivity enquiring into its own source.[52]

As an alternative approach Pannenberg suggests that the development of the individual, human self-consciousness is itself mediated through the historical process; the ego's identity is constituted through awareness of external objects; 'in the history of the individual, the development...of the perceptual field...precedes the emergence of the consciousness of the I.'[53] The significance of this is that it enables the Absolute to be conceived not only in terms of individual self- consciousness, but in terms of the individual's experience of objects and events in the world and the relations between them. The Absolute, far from being a projection of self-consciousness, is the source and the goal of all that is finite and subjective; 'the Absolute must be understood...precisely as the completion and perfection (*Vollendung*) of the relationship of the Infinite...to the existence of the finite...'[54] In other words, from a consideration of the nature of self-consciousness, the Absolute may be postulated not simply as the product of self- consciousness, but the constitutive ground and goal of it.

The theological significance of these abstract thoughts lies in the relationship between time and eternity and between the Infinite and the finite.

The general principle outlined above is worked out in Pannenberg's key ontological principle of the relationship between being and time, which in turn involves a particular view of the individual's experience of time. Following Augustine's analysis of the experience of time, the present moment cannot be isolated from that which precedes or follows it. The present is understood in relation to 'the *memoria* of the past and the *expectatio* of the future;'

---

[52] 'Feuerbach was right: if we begin with the thesis that self-consciousness is the "ground" and "truth" of all consciousness of objects, then every thought of an absolute ground of subjectivity must be the product of subjectivity...the Absolute could not be explicated...without immediately running into the suspicion that we are dealing with a merely human projection.'

[53] *Metaphysics and the Idea of God*, p.53. This idea is indebted to Henri Bergson's discussions concerning the nature of consciousness and the phenomenology of perception. See the preceding argument on pp.51, 52.

[54] *Metaphysics and the Idea of God*, p.62.

this constitutes a 'time-bridging present.'[55] At the heart of this experience lies a sort of 'extension of the soul' (*distentio animi*) in which the unity of the whole is appreciated at each particular moment. The human perception of duration is, in a limited sense, a 'picture or image of eternity.'[56]

From this perspective Pannenberg argues that the being and existence of all finite things is related to eternity, which is understood to be identical with the life and being of God. Here he links Augustine's interpretation of the experience of time with Plotinus's doctrine of eternity. The eternal is 'the whole of life (the "*diastasis...zoes*" or "spreading out of life") within the flow of time.'[57] The human soul lives in anticipation of its wholeness, yet it 'falls from eternity' because of its own 'desire to control itself.'[58] Human experience is constituted by separation of moments and parts of life; it is temporally broken and finite. From this perspective, the whole, the totality of life can only be understood in relation to a future goal; we travel through time to reach that goal. 'In short, when the theory of time is oriented toward the eternal totality, the consequence is a primacy of the future for the understanding of time.'[59]

---

[55] *Metaphysics and the Idea of God*, p.79. This is illustrated by human experience of listening to a piece of music in which each moment can only be fully understood in the light of the whole.

[56] *Metaphysics and the Idea of God*, p.80. To this point Pannenberg works with Augustine's view of our experience of time; constant reference is made to his *Confessions.*

[57] *Metaphysics and the Idea of God*, p.76.

[58] *Metaphysics and the Idea of God*, p.76

[59] *Metaphysics and the Idea of God*, p.77. 'the totality of existence is possible only from the standpoint of its future.'

It is significant that Pannenberg views Heidegger also advocating the primacy of the future for the understanding of time 'albeit in a reduced form.' The error attributed to Heidegger is that he lost the connection between time and eternity, preferring to relate it to the possible wholeness of a finite existence (*Dasein*). For Heidegger, *Dasein* is constituted from the future of its own death. Pannenberg offers a strong critique of this which will inform our conmparison with Jüngel's theology of death in the next chapter.

Pannenberg also contrasts his view with Kant who is seen to have replaced eternity with the 'subjectivity of the ego.' See the critique on pp. 83,84.

At this point it remains unclear how this relates to ontology. How is this understanding of the primacy of the future determinative for being?

Pannenberg's key move is to identify wholeness with essence. The wholeness of finite human existence is understood only in relation to eternity, which is itself understood as the totality of all life. This means that the present can only be interpreted in terms of participation in a future totality; 'the leading role in our consciousness of time belongs to the future understood as the source of possible completion.'[60] It follows that, since the future constitutes the totality of finite existence, it must also be seen as the source of its individual essence. 'As long as the future is the source of the possible wholeness of an individual human existence, then we must say that its essence, and thus "what it is," is determined by its future.'[61] This implies that being has a temporal structure.[62]

Viewed from within the course of time, each individual essence is determined from its own future. It follows that we might conceive of beings, in the present moment, in terms of anticipation of their essences; 'everything that exists is what it is only as the anticipation of its future in which the wholeness of each being might be established.'[63]

Hence we have a link between being and time. Contrary to Heidegger, the priority of the future for finite temporality cannot be grasped from the perspective of death; rather, 'the future is to be construed as the source of the wholeness of finite beings, and its being as the anticipation of its future.'[64]

---

[60] *Metaphysics and the Idea of God*, p.87.

[61] *Metaphysics and the Idea of God*, p.87. Once again there is indebtedness to the thought of Heidegger who viewed the 'wholeness of *Dasein*' in terms of its identity, its essence.

[62] Here the influence of Dilthey's analyses of history are significant. Note also how this relates theologically to Pannenberg's understanding of the Spirit as a field of force which, in essence, has a temporal structure.

[63] *Metaphysics and the Idea of God*, p.88. Note that future wholeness is only a 'possibility.' Pannenberg maintains the possibility of finite beings failing to attain final wholeness. Theologically this raises the important question of cause and effect; is the ontological primacy of the future when applied to God's relationship to humanity a form of predestination in reverse? We shall consider this later.

[64] *Metaphysics and the Idea of God*, p.88. Here it might be questioned to

Hence the idea of anticipation becomes central for this reconstruction of the concept of being.

Anticipation and Essence

The philosophical question which Pannenberg addresses here is the relationship between the idea of anticipation and the future totality towards which that anticipation is directed. Given that an anticipation is separated in time from its content, is the anticipation external to that content? Once again, the abstract nature of the question is shown to have theological significance in the context of Johannes Weiss's understanding of the relationship between Jesus' proclamation of the Kingdom of God and the future coming itself; in the proclaimed word, the Kingdom is present, but is an anticipation of the future consummation. It is likewise illustrated by regarding the resurrection of Christ as an anticipation of the eschatological resurrection of the dead.

> The structural parallel between Jesus' message of the Kingdom of God and the event of his resurrection is remarkable; in both cases the future...is viewed as already and actually having broken into history. The final reality is present.[65]

In developing his argument it is the structure of the concept of anticipation which is critical. In pointing towards a future reality, its anticipation is different from that reality; yet it has an identity with that reality. Thus 'the concept of anticipation...is able to unite both aspects - the identity with the thing and the difference from it.'[66] We should notice here close parallel with Pannenberg's exposition of the relationship between the infinite and the finite. The infinite is that which both stands over against the finite yet includes it and embraces its difference. Similarly, eternity is that which embraces all time as

---

what extent this can possibly be understood to be the framework for a general ontology, which is clearly what Pannenberg envisages; without contradiction he sees that Heidegger's relating of being and time becomes a 'point of access and the key to a general ontology.'

[65] *Metaphysics and the Idea of God*, p.95. Here is the ground for Pannenberg's view of truth as anticipatory; 'the future that will reveal the truth about the present remains open and ahead of us...the truth of this anticipation hinges on the still-absent future.' p.96

[66] *Metaphysics and the Idea of God*,, p.104.

well as the difference between the temporal and the eternal. The concept of anticipation is thus structurally and ontologically critical for Pannenberg's metaphysical description of God as infinite. It also underpins his assertion of the provisional nature of truth:

> the anticipation is not yet identical in every respect with the anticipated thing; it remains exposed to the risk of untruth, of a failure to grasp. Yet, given the presupposition that the thing will appear in its full form some time in the future, in the anticipation the thing is already present.[67]

It is in the relation between the ontological priority of the future and the concept of anticipation that Pannenberg finally arrives at a 'new definition of the concept of substance.'[68] If the primacy of the future is accepted, then the essence of a thing is decided retroactively; it becomes what it is from the end. Yet, that essence is already present in anticipatory form. Things are what they are 'from the outcome of their becoming on the one hand, and on the other in the sense of anticipating the completion of their process of becoming, their history.'[69]

In attempting to construct an understanding of the relationship between being and time Pannenberg takes care to distinguish his view from process philosophy. The temporal structure of being is constituted by the relation between the final, complete form of a thing and its anticipation. This relationship is viewed as a 'becoming' towards the goal, the final consummation. This is essentially an historical process which can only be understood in the light of the whole; for example, 'the historian cannot speak of the Thirty Years War in Germany or make it the object of his study until these thirty

---

[67] *Metaphysics and the Idea of God*, p.104

[68] *Metaphysics and the Idea of God*, p.107.

[69] *Metaphysics and the Idea of God*, p.107. Pannenberg develops this by adapting Aristotle's term 'completeness' (*entelecheia*) as motion towards a goal. Understood thus, the goal towards which motion is directed must somehow be already working within that motion. 'Entelechy therefore means both being at the goal and the way in which the goal is present...as something which is absent and not yet attained.' Yet, if the *telos* is identical to the essence of the thing then it can be argued that the essence is already present in the process of becoming. There is an anicipatory presence of the essence before its final completion.

years have passed.'[70] Yet every completed process such as this stands in an ever wider context, such that each is part of the final, universal whole of the historical process. Given the primacy of the future then it is the final totality which encompasses all finite events and processes which is determinative.[71] Hence, for Pannenberg, the whole is determinative for the parts.

By contrast, the process philosophy of Whitehead gives priority to the category of elementary events; these are the 'actual entities' out of which all enduring forms are constituted. In Whitehead's own words 'the ultimate metaphysical truth is atomism.'[72] Consequently, it is individual events which are the ground of their unity. 'In the end, in Whitehead's theory...the whole of the universe...has no inherent integrity of its own in the way that the monad- like events do.'[73] Pannenberg maintains that 'no atomistic idea can explain the unity of the many.'[74]

In the critique offered later in this chapter it will be questioned to what extent this emphasis on the priority of the universal over the particular is foundational for Pannenberg's entire systematic thought. In turn this may cause him to refer to the work of the Spirit in universal rather than particular categories.

The primacy of the future and the concept of anticipation are the foundational ontological building blocks for Pannenberg's description of the divine essence as Infinite. This also underpins his conceptualisation of revelation as proleptic disclosure and the associated notion of the provisional nature of theological truth

---

[70] *Metaphysics and the Idea of God*, p.141.

[71] The theological significance of this is that it enables Pannenberg to argue for the idea of the one God as the Creator of all that is finite and who is bringing all things to eschatological consummation. 'Without this reference to the totality of what exists finitely in the world...talk about God - the one God - would not be possible' (p.142).

[72] A. N. Whitehead, *Process and Reality*, New York, 1978 ed., p.35.

[73] *Metaphysics and the Idea of God*, p.120.

[74] *Metaphysics and the Idea of God*, p.72. Pannenberg's understanding of the relationship of the part to the whole informs his view of God's relationship to the world. 'In reflection on the most comprehensive whole of all finite reality, each particular finite thing in its concrete, individual definiteness is mediated with God...Correspondingly, theology is able, by means of reflection on the totality of finite reality...to show its relatedness to the reality of God.' (p.146)

claims. While the dependence of being upon time is a key feature, it remains uncertain that the ontological categories described here provide an adequate understanding of the idea of self-distinction which is the basis of Pannenberg's doctrine of the Trinity. The question which must now be addressed is whether the revised metaphysical concept of God as Infinite does indeed bear comparison with the nature of God asserted in the Christian tradition, most notably as a relational being whose definitive description is love.

The Love of God: Person and Relation

Pannenberg continues his discussion of the attributes of the divine essence through a discussion of the love of God. In this context he develops his trinitarian conception of divine love; from this he explicates the important concept of personhood in relation to the Trinity. Finally he attempts to expound the unity of the divine essence in terms of love which is viewed in its relation to God as Infinite. In this sense the idea of the divine love is 'the coping-stone' of Pannenberg's doctrine of God.[75]

The Trinitarian Love of God

From exegetical considerations the love of God is best understood in trinitarian terms. God's love is expressed in the sending of the Son; it is also expressed in the person of Christ himself (Gal. 2:20). Thus the Son both expresses the love of the Father and is the subject of the divine love towards creation.

In a similar way the love of God is 'shed abroad in our hearts' through the Holy Spirit (Rom. 5:5). This suggests that the Holy Spirit is also 'the subject of this love and remains so even insofar as it is at work in us and through us.'[76]

The New Testament statement that 'God is love' tells us not only that God has loved us in the sending of the Son, but that the divine essence is love. Pannenberg draws upon the work of Regin Prenter is stating that the Johannine phrase 'is not describing a quality of God but his essence or nature as love.'[77] The question which then must be

---

[75] Schwöbel, *Wolfhart Pannenberg*, 1989, p.281.

[76] *ST* 1, p.424.

[77] *ST* 1, p.424.

addressed concerns the relation between the unity of the divine essence as love and the trinitarian persons. This must be explicated in such a way that love is not defined in terms of a common quality or as some form of essence which lurks behind the three persons; Father, Son and Spirit must be 'love in the "unity of three persons" that can never be separated.'[78]

Pannenberg expounds his conception of trinitarian love in close debate with Jüngel's account in *God as the Mystery of the World.* As we have seen earlier, Jüngel attempts to express the love of God ontologically. However, in Pannenberg's view Jüngel fails to achieve this as a consequence of following Barth's notion of God as the subject of his own loving. This is expressed in Jüngel's contention that God is 'he who eternally loves himself.'[79] Pannenberg is critical of this view

> if the one loves self in the other instead of living the other as the other, then love falls short of the full self-giving which is the condition that the one who loves be given self afresh in the responsive love of the one who is loved.[80]

Pannenberg wishes to construct a view of divine love which is grounded fully in the mutual relations of the Trinity. To facilitate this he takes from Jüngel the concept of love as 'a power which shows itself in those who love and in their turning to one another.'[81] Love rises above persons, manifests itself in their mutual relations and grants them their selfhood. As each receives him or her self afresh from the other, the personhood of each is constituted by relationship to the other. The true basis of this personhood is the 'power of love that binds the two.'[82]

---

[78] *ST* 1, p.424, p.425, once again quoting from Prenter.

[79] *GMW*, p.329. In trinitarian terms Jüngel states that in the encounter between the Father who loves and the Son who is loved, God is seen to be the one who loves himself; in this encounter God is not yet love itself. Only with the sending of the Son may we say that God is love.

[80] *ST* 1, p.426.

[81] *ST* 1, p.426.

[82] *ST* 1, p.427. Here Pannenberg draws upon the well documented concept of the I-Thou relationship as expounded by Martin Buber who saw the personality of the I as being constituted by relation to the Thou. The basis of this was the 'mystery' which bound them together. Pannenberg sees love as the content of this mystery, especially as it applies to the trinitarian

Consequently, the divine love is the power that is manifested in the mutual relations of the Trinity and this in turn is identical with the divine essence. 'The two statements "God is Spirit" and "God is love" denote the same unity of essence by which the Father, Son and Spirit are united in the fellowship of the one God...the Spirit is the power of love which lets the other be.'[83] The unity of the one God is constituted by the mutual relations of the three persons.

In describing the Spirit as 'the power of love' it must then be shown in what way the Holy Spirit might be understood as personal.

The Person of the Holy Spirit

The three persons of the Trinity exist ec-statically. This means that their personal distinctness is constituted outside of themselves in their relations with the other persons; 'the persons are referred to the other persons...only thus do they exist as personal selves.'[84] The Father is the Father in relation to the Son; the Son is the Son in his obedience to and recognition of the Father. Their relations are constitutive for their persons.

It is through the work of the Spirit that the Father expresses his love in the sending forth of the Son; the Son embodies that love through his free self-distinction from the Father. The Spirit as a dynamic field is the essence of the Godhead. In this respect 'the dynamic of the Spirit radiates from the Father, but in such a way that the Son receives it as gift, and it fills him and radiates back from him to the Father.'[85]

Yet this does not express the personality of the Spirit. Pannenberg understands this in a different way from the personhood of the Son or of the Father. The Spirit is a separate hypostasis in that he 'comes over against the Son and the Father as the divine essence, common to both, which actually unites them and attests and maintains their unity

---

life of God.

[83] *ST* 1, p.427. This power which is at work in the trinitarian life of God is thus also the ground of creaturely existence - another form of 'letting the other be.'

[84] *ST* 1, p.427. p.430. The human individual is also constituted by reference to a social context, although the concept of human personhood is different, most notably in that it is not exclusively constituted by relation to one or two other persons.

[85] *ST* 1, p.429.

in the face of their distinction.'[86] Thus the Spirit is a distinct hypostasis yet is also the divine essence which is common to Father and Son. As distinct hypostasis the Spirit comes forth as the Holy Spirit; as essence the Spirit is the power of love.

Pannenberg argues that the essence of deity is also manifested, in different ways, in the persons of the Father and the Son. The three persons are thus 'concretions of the divine reality as Spirit...individual aspects of the dynamic field of the eternal Godhead.'[87] Thus Pannenberg grounds his understanding of the person of the Holy Spirit in his conceptualisation of the divine essence as Spirit which in itself is mediated by the relationship between Father and Son. The Spirit is a distinct hypostasis only in relation to the Father and the Son; 'the Spirit has full personal independence...only in his distinction from the Father and the Son in their differentiation.'[88]

The Unity of God

Since love is regarded as the concrete form of the divine essence, understood in trinitarian perspective, Pannenberg goes on to outline a second cluster of divine attributes which are viewed as expressions of the divine love. [89] The final link which Pannenberg strives to make is between the essence of God revealed as love and the metaphysical concept of the Infinite. He remains clear that any doctrine of God can only speak provisionally of the revealed God of love in terms of the one true God; 'only God's own acts in history and not doctrinal arguments can prove this.'[90] Pannenberg's purpose, as stated previously is to demonstrate the coherence of the Christian doctrine

---

[86] *ST* 1, p.429. By virtue of the fact that the Spirit is a separate hypostasis he can work within the creation.

[87] *ST* 1, p.430. Pannenberg prepares the way for this by discussing the different ways in which the Father and the Son represent the Godhead as a whole. This is interpreted relationally; the Father manifests the essence of deity as Spirit only through the Son. The Son partakes of deity in relation to the Father and through the Spirit. The reference of each person to the divine essence is 'mediated by the relations to the other two persons.'

[88] *ST* 1, p.430.

[89] These are expounded as God's goodness, grace, mercy, righteousness, faithfulness, patience and wisdom (*ST* 1, pp.432-442).

[90] *ST* 1, p.442.

of God with a renewed, philosophy of God as the Infinite: the compatibility of faith and reason.

The concept of the unity of God serves to focus the relationship between the essence of God as love and the true Infinite. From the perspective of biblical faith there is seen to be a link between the oneness of God and his love. In the claim to sole deity and the calling of a people to be his own, God expresses his love. As a result of God's reconciling action in the world his love embraces the world and 'bridges the gulf between God and the world.'[91] Thus the divine love, manifested in God's self-revelation manifests God's unity in relation to the world of the finite; we see a clear parallel with the idea of God as the true Infinite which transcends the finite and takes it up into itself. Once again, the true Infinite is not simply thought of as an antithesis of the finite, but also as 'the unity that transcends the antithesis.'[92]

Thus there is seen to be a structural parallel between the idea of divine love and the true Infinite. Yet Pannenberg goes further in seeing that both concepts may find common expression through the dynamic of the Spirit. As previously shown, Pannenberg understands the essence of God, from philosophical considerations, as Spirit, in the form of an infinite field of force; from consideration of revelation, the essence of God is also conceived as love. The Spirit is the power of love which unites the persons of the Trinity in their distinctions.

> Divine love in its trinitarian concreteness...embraces the tension of the infinite and the finite without setting aside their distinction. It is the unity of God with his creature which is grounded in the fact that the divine love eternally affirms the creature in its distinctiveness and thus sets aside its separation from God but not its difference from him.[93]

Here Pannenberg reaches a significant conclusion. With regard to the relationship between God and the world, God's freedom in the act of creation is retained, but as a result of this act his being is tied into creation:

---

[91] *ST* 1, p.445.
[92] *ST 1*, p.446.
[93] *ST 1*, p.446

> Because God is love, having once created a world in his freedom, he finally does not have his own existence without this world, but over against it and in it in the process of its ongoing consummation.[94]

The logical conclusion of this is that the essence of God as love comes to completion only at the end of all things.[95]

Critical Discussion

The following critique will focus on four significant issues that are foundational for Pannenberg's pneumatology. Consideration of his use of the infinite in relation to the essence of God will lead, secondly, to questioning whether the field concept is the most appropriate way of conceiving of God as Spirit. Critical discussion of the underlying ontology will then prepare the way for a consideration of the trinitarian distinctions and, in particular, whether Pannenberg adequately defines the Holy Spirit in personal terms.

God as the True Infinite

It is clear that the concept of the Infinite plays a decisive role in Pannenberg's theology. Infinity is that which both stands over against the finite yet which transcends and fulfils it; the infinite and the finite are, at the same time, mutually exclusive and mutually complementary.

The significance of this model is seen in Pannenberg's doctrine of the Trinity. It enables him to speak of the unity of the divine essence and the immanent Trinity. It also structures his understanding of the eschatological unity of the immanent and economic Trinity; it facilitates his argument that God may be understood to be the same in his eternal essence as he is revealed in his trinitarian acts of love towards the world.

Pannenberg is critical of theological models that make these connections on the basis of God as first cause. Yet Olthus has argued

---

[94] *ST 1*, p.447

[95] Properly understood Pannenberg wishes to assert that the being of God is certainly fulfilled through relation to his creation, yet he is not restricted by it. This lies at the heart of the trinitarian reformulation of the monarchy of the Father which is made dependent upon the outcome of the work of the Son and the Spirit.

that Pannenberg works in a similar manner in his methodology, replacing the first cause with the concept of the infinite; 'it is the internal dynamics of his system that speaks the decisive voice.'[96]

The implications of this are considerable with regard to other areas of doctrine. The notions of sin and fallenness are reinterpreted in terms of finitude and a turning away from participation in the divine infinity. This dictates Pannenberg's exegesis of Scripture; it is the 'affirmation of the creature in its limits...in face of its hardening of its finite particularity' which is 'the meaning of the overcoming of "the world" by the Son (John 16:33).'[97] Thus reconciliation becomes a participation in the infinity of God. This is particularly the work of the Spirit; 'The Spirit lifts us above our own finitude, so that in faith we share in him who is outside us, Jesus Christ.'[98] Olthus suggests that this constitutes a major redefinition of Christian doctrine. Understood thus, reconciliation is not at heart an act of mercy and grace; the fall and the existence of sin and evil become part of an overall cosmic process and in this sense they are 'domesticated' and lose their power.

This criticism must be assessed in the light of Pannenberg's later exposition of the doctrines of sin and reconciliation. He does tend to speak in a more orthodox manner when describing these in trinitarian language. Thus reconciliation is 'participation in the filial relation of Jesus to the Father' which 'frees believers for immediacy in relation to God as their Father.'[99] It is through the Spirit that believers are brought into fellowship with God 'as he [the Spirit] distinguishes himself from the Father and the Son, and with himself all those whose hearts he fills...'[100]

Yet in Pannenberg's exposition of sin it is human finitude in the context of the Spirit as the 'infinite ground of being' which lies at the heart of the discussion. In the nature of our finite being it is still the

---

[96] J. H. Olthus, 'God as the True Infinite: Concerns about Wolfhart Pannenberg's Systematic Theology Volume 1,' in *Calvin Theological Journal*, 27.2, 1992, p.322.

[97] *ST* 1, p.422.

[98] *ST* 2, p.451.

[99] *ST* 2, p.453.

[100] *ST* 2, p.453. Yet even here this is interpreted in terms of the finite existence of the believer; 'the Spirit completes our reconciliation with God by enabling us through faith in Jesus Christ to accept our own finite existence before God' (p.454).

presence of the infinite Spirit which enables us to be consciously aware of the interrelatedness of the I with the world. 'Awareness of the infinite as such in its distinction from the finite rests upon the fact that we are always "ecstatic" in relation to the other;' 'in grasping the finite there is always a non-thematic sense of the infinite as that which is other than the finite.'[101] Our fallen state is thus a failure to distinguish the infinite reality of God from the finitude of our own existence.

It would seem that Olthus's critique still carries weight in spite of the trinitarian content of Pannenberg's doctrines of sin and reconciliation; redemption seems to be an ontological necessity built into the process of creation. The practical implication of this for Olthus is that it plays down individual particularity in the context of universals. Human finitude is only properly comprehended in the light of the divine infinity. For Olthus this leads Pannenberg to construct a theology which seems remote from the concerns of the contemporary world; how are we to live for God in a culture of post-modern despair?

A further point regarding the structural importance of the Infinite is raised by Schwöbel.[102] To what extent is Pannenberg's adaptation of Hegel's concept of the 'truly Infinite' required by his understanding of the non-thematic awareness of the infinite which is constitutive for his religious epistemology? In his exposition of the unthematic awareness of the Infinite in the religions and also in his anthropology of the self-conscious awareness of the world, this certainly seems to be the foundational concept. Schwöbel asks whether the concept of the true Infinite is really required by the contents of the Christian Faith. It might also be questioned whether Pannenberg has employed the concept of the Infinite as a means of explicating the relation of God's transcendence and immanence in a way which is grounded in the Lutheran concept of the presence and absence of God. We will pursue this in comparison with Jüngel in the following chapter.

---

[101] *ST* 2, p.196. This is true in our fallen state when 'we do not glorify God.'

[102] Schwöbel, *Wolfhart Pannenberg*, p.286.

The Spirit as Field

Pannenberg's use of the field concepts of modern Physics are critical in his attempt to reconcile a doctrine of God based upon the trinitarian relations and the revised metaphysical view of God as the true Infinite. Consequently the concept of field is structurally important in the way in which Pannenberg conceives the essence of God and the immanence of God.

Yet from a scientific perspective it can be argued that this is an uncertain foundation for such an important metaphor to be built upon. Modern physics has moved beyond the concept of field, as initially developed by Farady, and replaced it with pure mathematical formulae. It is no longer clear that the field model is any more than a helpful and simplistic model. Pannenberg states that his intention is to use the field concept only as a model of reality; such theories can only be seen as 'approximations to reality.'[103] If that were true then there might be some justification for its use. Yet the way in which he utilises the concept indicates that he regards the dynamic field of the Spirit of God as, in reality, a field of presence which, in actuality, exists in this structure so that God is understood to be at work along the 'lines of force' in creation. The Spirit's work in creation as a 'dynamic field...connects the creatures to one another and to God.'[104]

It seems that Pannenberg intends this to be understood in terms of a real, essential action in creation and he thus might come uncomfortably close to what A. N. Whitehead called the 'fallacy of misplaced concreteness.'[105]

This is the essence of Hesse's early critique of Pannenberg where she suggested that his overly realistic interpretation of scientific theories was insufficiently aware of the diversity of field models available and suggested that a more critically perceptive approach to science would be appropriate.[106]

---

[103] *ST* 2, p.83.

[104] *ST* 2, p.84. Behind this lies the definition of a line of force as that which connects points of equal energy levels within a given field.

[105] A. N. Whitehead, *Science and the Modern World*, Cambridge, 1927, p.64. Keith Ward has used this phrase similarly of the tendency of scientists and philosophers to confuse a powerful model of reality with the true reality (*God, Chance and Necessity*, Oxford, 1996).

[106] M. Hesse, 'Retrospect,' in A. R. Peacocke (ed.), *The Sciences and Theology in the Twentieth Century*, Stocksfield, 1981, see especially p.285.

More recent criticism has taken a similar view. Worthing has suggested that Pannenberg conflates various field theories into one generalised concept. While he is closest to Faraday's field theory with its description of the field in terms of lines of force, he expounds this utilising Einsteinian notions of space and time. This highlights the dangers of over- simplification when a theological model is drawn from another source.[107]

Pannenberg's tendency towards an overly realistic interpretation of field theory may be illustrated by his description of all creaturely reality as that which is more than the sum of their elementary particles or events. These are themselves 'manifestations of fields' which constitutes the 'structural links that tie creaturely forms to the totality of creation.'[108] Such statements indicate that Pannenberg conceives the field activity of God as determining microevents in creation; there is thus a physical reality implied in field language which is neither commensurate with the understanding of modern physics nor compatible with any understanding of field theory as metaphorical.[109]

One further significant criticism concerns the description of the persons of the Trinity as 'concretions' of the field.[110] As a singularity

---

This brought a strong reply from Pannenberg in defence of his position but which did not fully meet the force of the critique.

[107] Worthing, *God, Creation and Contemporary Physics*, 1996.

[108] *ST* 2, pp.124-25. 'Although all material constructs are made up of atoms and their constituent parts and process, today...we have to ascribe to subatomic processes and conditions a holistic character...we may view the parts as local manifestations of a field that fills all space.'

[109] The course of the argument in the *Systematic Theology* follows through the implications of the field concept for the understanding of evolutionary biological processes. In earlier writing Pannenberg employed a different form of field theory to describe this. Drawing upon Michael Polanyi he postulated a 'morphogenetic field' as the agent of evolutionary process towards higher forms of life. This met substantial criticism on the basis that this type of field theory was not widely accepted by biologists. It is also of interest that Polanyi later moved away from this concept, deeming it unsatisfactory. In his later work Pannenberg has seemingly ignored this in favour of the electromagnetic field theory, but seeks to extend this to an understanding of biological processes.

[110] For example, the Holy Spirit is 'one of the personal concretions of the essence of God as Spirit.' (*ST* 2, p.83) 'The trinitarian persons are manifestations of the one divine essence' (*ST* 1, p.383).

within the field, the closest conceptual parallel might be with the scientific idea of a pole as a point of intense concentration of energy within the field. This again suggests an uncomfortable realism with which Pannenberg views the whole field concept. Beyond that it is extremely difficult to conceive of the trinitarian persons as concretions or manifestations of a field. Quite apart from the conceptual difficulty, this reintroduces the danger of regarding the divine essence as in some way separate from the trinitarian persons, which Pannenberg is most anxious to deny. The essence of God is, on the one hand, defined solely in relational terms so that it is identical with the trinitarian relations. One the other hand the persons are concretions of the divine essence. A certain ambiguity remains.

Regarding Pannenberg's employment of scientific concepts it might also be questioned why he prefers the field model to the greater emphasis upon discrete quanta of energy offered by quantum mechanics.[111] Given his prior commitment to the idea of God as the true Infinite and the concomitant thesis of the unthematic awareness of the Infinite in world religions, the choice of the field concept is understandable. The question is whether this is required by the dictates of his theological system rather than any inherent suitability of the concept over and above others which might prove equally fruitful.

Ontology: The Relationship between the Future and Anticipation

In this section it will be argued that there is an inherent ambiguity in Pannenberg's revised ontology. In brief it is highlighted by asking to what extent the future is determinative for events in the present and to what degree the concept of anticipation can be conceived in such a way as to carry ontological significance.

Molnar has offered a significant critique of the extent to which Pannenberg employs the concept of anticipation in ontological ways.[112] He correctly identifies that 'anticipation is a central category

---

[111] For a discussion of some aspects of quantum mechanics as applied to cosmology and theology see K. Ward, *God, Chance and Necessity*, Oxford, 1996. For a discussion of the way in which science and theology may interact by the use of models see M. Fuller, *Atoms and Icons*, London, 1995.

[112] P. D. Molnar, 'Some Problems with Pannenberg's Solution to Barth's "Faith Subjectivism," in *Scottish Journal of Theology*, 48.3, 1995, pp. 315-339.

of Pannenberg's theological and philosophical thought.'[113] Drawing upon Heidegger's idea of appearance as a 'fore-conception' (*Vorgriff*) of its future, Pannenberg understands the meaning of an event to be determined from its future. Thus it is the resurrection of Christ which defines the meaning of the incarnation.[114] This means that, from an epistemic perspective, the truth that Jesus is God and man is not yet a completed fact; this will only be seen to be true at the end of all things. Yet Pannenberg proceeds to extend this idea to an ontological level. He argues that it is history which is constitutive for the divine Sonship of Jesus; 'The eternal Son is first...an aspect of the human person. Hence his self-distinction from the Father is constitutive for the eternal Son.'[115] This must mean that the eternal Sonship of Jesus is grounded in his historical particularity.[116] This has profound significance for the doctrine of God, as we shall consider shortly, but the ontological issue is important.

Molnar argues that this illustrates a general problem with Pannenberg's thought. What is it that determines our concept of God? Is it the reality of God or the reality of God defined by our own subjective experience which is anticipatory in form? The path which Pannenberg seeks to follow is to assert the ontological priority of the reality of God, yet he does so by grounding our knowledge of God in our experience which anticipates that reality. The heart of the issue is shown in Pannenberg's understanding of the structure of the self-revealing activity of God in the world:

> the anticipation of the eschatological consummation by Jesus' proclamation of the coming Lordship of God in his own historical work, and the corresponding anticipation of the end time resurrection of the dead...is the basis of all that Christians affirm regarding

---

[113] 'Some Problems with Pannenberg's Solution to Barth's "Faith Subjectivism," p.322.

[114] The resurrection of Christ, is an 'anticipation' which 'takes on the character of an incarnation of God himself in the person of Jesus.' W. Pannenberg, *Metaphysics and the Idea of God*, p.96.

[115] *ST* 1, pp. 310-11.

[116] The argument is extended in Pannenberg's reinterpretation of the pre-existence of the Logos as retroactively defined: 'if the Father is from all eternity the One he is shown historically to be in relation to Jesus his Son...then we cannot think of the Father apart from the Son...the relation reaches back also to the time before his earthly birth...we must speak of a pre-existence of the Son' *ST* 2, pp. 367-8).

> God...the concept of revelation which is developed by the trinitarian understanding of God rests on an anticipation of the end of history in the person and history of Jesus Christ.[117]

Molnar sees that by using the concept of our experience as an anticipation, Pannenberg opens himself to the charge of subjectivism. Hence, 'the truth of revelation is grounded in the experience of anticipation and embodies the very subjectivism which Pannenberg criticises in Barth.'[118] Further, by interpreting revelation in terms of anticipation, the idea of mutual dependence which is part of created being is introduced into the immanent Trinity. Thus the deity of the Father is dependent upon the outcome of history. Molnar suggest that, contrary to Pannenberg's plea, this must be seen as compromising the freedom of God. Pannenberg 'grounds our knowledge of God, Christ and revelation in our human experience of anticipation and compromises his own view that only God can reveal God.'[119]

Now this criticism highlights the difficult relationship between ontology and epistemology in Pannenberg. In order to speak in ontological terms about the concept of anticipation we have noted how Pannenberg relates it to the primacy of the future. However, this then presents a different problem. To what extent is the priority of the future determinative for events within time?

As has been outlined, through his utilisation of Plotinus's concept of eternity and via his critical interpretation of Kant and Hegel, Pannenberg arrives at the concept of anticipation as that which receives its essence from the future; 'a zinnia is already a zinnia as a cutting and remains one during the entire process of its growth...even though the flower bears its name only on account of its blossom.'[120] Even if it was unique, it would still 'possess its essence through anticipation.'[121] This suggests a genuine ontological priority of the future. As Grenz states, 'Pannenberg's position would be simplified...were he only intending to speak epistemologically.'[122]

---

[117] *ST* 1, p.332.

[118] *ST* 1, p.330.

[119] *ST* 1, p.338.

[120] W. Pannenberg, *Metaphysics and the Idea of God*, p.105.

[121] *Metaphysics and the Idea of God*, p.105.

[122] S. Grenz, *Reason for Hope*, p.75. Grenz is clear that the *Systematic Theology* shows that Pannenberg intends an ontological primacy of the

That Pannenberg intends to speak of the future as ontologically constitutive for the essence of events in the process of time is clear from his understanding of the revelation of God in Jesus; 'The future of God is not merely disclosed in advance with the coming of Jesus; it is already an event...the future of God has already dawned.'[123] This can only make sense if the being of God in the future is, in some way determinative. As has already been argued, this in turn requires us to understand the future as the historically conditioned mode of God's being which, as eternal being, is co-present with all time. This historical determinism seems to be implied in Pannenberg's view of the incarnation as 'the self-actualisation of the trinitarian God in the world.'[124] Through the incarnation of the Son 'the future of God is already present in the world.'[125]

Such phrases suggest a strong divine causality from the future, which Polk has referred to as 'a kind of Calvinism set into temporal reverse.'[126] Yet Pannenberg cannot easily be accused of this since he envisages a real freedom within creation; human individuals are free to either accept the divine rule or reject it. 'We may turn aside from the revelation of deity, from the declaration of the divine will.'[127] Polk suggests that Pannenberg views this freedom as God willing to give creatures a share in deciding the future. Yet, as Polk argues, if God releases into the present the provision for other, created causal agency then it must follow that God himself is affected by this. By making the deity of God dependent on the outcome of the mission of the Son and the Spirit Pannenberg does appear to do this. 'Even in his

---

future.

[123] *ST* 1, p.247. 'In this special sense we can speak of an anticipatory revelation...of the deity of God.'

[124] *ST* 2, p.393. Pannenberg is quite explicit about this. 'To speak of a self-actualising of God in the event of his revelation naturally cannot mean that the trinitarian God has no prior actuality in himself. Taken literally...it names the self as both subject and object of the actualising. The self thus precedes the fulfilment of its own actualising...the self...must also be thought of as the subject of the action and therefore already actual at the very beginning.'

[125] *ST* 2, p.391.

[126] D. Polk, *On the Way to God. An Exploration into the Theology of Wolfhart Pannenberg*, 1989, p.286.

[127] *On the Way to God. An Exploration into the Theology of Wolfhart Pannenberg,* p.260.

deity, by the creation of the world and the sending of his Son and Spirit to work in it, he has made himself dependent upon the course of history.'[128] Yet, underlying this is the conviction that at the Eschaton, God will be revealed to be what he has been all the way through history. Thus Pannenberg does not wish to compromise the freedom of God by making the divine essence dependent on creation; '...God...did not have to create the world out of some inner necessity of his divine nature. If he did he would be dependent in his essence on the existence of the world.'[129] There is thus a dialectical account of the relationship between God and the world which does not fall to the relatively simplistic critique of Polk. However it may be asked whether Pannenberg successfully holds together the seeming ambiguity between God's freedom in creating on the one hand, and his involvement in creation in such a way his being is dependent upon the outcome of history on the other.

Polk's intuitive feeling that Pannenberg operates with a strong divine causality from the future might still be seen to retain force even when this is understood in trinitarian terms. The self-distinction of the Son is the basis for the distinctiveness of all creatures; the deity of the Father is made dependent upon the success of the mission of the Son as that is actualised in the field of the Spirit's presence in creation. Thus whatever degree of human freedom is granted, our existence and the decisions that are made, even if they turn away from God's self-revelation, are ultimately bound up with the trinitarian agency of God through which the creation is taken up into eschatological consummation.

The dilemma in Pannenberg's ontology is consequently this. If the concept of anticipation is asserted in a full ontological sense, then Molnar's critique comes into force and Pannenberg falls into a form of 'faith subjectivism' which he is anxious to avoid. If however, anticipation is mediated by the primacy of the future, as Pannenberg asserts, then, even within the trinitarian exposition of this, there remains the suspicion of a strong divine causality. This seems the import when Pannenberg asserts that the concept of anticipation contains within itself both the possibility of identity with its own fulfilment or a turning away from it. The priority of the future is structured such that this embraces the difference; whether or not the anticipation comes to fulfilment or falls short, the power of the future

---

[128] *ST* 1, p.329.

[129] *ST* 2, p.19.

will take it up and transcend the difference. In other words, God as the power of the future grounds the present contingency of events; the future remains ontologically determinative.[130]

Expressed rather differently, it is unclear that Pannenberg has adequately conceived the relationship between divine action and human freedom. As Olson comments, Pannenberg's doctrine of the Trinity, rather than shedding light on the ontology of the future, only seems to deepen the enigma.[131] This critique might also reflect the extreme difficulty and questionable method involved in attempting to construct a general ontology from a theological impulse.

One of the implications of a strong determinism in any form, which Polk identifies, is the problem of theodicy. If God still determines events from the future, then the problem of evil raises itself acutely. Pannenberg's response is to argue that the suffering of the world is taken up by the Son and eschatologically transformed. Despite Pannenberg's claim that this constitutes the only truly satisfactory theodicy Polk astutely asks whether it is acceptable to construe the end as justifying the means.[132]

The Person of the Holy Spirit

Three questions may be raised concerning the adequacy of Pannenberg's description of the personhood of the Holy Spirit. Firstly to what extent is the Spirit understood as the relation between the Father and the Son? Secondly, how is the self-distinction of the Spirit from the Father and the Son understood in the context of the field model? Thirdly, is the ascribed function of the Spirit as a principle of divine immanence in creation in its unifying of that which is distinct the most accurate and helpful approach to the trinitarian doctrine of creation?

---

[130] 'The action of the one God in relation to the world is...the determinative basis of relations between the Creator and the creatures.' *ST* 2, p.5.

[131] R. Olson, 'Wolfhart Pannenberg's Doctrine of the Trinity,' in *Scottish Journal of Theology*, 43, 1990, pp.175-206.

[132] Polk writes from a position of greater sympathy with process theology. He proposes an alternative theodicy on the basis of God sharing the suffering of the world; evil and suffering result more from God, in his will, deciding not to control the process of history.

As we noted earlier, the employment of the field concept to describe the Spirit does not easily lead to a conceptualisation of the Holy Spirit in personal terms. Yet from the perspective of the doctrine of the Trinity, Pannenberg speaks of the Spirit firstly in relational terms. It is the Spirit who unites the work of the Father and the Son in creation which is 'a free act of God as an expression of the freedom of the Son in his self-distinction from the Father...and of the Spirit who links the two in free agreement.'[133] This becomes clear in the context of the discussion of the love of God; 'the Spirit is the love by which the Father and the Son are mutually related.'[134]

This emphasis upon the Spirit as relation is apparent from Pannenberg's exposition of the work of the Spirit in lifting created being above its own finitude. It is the Spirit who manifests 'the relation of the Son to the Father' in the process of self-transcendence.[135] Understood thus we should question whether the work of the Spirit is better expressed as bringing about a union with Christ, rather than a manifesting of the Father-Son relationship.

Yet the third person of the Trinity must not simply be conceived as the love between the Father and the Son. Pannenberg is critical of Augustine's view of the Spirit as the love (*caritas*) that unites Father and Son; this tends to result in a doctrine of the Spirit which reduces the distinct personhood of the Spirit in favour of the '"we" of their communion.'[136] The specific criticism lies not in the idea of the Spirit as the union between Father and Son, but in the interpretation of this in terms of relations of origin. Pannenberg maintains that this fails to do justice to the full recipricocity in the trinitarian relations. Consequently Pannenberg emphasises the mutual self-distinction of the trinitarian persons. In terms of the Holy Spirit, this is conceived as distinct hypostasis 'as he comes over against the Son and the Father as the divine essence...and maintains their unity in the face of their distinction.'[137]

---

[133] *ST* 2, p.30. See Gunton's critique of the inadequacy of the field concept in describing the third person of the Trinity. C. Gunton, *The Triune Creator,* Edinburgh, 1998, p.161.

[134] *ST* 1, p.429. Pannenberg here refers clearly in this context to a distinct hypostasis of the Spirit who unites the Father and the Son in their distinction.

[135] *ST* 2, p.386.

[136] *ST* 1, p.316.

[137] *ST* 1, p.429. It is of note that here we see Pannenberg's

There is value in this description, particularly in the notion of self-distinction. In keeping with Pannenberg's desire to define persons relationally, the Holy Spirit is regarded as the distinct hypostasis who preserves and unites the distinction of the Father and the Son; the third person of the Trinity thus receives his own personhood by relation to the other two. Yet the problem lies in the proposed relationship between the divine essence as Spirit and the third person of the Trinity. Pannenberg maintains that the essence of God can only be understood relationally; but the three persons who are constituted by their mutual relationship, are also regarded as concretions of the divine essence. 'On the one side the Spirit and love constitute the common essence of deity, and on the other they come forth as a separate hypostasis in the Holy Spirit.'[138] The divine persons are 'individual aspects of the dynamic field of the eternal Godhead.'[139]

It is clear from this that Pannenberg only understands the personhood of the Holy Spirit by relation to his function in relation to the Father and the Son. Through the work of the Spirit in creation the kingdom of the Father, as mediated through the Son, is finally established; 'the Spirit...glorifies the Son...and in so doing glorifies the Father himself' and in so doing 'the monarchy of the Father in creation is consummated.'[140]

The description of the person of the Spirit in these terms might prove an interesting way forward, yet Pannenberg makes the development of this concept difficult by continually referring the third person back to the general dynamic of the Spirit in creation as a field of force. The result of this is that it leads him to speak of the Spirit more in terms of universals and as the unity of that which is distinct.

This becomes clear in the way in which the relationship between the Holy Spirit and the divine essence is expounded. The person of the Holy Spirit is 'one of the personal concretions of the essence of God as Spirit.'[141] Thus the Holy Spirit must not be confused with the

---

conceptualisation of the relationship between the essence of God as Spirit and the third person of the Trinity.

[138] *ST* 1, p.429.

[139] *ST* 1, p.430.

[140] *ST* 1, p.324. Once again the full ontological implications of this are asserted. The eschatological orientation of the monarchy of the Father is 'true not merely of the event of revelation.'

[141] *ST* 2, p.83.

field of the divine essence. Yet since the distinct hypostasis of the Holy Spirit is only manifest in distinction from the Father and the Son, the working of the Holy Spirit has 'the character of dynamic field operations.'[142] Whereas the Son mediates the 'distinctness and otherness of every creature,' the Spirit 'connects the creatures to one another and to God.'[143]

We are seemingly presented with a doctrine of the Holy Spirit understood in terms of a principle of divine immanence whose function is to unite that which is separated. Pannenberg is clear that 'this relates plainly to the specificity of the person of the Holy Spirit.'[144] Yet, by positing this, Pannenberg appears to want to express the personhood of the Spirit in universal terms. Whereas the *Logos* is regarded as the foundation of creaturely particularity, the Spirit becomes the principle of God's universal immanence in the world. It is the *Logos* who 'brings forth the particular *logoi* of specific creatures.'[145] It is the Spirit who connects creatures to God.

This tendency to emphasise the universal, uniting aspect of the Spirit is demonstrated further by an insistence on viewing the eschatological work of the Spirit as 'an expression of the power of the future.'[146] When placed alongside the statement that 'the oneness of God is the content of this future,' then Pannenberg's view of the Spirit in universal terms becomes clear.[147] This then reintroduces the problematic issue of how we are to conceive of the Spirit in his particular personhood.

Gunton has argued that a theology of the Spirit must give greater priority to the particularising work of the Spirit. It is through the Spirit that God comes into relationship with the world, but the Spirit may be better viewed as the one who 'maintains and even strengthens particularity.'[148] Just as the Spirit's function in the Godhead is to 'particularise the hypostases' so 'the Spirit's distinctive mode of

---

[142] *ST* 2, p.84.

[143] *ST* 2, p.84.

[144] *ST* 2, p.84.

[145] *ST* 2, p.63. In the person of Jesus Christ the Logos is 'fully one with the "flesh" of each individual person.'

[146] *ST* 2, p.98. Here it should be remembered that the priority of the future is the temporal expression of the totality of all created life, which is in turn an expression of God's infinity and eternity.

[147] *ST* 2, p.330.

[148] Gunton, *The Three, the One and the Many*, Cambridge, 1993, p.181.

action in both time and eternity, economy and essence, consists in the realisation of particularity.'[149]

Pannenberg tends to emphasises the universal, uniting aspect of the Spirit. This is a consequence of his relating the Spirit to the concept of a field of force, which in turn seems to be dictated by his decision to utilise the concept of infinity as foundational for his doctrine of God. As a result, despite some considerable efforts, his articulation of the personhood of the Spirit remains somewhat ambivalent. A greater emphasis on the particularising work of the Spirit might more easily facilitate this.

Summary

Pannenberg's attempt to formulate a way of speaking of the hypostasis of the Holy Spirit develops some potentially valuable insights but raises other serious questions. His understanding of person as relationally defined is of significance but the description of the trinitarian relations in terms of self-distinction, although interesting, marks a decisive break with theological orthodoxy. Similarly his attempt to derive the unity of the divine essence from the trinitarian relations is an important move which emphasises his determination to move away from an Aristotelian notion of substance, yet raises ticklish ontological questions.

Pannenberg's decision to reinterpret ontology as a basis for a philosophical doctrine of God as the true Infinite raises problems. We have also observed how his use of the field model raises certain problems in a conceptualisation of the Spirit.

It is not clear that Pannenberg's attempt to find a *via media* between the God so conceived and the trinitarian God of revelation is wholly successful. We have pointed to unresolved tensions within the ontological structure and discovered how this is reflected in Pannenberg's difficulty of conceiving the personhood of the Holy Spirit in an adequate way. It is his emphasis upon the universal, uniting aspect of the work of the Spirit which, though apparently demanded by his method, seems to prohibit a coherent and consistent view of the third person of the Trinity.

Given some of the unresolved tensions in his work, it might be suggested that 'even Pannenberg's philosophy of logic must be

---

[149] *The Three, the One and the Many*, p.190.

provisional given his commitment to the ontological priority of the future.'[150]

[150] R. A. Hinton, 'Pannenberg on the Truth of Christian Discourse: a Logical Response,' *Calvin Theological Journal*, 27.2, 1992, p.318.

PART 3

Revelation and the Spirit

Chapter 5

A Comparative Appraisal: Jüngel and Pannenberg on the Self-Revelation of God and the Doctrine of the Holy Spirit

Introduction

The purpose of this chapter is to compare the theology of Jüngel and of Pannenberg in such a way as to highlight both the contrasts and family resemblances between them. The comparison will be restricted to their understanding of the doctrine of revelation as self-revelation and the implications of this for pneumatology. Consequently the account is structured around certain key doctrinal loci, each of which will serve to highlight aspects of their respective understandings of the person and work of the Spirit. As part of this analysis, the influence of certain writers on both theologians will be identified, most notably Barth, Heidegger and Hegel. The impact of these writers has, to varying degrees, been noted elsewhere. We have previously indicated certain Lutheran aspects of the two theologians in question. For this reason this comparative analysis will give particular attention to the common Lutheran heritage. This will serve two purposes. First, it will facilitate a deeper understanding of the theological tradition from which both theologians draw their conceptual framework. Second, it will suggest that a more detailed examination of Luther's doctrine of the Spirit might prove fruitful for future work.

The Doctrine of Revelation

Contrasts

In some ways the contrasts between Jüngel and Pannenberg are most clearly defined in their approach to the doctrine of revelation. In interpreting Barth, Jüngel emphasises the correspondence of the being of God in his act for us and his being *ad intra* in the event of revelation.

The structural principle of correspondence, which Jüngel identifies as central for Barth, grounds Jüngel's own development of the notion of God's being in becoming. As event, the nature of revelation is expounded as the self-revelation of the being of God in encounter. God is uniquely revealed in the event of the cross and comes to the world anew in an event of justifying address. The often-noted echo of Kierkegaard in Barth with the emphasis on act, event and decision, is developed in Jüngel and mediated by his critical engagement with Heideggerian existentialism, partly as appropriated by Fuchs.[1] The constitution of humanity as authentic being in the word of address in its full ontological sense is clearly indebted to Heidegger's understanding of the two possibilities of *Dasein* as *eigentlich* (authentic) or *uneigentlich* (inauthentic). Consequently, the being of God as event is structured by the notion of repetition; God is event in threefold repetition.

This raises the question of the way in which Jüngel understands history as a process. For Jüngel, historical process can only be understood in terms of the working out of the possibilities of past historical events. Thus the significance of the history of Jesus cannot be 'limited to what we know of him historically (*historisch*).'[2] Rather, the history of Jesus must be properly understood in the light of the contemporary effectiveness of the past event of his life, and more particularly, his death; historical process is interpreted out of the category of event.[3]

---

[1] Barth echoes Kierkegaard in that the being of God is developed in relationship to an 'existentialist meaning of history constituted in dialectical encounter.' T. Bradshaw, *Trinity and Ontology*, Edinburgh, 1988, p.348. The approach taken to the structuring of this chapter follows to some degree Bradshaw's comparison of Barth and Pannenberg. For a summary of the influence of the hermeneutics of Fuchs on Jüngel and its relationship to the thought of later Heidegger see R. Spjuth, *Creation, Contingency and Divine Presence in the Theologies of Thomas F. Torrance and Eberhard Jüngel*, Lund, 1995, pp.41-46.

[2] E. Jüngel, 'Die Wirksamkeit des Entzogenen. Zum Vorgang geschichtlichen Verstehens als Einfürung in die Christologie,' in B. Aland (ed.), *Gnosis. Festschrift für Hans Jonas*, Göttingen, 1978, p.28.

[3] At the heart of this approach is Jüngel's concern to avoid any separation between an event and its subsequent interpretation. Christologically this grounds his understanding of the relationship between the Jesus of history and the Christ of faith.

Pannenberg's view is that this fails to do justice to the process of historical reality. By contrast, Pannenberg explores the concept of revelation in its historical development. This leads him to his examination of the nature of religions as the context for the debate about truth. Fundamental to this is his understanding of religion as a human attempt to explain the unthematic awareness of the Infinite. Pannenberg asserts that the resolution of rival religious claims to truth can only be found in the fact that the world is determined by God.

The historical development of Judaistic monotheism, and in particular the rise of apocalyptic literature, intensified the conflict between alternative religious truth claims. The God of Israel was the one true, universal God whose revelatory acts are regarded as a provisional unveiling of the final consummation of all history. In this context the person and work of Christ, and, most importantly, his resurrection from the dead, is interpreted as the proleptic disclosure of the eschatological reality.

This sets Pannenberg against the view that God can only be revealed in the form of the word. God's self-revelation is, rather, mediated through God's action which, in itself, is the content of the biblical understanding of the word of God as an acting, accomplishing word. Whereas for Jüngel, the divine-human encounter is grounded in the event of the cross and made actual in a word of encounter, for Pannenberg the particular event of the resurrection reveals the truth of the eschatological nature of reality and opens humanity towards the future. The particular historical event is a way of access into the universal reality.

An alternative way of putting this is to say that for Jüngel, history must be understood theologically in terms of the effective history of the event of the death of Jesus; for Pannenberg, the history of the resurrection of Christ is the essential horizon of theology since it discloses in advance the eschatological completion of the historical process.

These alternative views of revelation result in differing understandings of the relationship of God to time. For Jüngel, the unique event of the cross is the central locus of God's revelatory activity. History is a bringing into the present the possibilities of the perished past. In this sense any eschatological orientation is restricted to his assertion of the ontological priority of the possible and the recreation of humanity in the event of justification. The future is the temporal expression of the realm of the possible, and thus the power of the possible may be understood as the power of the future. Jüngel does not readily pursue this to the extent that Jenson does, and it could be argued that Jüngel remains close to Barth in what some have called a trinitarian 'gathering to the past.'[4]

By contrast, Pannenberg's thought is thoroughly eschatological and places a strong emphasis on the temporal process. The monarchy of the Father and, indeed, the whole being of God, to an extent that is hard to clearly define, is seen as dependent on the historical process.

This differing temporal orientation has a major impact on their respective understandings of humanity, as we shall show later. For Jüngel, humanity is ontologically defined by the event of the cross; for Pannenberg, our true identity is yet to be fulfilled eschatologically.

Resemblances

Although Pannenberg has expended much energy in distancing himself from certain aspects of Barth's doctrine of revelation, he remains indebted to him for certain key attitudes that are also found in Jüngel. Barth's approach to the dogmatic enterprise was to completely repudiate any way of thinking about God other than on the basis of his self-revelation. Theological epistemology is grounded in the continuum of revelation of which humanity is a part.

Jüngel follows this view and this grounds his doctrine of God who acts in his freedom to become the God of another. While he is more open to a natural theology than Barth, this is developed out of the revelatory event of redemption; we may only infer a natural knowledge of God from creation on the basis that creation itself receives its actuality out of the defining event of the cross. Humanity is enclosed within the overall history of God's dealing with the world in Jesus Christ.

Pannenberg is equally dismissive of a foundational epistemology which will ground the discussion of revelation. We are part of the history, the totality of which is the content of God's self-revealing act in Christ. We can have no standpoint outside this historical continuum; hence Pannenberg's theology is in an important sense a description of God's acts in history.[5]

---

4 C. Gunton, *Becoming and Being: the Doctrine of God in Charles Hartshorne and Karl Barth,* Oxford, 1978, p.182. Whether this is the case depends upon the view taken of the adequacy of Barth's doctrine of the Spirit.

5 This also explains Pannenberg's concern to locate his own proposals within the history of doctrine.

In this sense both Jüngel and Pannenberg show indebtedness to Barth, especially his concern to locate the being of God in his acts. This in turn provides the key for understanding the difficult relationship between epistemology and ontology in both writers. Since it is God we encounter in his act of self-revelation, our knowledge of God is an expression of the way in which God's being is. True knowledge of God, expressed theologically and linguistically, is true in so far as it reflects on the being of God in the act of his revelation. Thus while Jüngel may emphasise the event character, the particularity of encounter, and Pannenberg may emphasise the universal field of God's action in the totality of history, both are essentially descriptive theologies of revelation.

From the perspective of pneumatology, the presence of the Spirit is the means by which humanity is caught up with the presence of God in his revelation. Jüngel expresses this as the advent of God in the metaphorical word of address; Pannenberg prefers to emphasise the universality of the presence of the Spirit as a field permeating creation, with the activity of the Holy Spirit understood as a concretion of the field. Yet the common thread is to regard the presence of the Spirit as the possibility of any knowledge of God; we are within the realm of the Spirit and only thus are we able to speak of God as he unveils himself to us.

A further similarity may be noted in that both Jüngel and Pannenberg follow Barth in the deployment of an *analogia entis*. Jüngel prefers the analogy of advent in which God comes to the world in a word of encounter. Pannenberg rejects all notions of analogy; his entire doctrine of God and creation militates against this since there can be no vantage point within the unfolding process of history from which we can gain access to an analogical description of the being of God. He prefers to speak of theological language as doxological in a way that is remarkably similar to Jüngel:

> At the place where the old doctrine of analogy asserted a correspondence of the Word used to name God with God himself...there stands...the concept of revelation...he makes our metaphorical speech his own through his revelation and...gives our words of praise their ultimately valid content.[6]

---

[6] Pannenberg, *Basic Questions in Theology, Vol.1*, p.237.

Jüngel and Pannenberg express themselves very differently but share Barth's approach in exploring a specifically theological view of God's presence within human language.

This emphasis on God speaking through human language reflects to some degree the dialectical relationship between the presence and the absence of God, which both writers expound in differing ways. For Jüngel the theology of the cross facilitates a way of expressing absence as a mode of God's presence in and through death. More precisely, the notion of the *Deus Absconditus* operates for Jüngel as a further way of speaking of the correspondence of God with Jesus in his death; 'the very particular hiddenness of God in the darkness of the crucifixion of Jesus is not a contradiction of the divinity of the God who is himself light and in whom there is no darkness.'[7]

The importance of this notion for Pannenberg must be more carefully inferred. It seems to underpin his whole understanding of the structural relationship between the future and its proleptic appearance, most notably in the resurrection of Christ. In this event the future of God has already dawned; God is present, the Kingdom of God has arrived but the eschatological completion remains in the future. The reality of God and his rule is yet to be demonstrated openly and completely. Pannenberg is clear that it was at the cross that the divine absence reached a 'peak of intensity;' that absence now means that creatures are delivered up to the consequences of their own actions.[8]

We might also discern a form of the presence-absence dialectic in Pannenberg's use of the field model to describe God's creative presence within the world. The field pattern that Pannenberg envisages, with its lines of force, is structured by the variations in force in space. The lines of force represent the expression of points within the field which all have the same potential energy. At certain neutral points within the field there is a complete absence of potential energy. Hence the field structure contains within it the concepts of presence and absence. This would be the case whether or not the concept of field is understood metaphorically or, as we have argued Pannenberg seems to infer, in a more realist manner.

It is of interest that both approaches to the relationship between presence and absence draw to some extent on Luther's notion of the revelation of God in his hiddenness. As appropriated by Barth in his

---

[7] Jüngel, 'The Revelation of the Hiddenness of God,' in Webster (ed.), *Theological Essays,* Vol.2, 1995, p.130.

[8] *ST* 2, p.392.

assertion of the correspondence of the *Deus Revelatus* and the *Deus Absconditus*, Luther's development of the hiddenness of God arose from his theology of the cross. For Luther, the cross mediates an indirect, hidden revelation of God. Yet, as McGrath has pointed out, it is apparent that Luther used the phrase in at least two different ways.[9] Firstly, the *Deus Absconditus* is the God who is hidden in his revelation. 'The revelation of God in the cross lies *absconditus sub contrario*;' God's strength and power is revealed under the guise of weakness and death.[10] On this understanding the *Deus Absconditus* and the *Deus Revelatus* are one and the same; through faith they are seen as identical in the one event of revelation.

By contrast, the second way in which Luther employed the concept of the hiddenness of God was to view the *Deus Absconditus* as hidden behind his revelation. This implies that there are certain aspects of God which cannot be known; they are always hidden from us. This is a fundamentally different use of the concept and, as McGrath points out, arose mainly out of Luther's dispute with Erasmus. It is therefore a rather more polemical use of the phrase.

Jüngel's theological appropriation of this terminology lies much closer to Luther's first understanding, not least because it is grounded in a theology of the cross. It is clearly an adaptation since it is used to secure the correspondence of the being of God in his differentiation, as most clearly revealed at the cross. Pannenberg seems to operate with a model, of divine presence which, while containing within it notions of presence and absence within energy fluctuations within the field, is oriented rather differently to Luther's first understanding of the hiddenness of God. The presence and absence of God seems to be understood within a spatial and temporal structure such that both really co-exist within the field of the Spirit. By extrapolating the concept from the event of the cross, Pannenberg redefines it in realistic terms; the *Deus Absconditus* is an ontological part of the *Deus Revelatus*. It is no longer a matter of perceiving their epistemic identity, seeing God's power expressed through the weakness of the cross.[11]

---

[9] A. McGrath, *Luther's Theology of the Cross*, Oxford, 1985.

[10] *Luther's Theology of the Cross,* p.165.

[11] This represents a major shift from Barth's understanding; 'As far as our knowledge is concerned, God is hidden.' Sermon on Psalm 24 titled 'Open wide the gate,' in *Come Holy Spirit*, Edinburgh, 1934.

The Doctrine of Creation

Contrasts

Jüngel articulates his doctrine of creation within the context of his doctrine of God and, in particular, through an exposition of the way in which God reveals himself to be the mystery of the world. God is understood to be the mystery of the world in the light of his coming to the world, which, as we have seen, Jüngel expounds in trinitarian terms. Since God comes to the world, the world 'can never have itself.'[12] By this Jüngel affirms the distinction between God and the world. In coming to the world, God 'claims it as his creation anew and rights it.'[13] Thus creation is viewed within the same horizon as God's movement towards the world in reconciliation.

Jüngel persistently works through the dialectic of visibility and invisibility in trinitarian terms. From the perspective of the world, the doctrine of the trinity implies

> the self-differentiation of the invisible Father in heaven from the Son on earth, visible as man, and from the Spirit who reigns as the bond of unity and love between the invisible Father in heaven and the visible Son on earth and who produces in an invisible way visible results in us.[14]

In Jüngel's trinitarian language, the distinction between the Father and the Son in the Spirit in the coming of God to the world implies the fundamental distinction between God and the world. This distinction is grounded within the being of God; 'we are to understand the difference between God and the world on the basis of God's being...as...intrinsically the one who is coming.'[15]

To say that God comes from God is to speak of the 'absolute originality of God' which, in traditional terms, is to speak of God as Father.[16] This is to acknowledge God as sovereign of all being and therefore the creator. To speak of God coming to God as the eternal Son is to understand God as the end and goal of all being. In the Son, God

---

[12] *GMW*, p.378.
[13] *GMW*, p.379.
[14] *GMW*, p.375.
[15] *GMW*, p.380.
[16] *GMW*, p.381.

aims at himself in the becoming of creation. Thus the Son is the creative agent of the creator God; 'He is the original image of the creation in that God the Father aims at creation in him.'[17]

To say that God comes as God is to understand the Spirit as the actuality of God's coming. In the movement within God from source to goal, God remains God as the Spirit. Thus the Spirit is the giver of life and draws us into communion with the life of God. There is no doubt that while Jüngel pursues this relentlessly in terms of God's address to humanity, there is a cosmic dimension to this in which the whole being of creation is understood in the context of this eternal movement of the being of God out from himself in such a way as to embrace that which is other than himself. 'God goes on ways to himself even when they lead to other places, even to that which is not God...That other which God takes along with himself on his way is what the Bible calls his creation.'[18]

Pannenberg's doctrine of creation is, in many ways, more clearly articulated. This is, in part, due to his preference for understanding God's revelatory activity as an historical process. It is also a consequence of his abandoning of the filioque clause, which effectively facilitates a greater freedom for developing a doctrine of the creator Spirit.

Pannenberg expounds his doctrine of creation is fully trinitarian terms. The existence of the world is one expression of the goodness of God. As Father, God is 'the origin of creatures in their contingency by granting them existence.'[19] Yet creatures become objects of the Father's love because they are the locus for the manifestation of the eternal Son. Underlying this is a view that the mutual self- distinction of the Father and the Son is the ground of the distinction between God and creation. So far, parallels with Jüngel are apparent. Yet it is in the distinctive working of the Spirit in creation where Pannenberg diverges quite significantly. By stating that the Spirit is 'the element of the fellowship of the creatures with God and their participation in his life,' Pannenberg still shows affinities with Jüngel's trinitarian doctrine of creation. Yet it is in his particular expression of the relation between the Logos and

[17] *GMW*, p.384.

[18] *GMW*, p.159. In the same context Jüngel argues that proper theological thought is part of the process of being taken along by God; thus speech about creation is only responsible speech in so far as it reflects upon the reality of the world in the light of God's self-revelation.

[19] *ST* 2, p.21.

creation and of the Spirit as the creative working of God in terms of a field of force, that Pannenberg takes a different path.

For Pannenberg, the *Logos* is the ground of the specific *logoi* of creatures. In this sense the *Logos* is 'the creative principle of the cosmic order...who permeates the creation.'[20] This is only fully actualised in the person of Jesus of Nazareth. The existence of creatures distinct from God is grounded on the eternal distinction between the Father and the Son; yet because this path was 'first taken' by the man Jesus, we can now speak of 'an indissoluble relation between the eternal Son as the creative *Logos*...and the man Jesus in his relation to the Father.'[21] In this way the Son is the mediator in creation and the ground of the significance and particularity of every creature.

The Spirit is the over-arching field of presence which provides the connection, the means of communion between creatures in their mutual relationship and in their relationship to God. It is in this way that Pannenberg asserts that the Spirit's work in creation is 'more than a field of divine essentiality,' referring to the 'specificity of the person of the Holy Spirit in distinction from the Son.'[22]

The comparison with Jüngel is acute. While both conceive of creation in the context of God's movement towards the world, the temporal orientation of that movement is fundamentally different. For Jüngel, God moves from his own origin to his own goal without ceasing to be God, as Spirit, in the event of his coming. For Pannenberg, the eschatological completion is determinative for this movement, Hence the Spirit's activity in creation is understood temporally as the 'power of the future' which gives creatures their present and duration; hence 'only in the light of the eschatological consummation can we of the world understand the meaning of its beginning.'[23] Once again the temporal orientation is a place of dispute between Jüngel and Pannenberg.

A further contrast may be observed which results from their respective ontologies. For Jüngel, creation is the consequence of God's being as event; supremely at the cross the divine decision was made in favour of being over against the possibility of non-being. For Pannenberg, it is the whole as a summation of the historical process which underpins his view of created reality. There is a sense in which

---

[20] *ST* 2, p.63.
[21] *ST* 2, p.63.
[22] *ST 2*, p.84. As has been argued previously, the adequacy of this as a way of understanding the personhood of the Spirit is questionable.
[23] *ST 2*, pp.102, 146.

creation will not be complete until the Eschaton.[24] Thus their distinctive ontological commitments and temporal orientations result in different ways of articulating the manner of God's relationship to creation.

Resemblances

Yet there are remarkable resemblances in Jüngel and Pannenberg's approach to the doctrine of creation.

For both theologians establishing an ontology of createdness is of primary importance and this is grounded in their approach to the doctrine of revelation. God's self-revelation of himself as the Lord is the ground of the doctrine of the Trinity. By following Barth's orientation towards revelation as the being of God in his act as the guiding motif in their theologies, both inevitably integrate creation with revelation. The activity of God in creation is always the activity of this God who has revealed himself. In the same way that God's being is in the act of his revelation, such that it is self-revelation, the being of God is closely tied in with his activity in creating and sustaining the cosmos. Consequently, the doctrine of God contextualises their respective doctrines of creation. Hence both offer a trinitarian account of creation that carries ontological implications.

While both expound their doctrine of creation within the context of their all-embracing doctrines of God, both are anxious to affirm the freedom of God in creation; God was under no necessity to create. This is the import when Jüngel states that 'God is 'adequate to himself' and that God's coming to the world is 'understandable only as an expression of his grace.'[25] Similarly, Pannenberg states that God 'did not have to create the world out of some inner necessity of his own nature.'[26] To claim otherwise would be to make God's being in some way dependent on creation.

It is axiomatic for both writers that, given the existence of the world, then it can only be understood in relation to the being of God. Part of the foundation for this, once again, must be seen in Barth's decision to understand God's being in his act. It necessarily follows that creation is only capable of being interpreted within this framework of thought in terms of the being of God. Yet, there is also a common Lutheran heritage here. For Luther, the being of God was fundamentally related to

[24] '...it is only in the eschatological consummation that the destiny of the creature...will come to fulfilment.' W. Pannenberg, *ST 2*, p.139.

[25] *GMW*, p.384.

[26] *ST* 2, p.19.

the fact of creation. God is God because he creates and it is this that distinguishes God from humanity.[27] God is creatively present in all reality, yet the power of God is not consumed in the reality of the world. The whole divine nature can be 'entirely present in all creatures...and yet on the other hand may and can be circumscribed nowhere and in no being.' He 'embraces all things and is in all, but no one being circumscribes him and is in him.'[28]

The omnipresent working of God, as expressed by Luther, has been described by Althaus in terms of 'mystery.' By this is meant the concealed and hidden work of God as the sole causal agent who works behind the agency of his creatures. 'All creatures are God's masks and disguises; he permits them to work with him and help him create all sorts of things - even though he could and does create without their co-operation.'[29]

Consequently we can find in Luther the unfolding of a doctrine of creation in such a way which affirms the freedom of God and the non-necessity of creation, but which, given the existence of the world, can only understand creation in terms of the doctrine of God. Luther's concern to uphold the truth that God alone is the creator is inextricably tied to his assertion that God is God; in other words God's creative activity and on-going presence in the world is conceived in terms which preserve his transcendence and otherness from the world. This relationship is itself grounded in the concept of mystery, the hidden character of God's activity in the world.

The Person of Christ

Contrasts

Jüngel and Pannenberg express considerably different approaches to Christology which, in turn, reflects their very different theological methodologies.

Jüngel has inherited from Barth a strong christocentrism; he 'does not envisage Christology as merely one doctrine in a series of other doctrines. Rather it provides the platform for work in other areas, and is

---

[27] Luther often used the phrase 'Gottes Gottheit,' 'God is God' to denote the distinctive activity of God in creating and maintaining the world, eg. *WA* 31, 126.

[28] M. Luther, *WA* 23, p. 137; *LW* 37, p.60.

[29] P. Althaus, *The Theology of Martin Luther*, English translation by. C. Schultz, Philadelphia, 1966, pp.107-8, quoting Luther.

normative and regulative for the whole corpus of Christian teaching.'[30] The ground of this is the identification of God's self-revelation with the history of Jesus Christ; Christ is the content of God's self- revelation.

As previously noted, Jüngel expounds his Christology on the basis of the identification of God with the man Jesus, and most especially with the event of the cross. This identification is understood on the basis of faith in the resurrection, yet its significance applies retroactively to the history of Jesus and his proclamation.

The way in which this is expressed is by Jüngel's distinctive use of the language of an- and enhypostasia. As outlined earlier this serves to place a great deal of emphasis on Jesus' proclamation of the Kingdom and the ecstatic life of Jesus lived in obedient relationship to his Father. This relationship is grounded in the relationship between the *Logos* and Jesus which, in turn is disclosed by the resurrection. The historical being of Jesus was 'being in the act of the Word of the Kingdom of God.'[31] By using the terminology of an- and enhypostasia in this particular way, Jüngel is able to explore, through the idea of identification, how God can be understood as actually being in the world in the man Jesus, and most importantly, present in the event of the cross.

Consequently the relationship between Jesus and God, as expounded by Jüngel, understates the idea of incarnation or the role of the Spirit, and rather focuses on the relationship between Jesus and the proclamation of the Kingdom and the concept of the *Logos*. Equally, while the Chalcedonian two natures formula is not denied, neither is it emphasised. The hypostatic union is a history, albeit with the structure of event in repetition.

By contrast, Pannenberg constructs his Christology from the history of the man Jesus, understanding the deity of Christ in terms of the relationship between the man Jesus and God. The key to this relationship is not found in any principle of correspondence, so Jüngel's notion of identification is completely foreign to Pannenberg. He certainly gives due weight to the proclamation by Jesus of the imminent arrival of the Kingdom of God, seeing as implicit within this a claim to personal authority. Yet the message also looked forward to a future consummation which the church found to be confirmed in his resurrection from the dead. The resurrection, understood historically, announces God's confirmation and vindication of Jesus and his

---

[30] Webster, *Eberhard Jüngel*, p.37.

[31] E. Jüngel, 'Jesu Wort und Jesus als Wort Gottes. Ein hermeneutische Beitrag zum christologischen Problem,' in E. Busch, J. Fangmeier and M. Geiger (ed.) *Parrhesia, Karl Barth zum 80_Geburtstag*, Zurich, 1966, p.129.

message. For Pannenberg it is axiomatic that this meaning is inherent in the event itself.[32] This confirmation of the message of Jesus both implies the unity of Jesus with the future coming of the Kingdom, the future reign of God, and also works retroactively back into the earthly work and ministry of Jesus.[33]

Pannenberg approaches the question of the two natures from the perspective of the relationship between Jesus and God. Instead of seeking a formula to express the way in which deity became linked with humanity in the incarnation of the *Logos*, Pannenberg argues that Jesus demonstrates his Sonship through his obedience to the Father, through which he differentiated himself from the Father. Hence the deity of Jesus is secured on the relational basis of the concept of the self-differentiation of the Son from the Father as confirmed in the event of the resurrection.

The self-differentiation of the Father is secured by Pannenberg in two ways. Firstly, in the handing over of his Lordship to the Son, the Father differentiates himself from the Son. At the cross this Lordship is called into question; the Son suffers as he enters death and the Father suffers in the questioning of his Lordship. At the cross the Father absents himself in order that he might be revealed in the Son. Secondly, the role of the Spirit is to glorify the Father. In the sending of the Son into the world and in the process of glorification through the unfolding of the history of creation, God realises his own eternal being. The Lordship of the Father is seen as the result of the sending of the Son and the glorifying of the Spirit, yet this Lordship is also eternal. The life of the Trinity in God's involvement with the world is understood as a process of self-realisation. This is not to imply that God's being was in some way incomplete prior to this process, but rather points to the fact of God's movement towards the world as self-caused.

For the current purposes this complex system is thrown into sharp relief by comparison with Jüngel. For Pannenberg, Christology is grounded in the concept of trinitarian mutual self-distinction, and in this context he emphasises the glorifying work of the Spirit. The key historical event is the resurrection. For Jüngel, the person of Christ is

---

[32] Pannenberg's whole theological edifice works with this assumption; events contain within themselves their own meaning. This is contrary to any theory of inspiration *ad extra* which must somehow 'add' something to the historical reality.

[33] As Grenz points out, this way of arguing rests on Pannenberg's ontological commitment to the priority of the future. S. Grenz, *Reason for Hope*, p.119.

viewed in identification with God, a repetition of the event of self-revelation which is oriented particularly to the cross.

Resemblances

Despite the significant differences in their presentation of Christology, it is possible to find within both writers a common inheritance within the Lutheran tradition. In particular a brief summary of Luther's key christological principles will highlight these conceptual similarities.

While Luther stands firmly within the Chalcedonian dogmatic tradition concerning the person of Christ, one of his most distinctive emphases was the understanding of Jesus as true God. This amounts to more than an affirmation of the deity of Christ, which Luther accepted simply on the basis of his view of Scripture. 'Christ is the mirror of God's fatherly heart,' by which Luther means that God the Father can be found in and through Jesus Christ.[34]

Luther regarded Christ's coming to the world and his life and death as a totality; by emphasising the activity of God in Christ, our view of God is defined in terms of the human life of Jesus. 'If you can humble yourself...and hold to Christ's humanity - then the divinity will indeed become manifest. Then the Father, the Holy Spirit, the entire Godhead will draw you and hold you.'[35]

Luther's point cannot be understood in terms of the modern tendency to pursue Christology 'from below.' For Luther the deity of Christ was a given article of faith and his emphasis on the humanity of Christ was not intended to secure an understanding of Christ's deity. Rather, it was to provide a 'window' into the character and will of God in his movement towards us and in his will to bring us to salvation. The whole import of the relationship between Christ and God for Luther was understood in terms of the will of God as he turns towards us graciously to save us; thus the obedience of Christ is a central motif in understanding Luther's view of the relationship between Christ and God. Further, Luther's focus on the humanity of Christ already includes within it the whole

---

[34] Luther, *WA 30(I)*, p.192 (*BC*, p.419) Luther founded this view on his interpretation of Scripture, especially John and Paul; speaking of these two biblical sources Luther observed, 'they join and bind Christ and the Father so firmly together that we learn to think of God only in Christ.' (*WA 45*, p.519; *LW 24*, p.61)

[35] *WA 33*, p.154 (*LW 23*, p.102). Althaus traces this view back to Augustine's idea of human ascent from and through Jesus to the Father (*The Theology of Martin Luther*, p.183).

concept of incarnation and includes the notion of the pre-existence of Christ. Any concept of a movement from below to above is tempered by the metaphysical assumptions already inherent within Luther's theology.

Here we may see the ground of the similarities and also the differences between our two theologians in question. Jüngel, in following Barth's view of Luther, works conscientiously from the perspective of the otherness of God as revealed in Christ. Yet we find alongside this the interpretation of the deity of Christ in terms of his humanity. The key to Jüngel's Christology is the identification of God with the man Jesus. This is the theological foundation of Jüngel's whole enterprise to locate the being of God as present in the event of the cross. This is in full accord with Luther's close binding of Christ's deity with his humanity. For Luther, the man Jesus who dies on the cross is at the same time 'highest God...the deity itself is present with its power in the sufferings...'[36]

By contrast, Pannenberg works steadfastly from the history of the human Jesus to the deity of Christ; it is no longer possible for him to follow Luther's free acceptance of this deity as a matter of faith in response to Scripture. It has to be demonstrated. Yet Pannenberg takes Luther as his guide in that he makes the unity of will between the Father and the Son one of the foundational aspects of the relational unity in distinction between Jesus and the Father.

Consequently we can see that different aspects of Luther's Christology are used by Jüngel and Pannenberg. They both emphasise the humanity of Christ as the way into their respective trinitarian expositions of the person of Christ. In this sense they mirror Luther who, while accepting the two natures doctrine, viewed this as inadequate, since it did not deal with what, for Luther, was ultimately decisive - the communion between God and man in relationship through Christ.

With this thought we are led to consider the role of the Spirit in relation to the person of Christ. Since both writers develop their christologies in relational terms on the basis of the relationship between

[36] *WA 39 (II)*, p.279 and *WA 43*, p.579. This is allied with Luther's strong interpretation of the *communicatio idiomatum*. Christ in his humanity had the attributes of divinity freely available to him. Luther attempted to overcome the most obvious problems relating to this, such as the complete availability of omnipresence even in the human history of Jesus, by referring to varying degrees to which the Spirit 'possessed' or came upon Jesus. Yet, as Althaus points out, Luther is inconsistent on this point and there remains a contradiction in his understanding of the two natures. See discussion in Althaus, pp.193-198.

God and the man Jesus, the Spirit tends to be invoked to define the unity of the difference but in such a way as to define God as present in his coming to the world.

Jüngel expresses this as 'the coming in which God's being is.'[37] The Spirit is thus the means by which, through faith, the identity of God with the man Jesus is acknowledged; 'apart from the Spirit of God, God's identity with Jesus remains a past tense.'[38] The Spirit is thus the agent of our shared life in God; in the sense that the Spirit is understood as the bond of love which unites Father and Son, then through the same Spirit 'God and man will have love as their mutual future.'[39]

Pannenberg consistently refuses to regard the Spirit in any way separate from the process in which God acts in the world; the Spirit is not an 'added extra' but inheres within the historical process. Consequently, though for different reasons than Jüngel, Pannenberg tends to restrict the work of the Spirit to the on-going process of reconciliation and glorification. The apostolic testimony to the risen Christ is, by its nature, spirit-filled. It is through this work of the Spirit that the process of reconciliation is actualised in history.

God and Humanity in Communion: The Spirit and the Nature of Faith

Contrasts

Jüngel and Pannenberg attempt to ground the relationship between God and humanity in terms of divine action through which we are ontologically defined. This approach shows how their very different pneumatologies lead them to significantly different interpretations of this relationship.

The category of the word is central for Jüngel, not only in his exposition of the self-revelation of God in Christ but also in his understanding of the performative word of address. God is present in the word of address and in this justifying encounter; there is a dual effect which we will term destruction and definition.

The destructive power of the word is that it disabuses the human individual of any claim to self-righteousness; in this word, which has as

---

[37] *GMW*, p.388.
[38] *GMW*, p.388.
[39] *GMW*, p.389.

its content the death of Christ, we are brought face to face with the possibility of our own non-being, we transcend our existence here and now and are confronted with the consequence that all our attempts to live out of our own righteousness are brought under the judgement of God. On the positive side, in the event of justification we are defined anew. In so far as we live out of the death of Christ, who entered into and overcame the isolation which is the effect of sin, then we live out of the righteousness of God.[40] This is the outcome of God's activity in commandeering human speech; it is a coming to us from beyond to define us anew.

Consequently, faith is defined negatively as the overcoming of self-possession. 'Whoever possesses himself does not believe.'[41] Faith can never be self-belief in any human ability to do righteous deeds. Rather, faith receives God in his coming to the world and, in so doing, experiences a freedom and an actual opening and expanding of being. The believer is 'liberated from fixation on himself' and, in communion with God, comes to himself in ever new ways. To live in faith is to allow oneself to be 'taken along by God...in such a way that within the world new ways for humanity to come to itself become possible.'[42]

Pannenberg's understanding of the communion of God and humanity in the Spirit bears one close affinity to this view. He employs the idea of 'self-transcendence' to describe the manner in which this communion is experienced by humanity. Yet this concept is expounded with regard to the ecstatic nature of humanity that is already an intrinsic part of the created order. 'The Spirit lifts us above our own finitude, so that in faith we share in him who is outside us, Jesus Christ, and in the event of reconciliation that God accomplished in his death. Believers are "ecstatic," that is outside themselves, as they are in Christ.'[43]

This reconciling work of the Spirit in the act of faith is not understood as a form of inspiration, as God coming from outside of the historical process; there is nothing unnatural about it. The spiritual life of humanity 'may well be inherently "ecstatic" and may thus actualise in a special way the distinctiveness of living things.'[44]

---

[40] This lies at the heart of Jüngel's essay 'Living Out of Righteousness: God's Action - Human Agency,' in *Theological Essays,* Vol. 2, pp.241-263.
[41] *GMW*, p.390.
[42] *GMW*, p.391.
[43] *ST* 2, p.451.
[44] *ST* 2, p.451.

There is no doubting that this is supremely a work of the Spirit. It is the Spirit who 'brings fellowship with God;' just as the Spirit distinguishes himself from the Father and the Son, so too believers share in the communal life of God in so far as, through the Spirit, they distinguish themselves from God. The work of the Spirit in reconciling us to God is to enable us by faith in Jesus Christ 'to accept our own finite existence before God.'[45]

The particular contrast being drawn here is most significant. For Jüngel, the ontology of event leads him to construe the human communion with God in the event of justification as an encounter with finitude and death and a making new which is essentially a re-creation out of the unique event of the death and resurrection of Jesus Christ. For Pannenberg the focus is much more along the lines of self-distinction and otherness. It is the contrast between repetition and mutuality.

Further, this characterises their rather different ways of conceiving the presence of the Spirit. For Jüngel, the Spirit is the being of God in the event of his coming; the Spirit is the creative presence of God in the event of encounter who re-defines our being by actualising for us the past event of the cross. For Pannenberg the Spirit is only himself to the extent that he is in the other.[46] In viewing the presence of God in terms of the field model, and denying any activity of the Spirit as the coming of God from beyond as inspirer, he is left with the only option to construe the particular activity of the Holy Spirit in terms of a concretion of the field, a focus of activity. As we have observed earlier, this seems a rather inadequate way of speaking of the third person of the Trinity, and in the present context of the discussion of reconciliation, it seems even less appropriate as a description of the personal character of the Christian encounter with Jesus Christ.

Resemblances

As we have mentioned previously, the most notable similarity between Jüngel and Pannenberg focuses on the idea of the divine-human encounter as interpreted ontologically in terms of a transcendence of being. The origins of this thought might repay serious enquiry in the light of Macquarrie's exposition of the term 'transcendence' found in the philosophy of Heidegger. Here it is of note that in his early writing

---

[45] *ST* 2, p.454.

[46] 'Not in himself, but in the other, the Spirit is with himself.' *ST* 2, p.454.

Heidegger equated Being with 'absolute *transcendens*.'[47] While the meaning of this term is not entirely clear, Macquarrie points out that it is certainly impersonal and hard to reconcile with a theological view of God as personal. Of more interest is Heidegger's own allusion to the origin of this notion of transcendence within Christian theology. On the basis of a particular reading of the creation of humankind in the image of God, Heidegger finds in the writing of the Reformers an understanding of humanity as capable of transcending selfhood and being drawn towards God; 'the idea of "transcendence" - that man is something that reaches beyond himself - is rooted in Christian dogmatics.'[48]

The question of the exact relation of such existentialist thought to our two writers is more difficult to tease out, particularly in Pannenberg. Jüngel's indebtedness to Heideggerian metaphysics, although clearly in adapted form, is more readily apparent. This has already been noted in Jüngel's appropriation of the concepts of authentic and inauthentic being. The related notions of existential distancing and the expansion of being carry certain clear echoes of Heideggerian thought.[49]

Pannenberg cannot be regarded as sympathetic to existentialist thought, yet his use of self-transcendence is first expounded as part of his doctrine of creation, which is, interestingly, the dogmatic origin of the Christian notion of transcendence noted by Heidegger. Creatures can only continue to exist in so far as they are participating in God; 'the life of creatures as participation in God that transcends their own finitude is the special work of the Spirit in creation.'[50] It is in this context that Pannenberg draws his conceptual framework from a fusion of the evolutionary theology of de Chardin and the philosophy of Ebeling. The

---

47 J. Macquarrie, *Heidegger and Christianity*, 1994, p.60, quoting from Heidegger's 'Being and Time.'

48 *Heidegger and Christianity*, p.20, again quoting Heidegger from 'Being and Time.'

49 It has been argued that the most important aspect of Jüngel's interaction with Heidegger is that it opens the way for theology to pursue its tasks on its own grounds, rather than from the perspective of a predetermined metaphysics. Heidegger thus provides Jüngel with a hermeneutical key to unlock theology from the philosophical categories of modernity. M. C. Mattes, 'Towards Divine *Relationality: Eberhard Jüngel's New Trinitarian, Postmetaphysical Approach*,' PhD thesis (unpublished), University of Chicago, 1995.

50 *ST* 2, p.33. Pannenberg goes on, 'The immanent dynamic life of creation may be more precisely described as a process of the increasing internalisation of the self-transcendence of creatures.'

conceptual link to Heideggerian thought may be more easily traced back through these writers who have clearly been of importance to Pannenberg at this point in his own thought.

The point of similarity between our two theologians is the basically phenomenological, and in Jüngel's case existential, interpretation of the communion of God and humanity through faith offered by both writers. In Jüngel this is perhaps more to be expected; in Pannenberg it is somewhat surprising though it remains muted by his own philosophical realism.

A further similarity, which follows on from the above, is the tendency to interpret the whole area of the Christian doctrine of salvation and reconciliation in ontological terms. As noted previously, Jüngel's doctrine of justification is concerned with the redefinition of humanity rather than forgiveness of sins. So too within Pannenberg, the experience of faith is related to the transcendence of human finitude. Indeed, Pannenberg offers a critique of what he perceives as an over individualistic notion of the gospel by the Reformers to the extent that they emphasised the forgiveness of sins to the exclusion of other important elements. To restrict the content of the gospel to the forgiveness of sins 'is not in keeping with the message of Jesus...it is a matter of life and death.'[51] By this he means that the gospel is far more to do with the establishing of the Kingdom of God, with all the ontological overtones which that carries for Pannenberg's doctrine of God.[52]

This similarity need not necessarily be construed as a weakness; however, it should alert us to the significant reconstruction of key theological issues which is required when Christian Theology is unfolded as a vast doctrine of God.

As a final point of similarity it will be useful to turn again to the Lutheran inheritance. Luther's understanding of the relationship between word and Spirit is of great importance to both theologians, although they apply it very differently. Luther never tired of asserting that the Spirit was closely bound to the word; this was in part due to his opposition to the enthusiasts of his day. The Spirit always works within the given means, which he understood to be the word. 'Faith comes only

---

[51] *ST* 2, p.461.

[52] This view would find support in contemporary New Testament studies, the same point being made most recently in N. T. Wright, *Jesus and the Victory of God,* Oxford, 1996.

through the work of the Holy Spirit and that is done only through the external word.'[53]

Jüngel tends to follow this quite closely since his is supremely a theology of the word. In interpreting and developing Barth's threefold form of the word as a revelatory scheme, Jüngel at times seems to subsume the person and work of the Spirit under a theology of the word. Pannenberg, on a cursory reading, seems to approach this differently. His emphasis is much more on revelation within the historical process, yet his indebtedness to Luther is clear to the extent that he ties the activity of the Spirit within that process. The Spirit is not an 'extra' which comes to the events of history or even to the word, as an outside agent, somehow supernaturally activating the word. The Spirit inheres within the process, just as for Luther the Spirit and the word as closely tied together.

Once again Luther is seen to be a useful interpretative tool for both theologians.

The Person of the Holy Spirit

Contrasts

We have argued that Jüngel's theology offers promise for pneumatology, but that this remains a relatively unexplored option in his own work. As mentioned previously, the theological tenor of Jüngel's approach tends to subsume dogmatic categories normally associated with the person of the Holy Spirit under the guise of the self-revealing activity of God in his word. The Spirit is consequently interpreted in terms of the advent of God in his encounter with the world; the Spirit is event. He is the manner in which God is conceived as present, in movement from his eternal being towards to the world, even in the midst of perishing; 'God is indestructibly his own origin and irrevocably his own goal.'[54]

This statement means at least three things. First, in the event of the cross, viewed in the light of faith in the resurrection, God is still God even in his encounter with death. God is still God in the act of perishing. Second, God's being is moved being in the sense that he is overflowing from his own being to the world and returning to himself in and through the Son. Third, in this movement God remains related to himself; God is

[53] *WA 17 (II)*, p.459.
[54] *GMW*, p.387.

his own mediation, which is 'the third mode of being of God, God the Holy Spirit.'

Further, the doctrine of the Trinity conceived in this way facilitates Jüngel's interpretation of the Holy Spirit as the 'bond of love,' which is an 'overflow' of the being of God. 'As the "bond of love" the Holy Spirit is simultaneously, the "vehicle of eternity" (*vehiculum aeternitatis*).'[55]

In the advent of the Spirit humanity is drawn into the triune life of God; this share in the divine life is not understood merely relationally, but in terms of a 'power' which confronts and interrupts in order to open up a new future for us. One main feature of the effect of the Spirit upon us is to align us eschatologically towards a future which we have already been defined by in the events of the cross and resurrection.[56] Through the Spirit we are taken along by God in the new path of love; this is life out of death, supremely the death of Christ as its effects are 'perfected' in our own beings. For Jüngel, this is the closest he comes to explaining what it means to be 'in Christ.' As we enter the realm of the Spirit, the negation of being suffered by Christ in his death is 'perfected in our mortal bodies' as 'the victorious power of love' so that God 'makes a place for us to live within his own being.'[57]

The emphasis in the work of the Spirit is ontological and soteriological; this model of the Spirit informs Jüngel's doctrine of God and is grounded in his analogy of advent. What is less clear is how the Spirit of God is related to creation and the idea of providence. Jüngel clearly intends to ground his doctrine of creation in the event of the cross and relate it to the being of God in that event. Yet once again we are faced with the difficulty in expanding a basically punctilliar, context-less view of the activity of the Spirit into a consistent doctrine of God's abiding presence in space and time.

Closely linked with this problem is the previously noted tendency to conflate language about God as Spirit with the doctrine of the Holy Spirit as the third person of the Trinity. The descriptive categories outlined above are not conducive to ascribing personhood to the Spirit. Further, given the strongly existential character of Jüngel's theology, it

---

[55] *GMW*, p.388. On this basis it is as the Spirit of love that Jüngel interprets the eternity of God as the one 'who is' and 'who was' and 'who is to come.'

[56] *GMW*, p.389, 'The spiritual giving of a share in God's own future means...the giving of a share in the future...toward which we are going because we are already defined by it.'

[57] *GMW*, p.389.

is notable that his own pneumatology remains significantly under-characterised.

While Jüngel's difficulty may be one of under-statement, Pannenberg has no such reticence. His greater awareness of the inter-connectedness of different doctrinal loci facilitates a richer description of the person and work of the Spirit in revelation, within the Trinity and in creation. Apart from the obvious contrasts with Jüngel, the critical question that remains to be addressed concerns the inner conceptual consistency of Pannenberg's pneumatology.

As noted previously, Pannenberg develops his doctrine of the Trinity through using the concept of mutual self-distinction. It is the self-distinction of the man Jesus from the Father that is constitutive for his fellowship with the eternal God as the Son. The self-distinction of the Father from the Son is seen in the handing over of the Kingdom from the Father to the Son; the deity of the Father is dependent upon the outcome of the mission of the Son. The self-distinction of the Spirit is grounded in the resurrection of Christ:

> The Spirit manifests Jesus as the Son. He thus completes the revelation of the Father by the Son...Glorifying the Son, the Spirit also glorifies the Father and their indissoluble fellowship. Here, then, we have a self-distinction which constitutes the Spirit a separate person from the Father and the Son and relates him to both.[58]

Central to this understanding is the idea that the Spirit is the creative origin of life. This is seen supremely in the resurrection of Jesus from the dead in which the Father and the Son are referred to the working of the Spirit. Equally clear from the above quotation is the revelatory significance of the Spirit, who 'manifests' Jesus and, in so doing, glorifies the Father through the Son. Further, while ascribing this self-distinction to the person of the Spirit, Pannenberg at the same time ascribes to the same Spirit the means of the fellowship of Father and Son, which he understands as love. The Spirit is the agent of communion and 'only on this basis may the imparting of the Spirit to believers be seen as their incorporation into the fellowship of the Son with the Father.'[59]

The contrast with Jüngel consists firstly of the use of the language of self-distinction. Whereas Jüngel's analogy of advent tends to reinforce Barth's preference for the language of modes of being as against

---

[58] *ST* 1, p.315.
[59] *ST* 1, p.316.

persons, Pannenberg's doctrine of the Trinity is built upon the principle of mutuality in distinction. The persons are constituted only in terms of their relations, as revealed in their mutual self-distinction. This has an important consequence for Pannenberg's doctrine of the person of the Spirit; he does not understand the Spirit as person in the same way that the Father and Son are persons because 'self-distinction does not mean exactly the same thing for each of the three persons.'[60] From the point of view of the Son, the Father is the only God and thus he must subject himself to him. Yet the Spirit both teaches the confession that 'Jesus is Lord' and that God is Father. This means that the personhood of the Spirit might be expressed differently than any understanding of personhood which is immediately available from the event formulation offered by Jüngel.

Pannenberg develops the concept of the personal self-distinction of the Spirit in his doctrine of creation and in the context of his use of field theory to describe the presence of God in the Spirit. The description of the essence of God in terms of Spirit leads Pannenberg to the use of the field model, with some of the attendant difficulties already noted. The question which must be asked is how does this facilitate a deeper insight into the person of the Spirit? The Holy Spirit is understood as a 'personal concretion' of the essence of God as Spirit; the Holy Spirit is not understood in this personal sense as the field, but as a 'unique manifestation (singularity) of the field.'[61] Yet since the Holy Spirit can only be understood in distinction from the Father and the Son, the working of the Spirit in creation has 'the character of dynamic field operations.'[62]

By using this phrase Pannenberg appears to mean that the specific work of the Spirit is to relate in fellowship that which is distinct. The Spirit is specifically personal only in distinction from the Son who is understood to mediate the particularity of creatures. The Spirit is the 'positive relation' which is 'the fellowship of what is distinct, and also the associated dynamic.'[63]

---

60 *ST* 1, p.321.

61 *ST* 2, p.83.

62 *ST* 2, p.84.

63 *ST* 2, p.84. The meaning of the 'dynamic' which is ascribed to the Spirit seems to refer to the active movement of the Spirit in preserving creation and in drawing creatures into the reconciling work of God. It is the dynamic of the Spirit's working which has to 'overcome the rifts' caused by the self-seeking of the creature for independent existence.

Here Pannenberg struggles to articulate a view of personhood in relational terms. To speak of the Holy Spirit in terms of fellowship is required by the trinitarian grounding of the term 'self-distinction.' Yet this remains an impersonal concept; to what extent is the Holy Spirit more than a relation? In answering this Pannenberg employs the language of concretion within the field, yet the third person of the Trinity acts in a way consistent with the dynamic of a field. He wishes to say that the work of the Spirit in creation is 'more than a field of divine essentiality,' by which is implied a greater specificity of action than is implied by the divine essence as field. Yet even here there seems a tendency to conflate the idea of God as Spirit with the person of the Holy Spirit. As Spirit the essence of God has extensivity in space and time; as Holy Spirit that extensivity achieves localised specificity of action, as the individuality of creatures, which is mediated by the Son, is brought into fellowship with the life of God.

This tendency to bring together the different concepts of God as Spirit and the third person of the Trinity may be viewed as a consequence of the decision to ascribe to the Son the role of mediator of creaturely particularity. Ascribing this function to the Son requires that the role of the Spirit be understood primarily in terms of uniting what is distinct; the definition of the person of the Spirit is then expressed in terms that are overwhelmingly relational. This inevitably tends to play down the particularising role of the Spirit. In Pannenberg's theology the interpretation of the essence of God as Spirit in terms of an all-encompassing field can only serve to highlight the relationship between the concepts of Spirit and universality. It is doubtful whether the subsequent use of the idea of concretion within the field is strong enough to carry the weight of conceptuality necessary to articulate a personhood of the Spirit.

This brings out the most significant contrast with Jüngel's theology of the Spirit. Pannenberg tends to stress the universal, uniting aspect of the Spirit with some cost to the specific and the particular. Jüngel's preference for event terminology gives him the conceptual framework with which to speak of the Spirit in terms of the particular, but, restricts his ability to explain how the Spirit might be at work in the processes of history. The concomitant result is that, for different reasons, both fail to adequately distinguish between the idea of God as Spirit and the third person of the Trinity.

Resemblances

Spirit of Life

In orienting his doctrine of God to the event of the cross, Jüngel speaks of God as revealed in death as the eternally living one. It is the Spirit who brings life out of death; the Holy Spirit is 'the creative power of renewal which reverses the movement from life to death by which earthly existence is defined, and leads from death into life, from non-being into being.'[64] The Spirit gives life; the Spirit is 'God Himself...who creates life in freedom, who gives life from the dead.'[65]

This life giving activity of the Spirit *ad extra* is grounded in God's own life in the Spirit *ad intra*. As Spirit, God is united in that he remains God who is both the beginning and also the goal; God is 'the one who begins something with himself.'[66] On this basis God is able to 'start something new' with us; as the gift of the Spirit is given, we are made new creations in Christ. We participate in this capacity to begin again in freedom, which is itself characteristic of the being of God as Spirit.

Linked to this concept of the Spirit as the giver of life is the idea of the being of God as moved being. This is most clearly expressed in Jüngel's analogy of advent; God comes from God, to God, as God, which is his trinitarian interpretation of the thematic concept that God's being is in becoming. There is an eternal movement within the being of God which finds expression within time as a movement from beginning to goal. The repetition in eternity which characterises the being of God as event is worked out in God's relationship to the world in that God aims at humanity in and through the Son. The relationship between the Father and the Son is constituted as 'eternally new' through the event of the cross and resurrection. This eternally new relationship is implemented for us in and through the Holy Spirit as we are caught up into the divine life.

---

[64] Jüngel, 'The Emergence of the New,' in *Theological Essays,* Vol. 2, p.55. Distinctively, Jüngel understands the renewing effect of the Spirit as grounded in the creative power of God 'in and through non-being,' as defined in the death and resurrection of Jesus Christ.

[65] 'The Emergence of the New, p.56.

[66] 'The Emergence of the New, p.58. The rather obtuse language here comes from an interaction with Pre-Socratic philosophy which defined human death in terms of the human inability to link the beginning with the end. God is able to do this because he is eternal and thus God 'does not cease to be the one who begins.'

For Pannenberg the Spirit is the giver of life, which is also understood by reference to the idea of movement. On the basis of the resurrection of Christ the Spirit is 'the creative origin of the new life of resurrection.'[67] The Jewish understanding of the Spirit as the origin of life is placed in a new eschatological perspective as a result of Christ's resurrection. In this sense the Spirit is the dynamic creative force which moves creation towards the final consummation. This is the inner logic that drives Pannenberg's view of the Spirit as a dynamic field which in time gives creatures duration and their own present, and in space grants simultaneity of existence.

The Spirit is thus the origin of all life in that creation is moved towards the eschatological consummation in being taken up into the divine life. This is apparent from Pannenberg's doctrine of reconciliation. The salvation secured through the death of Jesus 'consists of fellowship with God' and a related renewal of fellowship with others.[68] This is to have a part in the divine rule, to enter the Kingdom of God. It is this eschatological message of salvation which makes explicit the relation of human salvation to the future Lordship of God; 'the relation of the future of God and his lordship decides the final salvation (or not) of human life.' In other words, human salvation is dependent upon the future, as proclaimed by Jesus and anticipated in the lives of believers. In this anticipation of the eschatological reality, it is the life- giving Spirit who draws us into the movement towards the goal. The Spirit 'gives believers...the beginning of a new filial life in the Spirit, in a fellowship that has a part in the filial relationship of Jesus Christ to the Father.'[69] This is the work of the Spirit in adopting and in drawing humanity into the glorification of the Father and the Son.

Two things can be said with reference to both theological affirmations of the Spirit as the giver of life. First, this is closely related to the events of the death and resurrection of Christ and as such they both follow orthodox Lutheran and Reformed tradition. Second, both go beyond these traditions by tying the immanent life of God closely to the working out of God's purposes in creation. One reflection of this is the way in which they relate the immanent and economic trinities. In this regard the agency of the Spirit is a vital concept and it is therefore not surprising that the idea of movement is important for both. This is interpreted as the divine movement which takes creation up into

---

[67] *ST*, 2, p.98.

[68] *ST* 2, p.398.

[69] *ST* 2, p.395.

fellowship with the triune being of God while still distinguishing God from the world. God does not need the world; creation is a free act. Yet, given the existence of the world, God works in and through the world, this divine movement being expressed pneumatologically in terms of the life-giving work of the Spirit. Consequently, this aspect of the work of the Spirit is interpreted in terms of the triune being of God with respect to human life and our relationship to Christ.

Spirit of Love

In their respective views of the Spirit both writers utilise the concept of the love of God as the 'coping stone' of their doctrine of the Trinity. From the perspective of his theology of the cross Jüngel unfolds the notion of love to articulate the relation of the triune God to the world. As Spjuth has argued, Jüngel describes love dialectically in terms of the relation between having and not-having, self-having and surrender, life and death.[70]

The statement 'God is love' is understood, from the perspective of the cross, as God's involvement with nothingness. This is not to say that God became love in that event, but that in the unique event of God's identification with the crucified Jesus, God 'expresses himself as the one who he has always been, in himself.'[71] This self-expression of God is explicated in terms of 'overflowing being' which affirms that God's being is not to be understood a priori as possession but as a 'going with himself beyond himself.'[72] This is the basis of God's entering into nothingness in order to create *ex nihilo*. 'God is Creator out of love and thus Creator out of nothingness.'[73] The love of God is thus the ground of all created reality.

In that this concept of God's love grounds Jüngel's understanding of the way in which God is related to creation, it is important for him to explicate this notion of love with regard to the Trinity, most especially

---

[70] See the discussion on God's presence in absence and its relationship to Jüngel's concept of love in R. Spjuth, *Creation, Contingency and Divine Presence in the Theologies of Thomas F. Torrance and Eberhard Jüngel*, Lund, 1995, pp.189- 193.

[71] *GMW,* p.220.

[72] *GMW*, p.222.

[73] *GMW,* p.223. The importance of the relation between God's act and being should be noted here. The creative act of God is 'nothing more than' God's being.

with regard to the Spirit. This he achieves through a consideration of the unity of the Father and Son in their distinction at the cross. In such great differentiation in the being of God the Holy Spirit relates the Father and Son. He is the unity of the giving Father and the given Son in the event of giving; this is an event of love. Here the Spirit constitutes the relation between Father and Son as love; it is as Spirit that God's triune being is understood as love. Consequently, Jüngel's notion of the love of God gathers together a cluster of ideas. It is the controlling motif in Jüngel's affirmation of divine freedom, it is the leading category with which he seeks to expound the relationship between God and creation in terms of *creatio ex nihilo*, and it formulates his understanding of the essence of the triune God.

Pannenberg similarly grounds his concept of the love of God solely on the basis of the historical revelation of God in Christ. It is in the context of his exposition of the divine love that Pannenberg explicates his understanding of the unity of God, which is not viewed as a quality or a number, but as singularity and uniqueness. This unity is the content of the revelatory action of God, not merely its presupposition. The love of God reaches out to creation and 'bridges the gulf between God and the world.'[74] This is interpreted characteristically as constituting the unity of the true Infinite which 'transcends the antithesis to what is distinct from it.'[75] Here Pannenberg attempts to bring together the two sets of divine attributes which he has classified according to philosophical reflection and revelatory action. The philosophical idea of God's infinity includes within it the idea of the unity that transcends the antithesis between the true Infinite and finitude. For Pannenberg this can only be articulated without paradox through the idea of Spirit as a dynamic field. Yet this remains an abstract formulation which is only given content by reference to the idea of the divine love which is grounded in the revelatory acts of God. Consequently divine love is made concrete in the trinitarian relations which constitute the being of God and which explicates the form of the relation between God and the world; it is divine love 'in its trinitarian concreteness,' which 'embraces the tension of the infinite and the finite without setting aside their distinction.'[76]

The significance of the concept of love for Pannenberg is that it provides the conceptual link between the main threads of his systematic

---

[74] *ST* 1, p.445.
[75] *ST* 1, p.445.
[76] *ST* 1, p.446.

synthesis. It is the ground of the relationship between God and the world that asserts both the freedom of God and the idea that God's existence is now closely bound up with the historical process.[77] It is the thought of the divine love that conceptually grounds the relationship between the economic and immanent trinities; this is because the trinitarian life of God is understood as 'an unfolding of his love.'[78] In a way which bears considerable similarity to Jüngel, the concept of the love of God grounds the relation of the God to the world and is the supreme expression of the doctrine of the Trinity.

Spirit of Truth

Biblically the Holy Spirit is the one who will lead the disciples of Jesus into all truth. The idea of the truth of the Christian Faith lies at the heart of much of the theological agenda pursued by Jüngel and Pannenberg. It is the concern to speak responsibly about God as God, in the context of the dispute with atheism and other religious world views, which leads both to develop distinctive and yet related ontologies.

Jüngel's linguistic ontology, which is oriented to the priority of the possible, reflects the degree to which he is unwilling to work with a notion of truth as a simple correspondence between ideas and reality; rather, truth is understood from the perspective of the expansion of the actual. Truth is discovered beyond the realm of actuality in the word of address; it is the nature of metaphor to bring to speech that which is more than actual. Understood in this way, truth is an event which is defined in terms of discovery or uncovering ('*Entdecken*').[79] Metaphors state that which is more than is actual; that which is actual lets itself be

---

[77] 'Because God is love, having once created a world in his freedom, he finally does not have his own existence without the world, but over against it and in it in the process of the ongoing consummation.' *ST* 1, p.447.

[78] *ST* 1, p.447.

[79] Here Jüngel draws upon Nietzsche's critique of any proposed correspondence between the ego and actuality; for a summary of Jüngel's critical engagement with Nietzshe see R. Spjuth, *Creation, Contingency and Divine Presence*, pp.101-105. Jüngel's use of Heidegger is apparent here in his adaptation of the notion of truth as an event of discovery. Over against Heidegger, Jüngel emphasises the nature of truth as an event in which being 'lets itself be discovered.' See the discussion in *Metaphorical Truth*, pp.53-57 and especially footnote 101, p.56.

discovered. Being is transferred into language and 'the event of truth is an absolute metaphor.'[80]

The theological significance of this is readily apparent to the extent that this account of truth closely parallels the doctrine of revelation. Truth is an encounter in which we are addressed and defined by God. In this event we experience a 'gain to being,' by which Jüngel implies the coming of God to the world, who enters our worldly context and gains space for himself, expanding our sense of actuality by addressing us with that which is more than actual. This typically abstract way of formulating the presence of God in the event of encounter is given content in terms of the 'renewing power of the Holy Spirit.'[81]

For Pannenberg, the truth claims of the Christian Faith are understood to be contestable until the Eschaton. In the historical revelation of God in Christ, and particularly through his proclamation of the Kingdom and resurrection from the dead, this truth has arrived proleptically. Those who encounter God in the Spirit can have a degree of certainty in the present, yet the fundamental, non-negotiable truth of the Christian view of God will only be fully manifest at the end of the historical process.

Again, the relation between truth and ontology is apparent. On the basis of his future ontology Pannenberg argues that the future outcome of the acts of God in history will demonstrate the universality of the truth that the God of Jesus Christ is the one true God. Yet his dialectic of appearance and arrival, prolepsis and eschatological consummation, grounded in the relation between God and the world, facilitates this historically mediated understanding of truth as faithfulness to the end.

The similarities are clearest in their respective attempts to renegotiate a relational ontology. Jüngel attempts this from the perspective of the possible; Pannenberg from the priority of the future. For Jüngel, the activity of God in coming to the world in the present is defined out of the possibilities of the past event of the cross. What is positive about the perished past is the possibility which inheres within it. For Pannenberg, the eschatological Lordship of God has retroactive significance in the unfolding of the being of God in relation to world history. The two ontological systems, while displaying differing temporal orientations that we have noted before, bear close resemblances.

Jüngel's priority of the possible, with its orientation to the cross enables a particular interpretation of the way in which God comes to the

---

[80] *Metaphorical Truth*, p.56.
[81] *Metaphorical Truth*, p.71.

human individual in an event of reconciliation. Further, this event is given content since the analogy of advent makes clear that it is truly the God of Jesus Christ who encounters us; Jüngel's christocentrism and indebtedness to Barth and Luther means his brand of theological existentialism does not lead readily to mysticism. Yet, in orienting the event of encounter to the past event of the cross, Jüngel seems to offer a restrictive account of the way in which the Spirit might abide within the process of on- going world events or human living. Equally it appears to play down the eschatological thrust of the work of the Spirit in the process of glorification and consummation. The category of the possible does not rule this out; indeed, Jüngel makes some references which indicate an awareness of the eschatological openness of his conceptual scheme.[82] We shall pursue this possibility in the final chapter.

Pannenberg's eschatological positing of the unity of God and his understanding of the ontological priority of the future lend themselves to the dynamic field model of the Spirit as a way of describing the manner of God's presence in creation, in space and time. This offers one particular way of viewing the activity of God within historical processes, but given the noted tendency towards an unintended realism, noted in our critique, this could leave Pannenberg open to the charge of a vague pantheism, which is far from his original proposal. It also tends to emphasise process at the expense of the particular and this is reflected in his tendency to ascribe to the Holy Spirit the functions of universality and relationship over against personal address and encounter.

---

[82] Perhaps his most interesting move in this direction is in the essay 'The Emergence of the New,' in *Theological Essays, Vol.2*, where he states that 'the Eschaton...determines everything which occurs in time.' (p.54) This rather bald assertion is subsequently expressed in a more nuanced form in which Jüngel speaks of the Spirit as the power of renewal.

This comparative study tentatively suggests that trinitarian pneumatology must seek to embrace both the particularising aspect of the activity of the Holy Spirit and the concept of communion, the establishing of relationship between that which is distinct.

CHAPTER 6

Participation in God

Introduction

In tracing the pneumatological implications of the theology of Jüngel and of Pannenberg a number of critical points have emerged. In developing Barth's doctrine of the Trinity, Jüngel employs the language of event to describe the interruptive nature of God's address to humanity. One of the purposes of *God as the Mystery of the World* is to show in what sense this address is constitutive for the world; Dalferth is correct in seeing in Jüngel an attempt to show that the world and the church live by the same mystery. The church celebrates that which remains concealed in the world.[1]

The consequence is that Jüngel's implied doctrine of the Spirit is either expressed rather nebulously in terms of 'mystery' or is focussed upon the event of new creation, the justification of the godless. Yet it is precisely here that Jüngel's understanding of the nature of theological language as address provides potentially fertile ground for an understanding of the Spirit as the agent of our participation in the event of our being addressed - as the giver of life. This is still a restrictive theology of the Spirit especially with regard to any understanding of the way in which God might be present in creation, and through the historical process in a more general sense. Spjuth's critique is apposite; Jüngel would benefit from a pneumatology which 'can assert divine presence both in perpetual and diachronical movements and in interruptive disruptions.'[2]

Pannenberg's attempt to forge a systematic *via media* between the concept of God derived from revelation and the metaphysically derived notion of God as Infinite initially seems to give greater scope for a more nuanced pneumatology. By interpreting the self-revelation of God in the

---

[1] I. Dalferth, *Existenz Gottes und christlicher Glaube. Skizzen zu einer eschatologischen Ontologie*, Munchen, 1984.

[2] R. Spjuth, *Creation, Contingency and Divine Presence in the Theologies of Thomas F. Torrance and Eberhard Jungel*, Lund, 1995, p.220.

historical self-distinction of Jesus from the Father as a manifestation of the eternal mutual self-differentiation of the Son and the Father, Pannenberg is able to develop a strong theology of trinitarian distinction within God. Yet, it is really only by considering the resurrection of Christ that he is able to develop an understanding of the Spirit. It is here that the Father and the Son are mutually dependent on the Spirit as their medium of communion. Yet in attempting to relate this concept of the trinitarian distinction within God, grounded in the self-revelation of God in history, with the unity of God as Infinite, understood independently of revelation, it is not at all clear that we have a truly trinitarian solution to the problem of God's unity in the present. Positing the unity of God as the eschatological goal while deciding to employ the metaphysical category of the Infinite contextualises Pannenberg's use of field theory as a model of the Spirit. As we have argued, it is open to question whether the use of this model simply serves to reinforce the prior decision to understand the unity of God in terms of the Infinite.

It is apparent that both theologians have significant difficulty in their exposition of a coherent, fully trinitarian doctrine of the Spirit. Jüngel's problem is one of restriction; by developing and interpreting Barth's 'revelation model' his implied pneumatology gives emphasis to the defining, interruptive address of God. His understanding of the ontological importance of language, especially metaphor, is his most significant attempt to give content to Barth's model, yet the pneumatological implications of this are relatively unexplored. Pannenberg's greater emphasis upon the resurrection and of God's presence in creation gives wider scope for a theology of the Spirit. Yet his attempt to regulate the concept of God derived from revelation by reference to the fundamental idea of God as Infinite leads to a particular model of the Spirit that is difficult to equate with certain biblical statements concerning the Spirit. In both theologians there remains the tendency to conflate the concepts of God as Spirit and the third person of the Trinity.

This concluding chapter will suggest that a more fruitful foundation for a trinitarian theology of the Spirit might be a more profound understanding of the term 'communion.' This will be explored with specific reference to a number of contemporary theologians and will entail a suggested theological rehabilitation of the term 'inspiration.' It will be concluded that a fully trinitarian doctrine of the Spirit will be eschatologically oriented, christologically grounded, creative and redemptive in significance and will imply a distinct type of action to the person of the Holy Spirit which is best understood in terms of participation.

Revelation and Communion

Contemporary Lutheran theology is indebted to Barth for his insistence on the *a posteriori* nature of the theological task. Theology properly speaks of God in the light of his self- revelation. Yet, Barth's insistence on grounding his doctrine of the Trinity on the threefold structure of revelation has drawn sustained criticism. For example, Torrance has argued that Barth's 'revelation model' has serious limitations when used to articulate a concept of triune personhood.[3] Barth's decision to employ the term '*Seinsweise*' to speak of the differentiation within God was due to his overriding concern to speak of the identity of God. The God who reveals himself is identical with his act in revelation and also identical with its effect. When God addresses humanity and reveals himself, we meet with the person of God, 'the identical divine Subject in his singular totality.'[4] Barth's concern is with the divine identity; this is reflected in his use of the terms 'repetition' and 'reiteration' with respect to the being of God. As Torrance points out, this inevitably underplays the concept of the being of God in communion.

Torrance, after lengthy engagement with Zizioulas, Moltmann and Jüngel, suggests that a theological model based upon doxology, or communion, might offer a more integrative approach to trinitarian personhood. In particular, Zizioulas is critically appropriated in the light of his interpreting of revelation in the context of the divine communion and human participation in the divine life.

By placing greater weight upon the idea of communion and participation, the role of the Spirit is brought into prominence. In his own exposition Torrance concentrates effectively on the relationship between doxological participation and semantic participation in Christ; the reality is mediated by language. Revelation is understood as 'communication-within-communion;' by the Spirit we participate in an event which, through the 'functionality of the language of revelation'

---

3 A. Torrance, *Persons in Communion*, Edinburgh, 1996. The critique of Barth offered by Torrance is best understood as an adaptation to the approach of *CDI/1*. The perceived weakness of Barth's 'revelation model' is its narrowness and consequent restrictiveness when applied to trinitarian personhood and ecclesiology.

4 *Persons in Communion*, p.214.

grants to us reality and truth, and which draws us up into the communion which is characteristic of the divine life as we participate in Christ and he in us.[5] Torrance is certainly alert to the pneumatological implications as is shown in his own exposition of the work of the Spirit in our participation in the event of revelation.

> ...the grace of the triune God is to be conceived in terms of the full 'vitality' of its perichoretic energy, that is, as denoting the two-way movement grounded in the mutuality intrinsic to the Trinity and opened to humanity in the revelation event. The movement here is...a dynamic personal co-presence...which takes the form of a simultaneous and participative drawing and meeting, a vicarious presenting of the human person to the Father and the Father to the human person in and through Christ by the Spirit.[6]

One advantage of this emphasis on communion, as put forward by Torrance, is that it offers a more adequate integration of the immanent Trinity and the divine economy and thus enables greater emphasis to be placed upon human participation in the divine life, through the Spirit.

In the context of this study we see that that this approach provides a much more specifically pneumatological content to Jüngel's theology of address and contrasts sharply with Pannenberg's alternative metaphysical/revelation model. It is also consistent with the Lutheran tradition which has placed great theological importance on human participation in Christ. The question which must be addressed is how the doctrine of the Spirit might be expressed so that greater emphasis is given to participation and communion. Is it necessary to restrict a theology of the Spirit to the ontological category of event? Can we express the nature of the immanent triune life and human participation in Christ, and Christ in us, in such a way which encompasses the notion of semantic participation as well as giving wider scope to the work of the Spirit, typified by Pannenberg's detailed, yet ultimately problematic attempt

God the Spirit: Participation and Public Personality

One interesting, though limited attempt to do just this, is offered by Welker. In his introduction to *God the Spirit*, he sets out his central

---

[5] *Persons in Communion*, p.364.
[6] *Persons in Communion*, p.222-23.

affirmation that a theology of the Spirit which pays close attention to biblical testimony will emphasise the power and presence of God in the world.[7] The Spirit of God is described as the power of God which works in the world towards the establishment of justice, mercy and the knowledge of God, enables prophetic community and renews that which is perishable and finite, bringing new life within the context of community. This same Spirit is the Spirit of Christ, the 'selflessly delivering power of the Crucified One...'[8]

In the subsequent development of his own theology of the Spirit, Welker identifies a number of key themes. Firstly, the power of the Spirit is expressed in terms of selflessness and redemption; this contrasts with what is seen as the negative influence of Aristotelian metaphysics which viewed Spirit in terms of self-relation and self-potentiation. The Spirit of God brings into actuality the freedom from selfishness and sin which characterises the world in its godlessness; this is the actualisation in human experience of the benefits of the sacrifice of Christ. 'The Spirit of God effects a domain of liberation and of freedom, a domain not determined by self- relation, exercising control.'[9]

Secondly, there is a strong emphasis placed upon communion and participation. By the Spirit we are brought into communion with Christ. We are in Christ and He is in us; 'in constantly new ways the Spirit leads people into communion with the resurrected Crucified One.'[10] The reference to Christ as crucified and risen is helpful in holding together what we would term the destructive and renewing work of the Spirit. In entering into communion with Christ we are confronted with our sinfulness and unrighteousness; it is this which is taken and crucified in Christ. In exchange we receive the life of the risen Christ, by the Spirit. He lives in us; we live in Him.

Neither is this strong emphasis merely individualistic in scope. Welker extends the participatory function of the Spirit to the constitution of community. The Spirit brings us into relationship with God and with one another, not simply for mutual benefit, but for the sake of the world. This community is a prophetic body, brought into being for the sake of a godless world. The Spirit of God 'places people

---

7 M. Welker, *God the Spirit*, translation by J.F. Hoffmeyer, Minneapolis, 1994. This emphasis is also central to Fee's recent analysis of the Holy Spirit in the letters of Paul. See G. Fee, *God's Empowering Presence*, Peabody, Massachusetts, 1994.

8 *God the Spirit*, p.222.

9 *God the Spirit*, p.296.

10 *God the Spirit*, p.336.

in the community of conscious solidarity, the community of responsibility and love of persons;' such a community lives for the benefit of others.[11]

The work of the Spirit as the agent of participation and communion is clearly central to Welker's pneumatology. There is no abandonment of the *a posteriori* theological principle; God is known as he gives himself to be known. Yet the concept of participation contextualises the revelatory activity of God. Further, whereas Torrance speaks in general terms of doxology, here there is greater emphasis upon the prophetic, missionary character of the community. We participate in Christ and we are part of the new community of the Spirit for the sake of the world. This does not detract from Torrance's model, but may add a further dimension to it.[12]

Yet, to this point, Welker's understanding of participation remains oriented towards human participation in the triune life of God. We participate in Christ and are brought into communion with one another through the Spirit, but the intra-trinitarian agency of that participation remains unexplored. Here Welker turns to the concept of the Spirit as a 'force field,' but in a manner which is markedly different from Pannenberg.

For Welker, 'force field' is a metaphor for the presence and activity of the Spirit and the ground for what he terms 'public force fields.'[13] The intended meaning here is of the Spirit as the ontological ground for public 'force fields' of knowledge. Faith is therefore understood as a public field in which we participate through the Spirit. Our participation in Christ remains at the heart of this; our experience of faith is grounded in the vicarious faith of Christ in which we participate through the Spirit. Yet, if we are to give fuller expression to the idea of a public force field which is called 'faith,' there has to be a means of communicating the content of that faith. Here we return to the centrality of language. For Jüngel we encounter God in a speech event which conveys the reality of which is spoken; in Torrance's view our participation in Christ through the Spirit is mediated semantically

---

11 *God the Spirit*, p.282.

12 Torrance does not ignore the prophetic aspect but expounds this in the context of the meaning of semantic participation. Here we participate in the Father's 'Word of grace to the world - participation in that One proclamation that is his Self-proclamation by the Spirit in and through the Body.' Torrance, *Persons in Communion*, p.360.

13 'The Spirit is a force field that constitutes public force fields.' M. Welker, *God the Spirit*, p.242.

through the doxological and communal life of the Church. The individual reality of the indwelling of the Spirit, our being in Christ, is at one and the same time a real participation in Christ's worship and knowledge of the Father, and also a semantic participation in Christ's articulation of reality. Welker opts to describe this by the metaphor of a public field of force. Our participation in Christ is supremely a work of God's grace brought into reality by the Spirit; our semantic participation is equally a work of the Spirit, working through the words of the ecclesial community, grounded in the eternal Word. Yet this is a public reality; we share in the common faith of the Christian Church, to the extent that it is grounded in the eternal Word of God. Thus, by employing the metaphor of force field Welker conveys both the public and semantic nature of the participatory work of the Spirit. Yet, by grounding these public fields of force in the overarching metaphor of the force field of the Spirit, Welker develops a model which expresses the reality of the triune life, the being-in-communion of the one God which is the sole ground of our human participation in the divine life through the Spirit. Further, this model might give greater scope for the wider presence of the Spirit in creation. The Spirit is not restricted to the life of the Church.

The advantages of Welker's use of the metaphor of field are twofold. Firstly, as we have seen, by using the concept of a public field, distinct from yet grounded on the overarching field of the Spirit's presence, we can develop and utilise the notion of participation as the key concept in pneumatology. We can develop within this the importance of semantic participation and doxological participation, as Torrance is keen to do, yet ground both in the overarching concept of a fully trinitarian theology of the Spirit. Secondly, Welker seems more alert to the risks of realism than Pannenberg. His use of field theory is less scientifically governed and is more openly metaphorical in nature. Through its use Welker simply asserts the Spirit to be the ontological ground of our participation in Christ as well as the selfless presence of God in his creation. This latter path remains unexplored by Welker, but might prove more fruitful than Pannenberg's deployment of the concept.

Yet there remains a major disadvantage of Welker's use of field theory is the remaining tendency to undercharacterise the personhood of the Spirit. He seeks to address this through the concept of the Holy Spirit as a 'public person.' What is meant by this can only be understood once again from the key perspective of participation in Christ. As the Holy Spirit brings us into union with Christ we enter into an individual reality; each individual brings their own life story and testimony. We are taken up into Christ and our experience is personal and individual to the extent that each human being is a created particularity. In this respect the revealing and redeeming activity of the Spirit is the making new of each individual; we are born from above. The Holy Spirit is the creator of true personhood and individual particularity. Yet, at the same time, each person who is born anew of the Spirit is brought into communion with the one Christ in the one Body. To the extent that the Spirit manifests Christ in us, to the extent that we participate in the prophetic, redeemed community, the Spirit is 'the public person corresponding to the individual Jesus Christ.'[14]

There is some value in this conceiving of the Spirit as 'public person,' but it carries a significant disadvantage. To ascribe to the Holy Spirit the function of the creator of personhood and individual particularity is attractive. Biblically we are made new through the coming of the Holy Spirit[15]. Equally, we might see in the intra trinitarian life a function of the Holy Spirit not only to unite the Father and Son in their distinction, but, in the language of perichoresis, to be the agent of their mutual self-giving and inter-penetration. Equally, the Spirit as the agent of participation constitutes our union with Christ; in our created particularity we are brought into union with the eternal Word, the ground of all creation. The Holy Spirit is thus the eternally self-giving agent of communion, who, in the coming of God to the world is the public person who enables participation in Christ. This seems to be the direction in which Welker moves; it is in and through the Spirit that 'individuality and world- overarching universality are held together.'[16]

The primary disadvantage in this view of the Spirit as 'public person' is the risk of confusion between the active indwelling of the Spirit and the action of the human person which is recreated and renewed by the Spirit. There is the ever-present risk of ascribing initiative to the human endeavour in our coming to faith. Indeed, Welker comes close to this in stating that the unity brought about by the Spirit is something which we 'help to constitute.'[17] Welker is surely correct in regarding participation and communion as key concepts in describing the work of the Spirit; his particular use of the metaphor of field and the 'public field' of faith, provided it is given semantic content, may be helpful. The extent to

---

14 *God the Spirit*, p.314.

15 For example, Rom. 8:11; 2 Cor. 5:17; Titus 3:5-7

16 *God the Spirit*, p.248. It is interesting that Welker sees this as reflecting the Heidelberg Catechism; the Holy Spirit inspires faith which binds the individual to the whole church.

17 *God the Spirit,* p.314.

which the idea of the 'public personhood' of the Holy Spirit is either necessary or helpful is open to question. The related idea that the Holy Spirit is the creator of personhood and that this comes about as the Spirit selflessly gives of himself in bringing us into participation with Christ certainly has considerable potential and, as we have indicated, would benefit from engagement with Torrance's work on semantic participation.

Inspiration and Trinitarian Pneumatology

We have seen that one approach to the systematic relationship between revelation and the doctrine of the Trinity is set out by Torrance. In this section we shall draw upon Torrance's view of the intrinsic relation between revelation, participation and the doctrine of the Trinity. In order to push the argument further we shall draw upon recent work by Dalferth.

We have seen that Torrance maintains that an 'intrinsic relation' in the event of revelation.[18] God's act of self- revelation involves a 'semantic *ekstasis* of the Spirit' which occurs as we are addressed.[19] Intrinsic to this is our participation in the event of revelation, an engendering of union with the Word. This is the essential implication of understanding revelation as God's being-in-act. In this event we do not have to do with a structure of revelation; we have to do with the very being of God through the Spirit.

The whole thrust of Torrance's argument is to expound the parallel relation between revelation and our participation in the triune life of God in and through the Spirit. As Torrance expresses it, 'the communion which is intrinsic to God and to the second Adam is seen to be intrinsic to the New Humanity, to the Body of Christ.'[20] We would strongly affirm this increased emphasis upon participation as a way of interpreting the doctrine of the Trinity, out of which would emerge a trinitarian theology of the Spirit. The doctrine of the Trinity understood in these terms then ceases to become a speculative theory but a practical doctrine, in so far as it seeks to be true and faithful to the individual and ecclesial experience of God. It remains to consider how this perspective on the doctrine of the Trinity might be expressed and what implications this would have for pneumatology.

---

18 A. Torrance, *Persons in Communion*, p.363.
19 *God the Spirit*, p.364
20 *God the Spirit*, p.364.

Dalferth offers one constribution that will help to amplify the pneumatological implications of our intended emphasis upon participation.[21] For Dalferth, this participation is eschatological in nature. Here the eschatological reality is quite specifically defined as the new life into which we are drawn by our participation in Christ through the power of the Spirit. We enter into the saving knowledge of God as the Spirit draws us into communion with the risen Christ. It is the 'self-disclosing and self-communicating presence of God's creative love' which is the eschatological reality in which and through which we have our being in Christ through the Spirit.[22] The fundamental eschatological contrast is between the old and the new, between life lived outside of the eschatological reality, and the new life circumscribed by our participation in Christ; 'our human situation and the destiny of creation is rooted in the resurrection and results from being drawn into the savong presence of God's love by the power of the Spirit.'[23] Dalferth argues that there are three features that are essential to this eschatological reality; its divine constitution, its christological determination and the experience of radical newness of life. These may be understood as three aspects of one complex divine activity and provide Dalferth with a way into a trinitarian description of God.

To say that God constitutes the reality and actuality of everything that is not God is to affirm that God is Creator. In disclosing his purposes for creation in terms of his outward moving love in Christ, God reveals and redeems. In his action to enable us to understand and receive his love God is affirmed as the one who inspires and draws us into this eschatological reality. Dalferth is quite clear that these three types of divine activity cannot be reduced to anything more basic. Neither do they imply three distinct divine agents; rather, they are 'three distinctive though internally related types of action of the one divine activity.'[24]

In trinitarian terms, these centres of agency of the one God may be referred to as the Father, the Son and the Holy Spirit. The Father is the ultimate source of all there is that is different from God. Jesus Christ, the Son, reveals through his life, death and resurrection, the character of

---

[21] I. Dalferth, 'The Eschatological Roots of the Doctrine of the Trinity,' in C. Schwöbel (ed.), *Trinitarian Theology Today*, Edinburgh, 1995, 147-170.

[22] *Trinitarian Theology Today*, p.160. Notice the combined emphasis upon revelation and participation in Dalferth's terminology here.

[23] *Trinitarian Theology Today* , p.160.

[24] *Trinitarian Theology Today*, p.162, quoting C. Schwöbel, 'Divine Agency and Providence,' *Modern Theology*, 3:225-44, 1987, p.240.

the God who is Father and who not only creates out of his own inexhaustibility, but loves sacrificially and selflessly; 'incomprehensible creativity and comprehensible love are central features of the Christian understanding of God.'[25] The third feature of this eschatological reality is the radical breaking in of this reality into our lives. Our old orientation to the world is undermined and replaced by a radical newness; our whole view of reality changes as a result of this 'new creation' which is the inspiring work of the Spirit.

It is interesting that Dalferth here employs the language of inspiration. This has generally been rejected by contemporary Lutheran theology; Jüngel's theology is more susceptible to its use than Pannenberg's approach where the term is rejected as a relic from a 'supernatural' age. It may prove helpful to further theological reflection if we rehabilitate this term within the context of our participation through the Spirit in the triune life of God. If the activity of the Spirit is understood in terms of a radical disruption and reconstruction of ourselves, if the Spirit brings us into this eschatological reality which is ontologically and epistemologically constituted by God alone and christologically determined, then the term 'inspiration' is as appropriate as any. Here we are referring to the activity of the one triune God, whose presence breaks into our existence and 'shatters the continuities of our life,' and brings in its place a 'new orientation both in the individual life of faith and the life of the Christian community.'[26] This is the biblical and theological new birth; it is a new creation effected in its entirety by God but which affects all that we are and do. Dalferth's presentation of the doctrine of the Trinity consequently rests on the central eschatological reality, our participation in Christ through the Spirit; this is the true and ultimate reality in which we have our being.

From a consideration of Dalferth's trinitarian model a number of principles emerge for a trinitarian pneumatology that will take as its guiding motif the theological notions of participation and communion.

Firstly, a trinitarian pneumatology will be eschatologically grounded. In drawing us into communion with the triune life of God, us in Christ and He in us, the full and ultimate reality of our human condition and the true nature of God are both revealed and experienced. Through the Spirit, God is co-present with us and in us, this presence being mediated through Christ. This eschatological reality into which we are drawn through the Spirit bears testimony to the divine constitution of that reality; this is entirely a work of God's grace.

---

[25] *Trinitarian Theology Today*, p.164.

[26] *Trinitarian Theology Today*, p.163.

Secondly, in that the work of the Spirit is to bring about what Torrance refers to as 'communication-within-communion,' trinitarian pneumatology will find expression as revelatory and redemptive participation in Christ. Expressed in terms of the trinitarian relations, the life, death and resurrection of the Son reveals the Father and is the ground of our new, redeemed life in the Spirit. The eschatological reality of this new life depends on its christological orientation; the Spirit of God is the Spirit of Christ who died for the sin of the world. Through the Spirit we are brought into a knowledge of this reality. This christological determination of the agency of the Spirit is essential if our experience of God and our God-talk is to be truly Christian. We will explore this in the next section.

A third area in which trinitarian pneumatology will be expressed is in the doctrine of creation. This follows from our understanding of God as the all-determining reality who is the ground of all that is not God. Expressed in terms of trinitarian relations, again following Dalferth, we may summarise this through the Father-Spirit relationship. Through the Spirit we confess Jesus as Lord and call upon God as Father. The Father-Spirit relationship serves to remind us that God is at work beyond the confines of the history of Israel and the Church; God is at work in creation. God is not 'the private deity of the Christians but the Lord of all there is.'[27] This may not be known or acknowledged; indeed our emphasis upon the Spirit as the agent of participation and communion would emphasise that a true understanding of God's presence in creation can only be articulated from within this framework. This is vital if the christological determination of our doctrine of the Spirit is to be retained.

One way forward here might be to appropriate the notion of the Spirit as a field of force, but tending towards Welker's use of the metaphor rather than Pannenberg's. As the field which grounds public fields of force a relationship is retained between the public and ecclesial language of faith, which, in turn, is grounded in the eternal Word. The value of this metaphor is that it enables some form of conceptualisation of the extensivity of the Spirit; God's presence in creation is not tied to temporal or spatial locality. Ultimately, whether this metaphor is employed or not, any doctrine of the Creator Spirit must come out of the eschatologically grounded, christologically determined pneumatology developed out of our participation in the triune life of God. This itself is semantically mediated through the ecclesial community; whether the

---

27 *Trinitarian Theology Today*, p.168.

language of force fields can be a true vehicle for modelling a greater intelligibility of God's presence in creation will depend upon the extent to which this metaphor can be related to the eternal Word, through whom all things came into being.

Fourthly, a trinitarian theology of the Spirit will give due weight to the disruptive and re-orienting agency of the Spirit in effecting in us the eschatological reality of God's presence. This will include an understanding of the destructive mode of the Spirit's work, in revealing and destroying in the crucified Christ our old, selfish, distorted pattern of life.

It will also view the Spirit as the agent of our renewed personhood, the active agent of our participation in Christ and he in us. This 'inspirational' work is both the summary and foundation of trinitarian pneumatology.

Important questions will need to be addressed in any subsequent pneumatological enquiry. Most significantly, the personhood of the Holy Spirit remains undercharacterised; Torrance's work provides a foundation for greater exploration here and Welker's notion of public personhood might offer scope for further development, particularly in an ecclesiological or community direction. It remains to elucidate the significance and meaning of the concept of participation in a more fully trinitarian manner and in ways which will start to address the questions posed at the beginning of our study.

Spirit of Life, Spirit of Truth

We have indicated that one approach might be to ascribe to the Holy Spirit the function of creation of personhood. Within the context of a trinitarian pneumatology which is guided by the principle of participation and communion, the Holy Spirit is primarily the agent of our re-creation in Christ. In this sense we might then suggest that the personhood of the Holy Spirit has to be understood in terms of creative agency, the realisation and enabling of true personhood in the other. In and through the Spirit the Father and the Son express and have their personhood in the triune life of love. Through the same Spirit human participation in Christ is mediated in such a way that we come to full and true personhood. Part of that re-creation involves our conscious and willing participation in communion with and for others as the Spirit draws us into the eschatological reality of the divine action within the Body of Christ and towards and for the sake of the world. The gift of the Spirit is life, which liberates us to live in the freedom of relationship with the triune God. The Spirit of life is the Spirit of Christ who liberates us from the past and who frees us for participation in God's future.

The development of trinitarian pneumatology must seek a clear articulation of several distinctions which, we have noted, are frequently confused. To distinguish the idea of Spirit as divine essence from a doctrine of the Holy Spirit as third person of the Trinity is as important as carefully delineating differing forms of participation. Is there any significant difference between participation in Christ and participation in God? Simply using the two phrases interchangeably runs the risk that we repeat the conflation of concepts of which we have already been critical in our two theologians.

When we speak of God as Spirit, we are most clearly affirming our understanding of God as being in communion. Father, Son and Holy Spirit share their common life, united in their difference in an open relationship of love. To participate in the divine life, through the agency of the Holy Spirit is to be drawn ecstatically into this relationship, while retaining personal distinction from God. Individual personhood is constituted in renewed form by participation in the communion of God's being in such a way that humanity is not simply taken up into God and God is not dissolved into the world. To speak of the Holy Spirit is to identify the common life of the Father and the Son, standing over against them as distinct, opening up new possibilities for the future of God and creation. The Holy Spirit frees the Father and the Son for each other and opens up humanity to ever new possibilities, standing over against us as a disrupting, creative and life-giving energy.

This implies a distinct agency of the Holy Spirit, yet not in any sense that denies any ongoing action by the Father and the Son within creation. If the Holy Spirit is viewed simply as a 'filler of gaps,' the bearer of Christ's finished work of salvation into the present, then we run perilously close to a form of dispensational theology. The triune God is ever at work in the world, creating, redeeming, and opening up new possibilities for the future in an eternal movement of love. Yet here we are faced with the question of the particularity of the Christian claim to truth.

The concept of participation in God aids our understanding of God's presence in creation. Fiddes has pointed out that there are two ways of expressing this; either we begin with the universal and view creation, in a metaphorical sense, as God's embodiment, or we affirm the particularity of the incarnation. Taking the former view can lead either to a form of pantheism, or to a type of creation spirituality which views the cosmos as God's body in some sacramental sense. The latter view, and the more orthodox, is to see in the incarnation a unique depth of participation of the Father in the man Jesus and of Jesus in his response to his Father. 'Here, and only here the divine and human 'yes' to the Father were one voice.'[28] It is the particularity of the incarnation that grounds all that can be said concerning the presence of the triune God in creation. It is this very particularity which preserves the diversity within the created order and enables us to see God in the wonder of the universe.

By affirming the unique embodiment of God in the human Jesus, we can conclude that participation in Christ says something about God's knowability and the truth of the Gospel. In the particular birth, life, death and resurrection of the man Jesus, God has given himself to be known. Yet God already knows himself in the mystery of the trinitarian life; God knows himself in the mutual life of Father, Son and Holy Spirit as the Spirit frees the Father to find himself in the Son and in the Spirit the Son knows himself to be loved. To participate in Christ, through the Holy Spirit, is to participate, all be it in temporal and different ways, in Christ's self-knowledge which is precisely the self-knowledge of God. As expressed by Jenson, 'God says at once to himself and to us, who I am is the Father of that man Jesus. Because he says it first to himself it is true when he says it to us.'[29] Put pneumatologically, we share in the knowledge of God by the Spirit of Christ for 'the Spirit is Christ's Spirit and yet other than he, who shares Christ's ability to speak truly of God when and where he is pleased to do so.'[30]

Conclusion

The emphasis upon participation in Christ as a ground for a doctrine of the Trinity, and subsequent trinitarian pneumatology, has at least two important consequences. Firstly, the doctrine of the Trinity and our formulation of the doctrine of the Spirit is essentially practical rather than speculative or metaphysical. Our knowledge of God and the saving reality of his presence in Christ through the Spirit sustains a free response of conversion, worship, confession and prayer.

---

[28] P. Fiddes, *Participation in God*, London, p.288

[29] R. Jenson, *Systematic Theology*, Vol.1, p.229

[30] R. Jenson, *Systematic Theology*, Vol.1, p.229

Secondly, by insisting on an intrinsic relation between our theological talk about God and the eschatological reality which has broken into our lives through the disrupting, renewing presence of the Spirit, we are reminded that there remains an important difference between our models of God and God. To the extent that our models speak faithfully of that which God has disclosed to us in Christ, through the Spirit, then our language lives and mediates that reality solely out of the grace of God. The love of God revealed to us is comprehensible and can be received and experienced; yet 'the creativity of his divine love is greater than anything we can conceive.'[31] Our language and the understanding of God mediated through it possesses an 'intrinsic provisionality, inadequacy and incompleteness under grace.'[32] Yet as we participate in Christ we live in freedom and speak confidently of the hope which is grounded in the reality of the triune God who comes to us and dwells within us through the presence and power of the Spirit who leads us into all truth.

---

31 I. Dalferth, 'Eschatological Roots,' p.170.
32 A. Torrance, *Persons in Communion*, p.370.

Select Bibliography

Primary Sources

Works by Eberhard Jüngel

Jüngel, E.

- *Death. The Riddle and the Mystery* (Edinburgh: Scottish Academic Press, 1975
- 'Die Wirksamkeit des Entzogenen. Zum Vorgang geschichtlichen Verstehens als Einfürung in die Christologie,' in *Gnosis. Festschrift für Hans Jonas*, edited by B. Aland (Göttingen,1978)
- *The Doctrine of the Trinity: God's Being is in Becoming,* English translation by H. Harris (Edinburgh: Scottish Academic Press, 1976)
- *God as the Mystery of the World,* English translation by D.L. Guder, (Edinburgh: T&T Clark 1983)
- *Karl Barth: A Theological Legacy*, English translation by T P. Garrett, (Philadelphia: Westminster Press, 1986)
- *Theological Essays Vol.1*, edited by J.B. Webster, (Edinburgh: T&T Clark, 1989)
- *Theological Essays Vol.2*, edited by A. Neufeldt-Fast and J.B.Webster (Edinburgh: T&T Clark, 1995)
- 'The Church as Sacrament,', in *Theological Essays, Vol. 1*
- 'The Effectiveness of Christ Withdrawn,' in *Theological Essay Vol.1*
- 'The World as Possibility and Actuality: The Ontology of the Doctrine Justification,' in *Theological Essays Vol. 1*
- 'Metaphorical Truth,' in *Theological Essays Vol. 1*
- 'The Emergence of the New,' in *Theological Essays Vol. 2*
- 'The Dogmatic Significance of the Question of the Historical Jesus,' in *Theological Essays Vol.2*
- 'The Revelation of the Hiddenness of God,' in *Theological Essays Vol.2*
- 'Value-Free Truth,' in *Theological Essays Vol.2*
- 'Living Out of Righteousness,' in *Theological Essays Vol.2*
- 'On Becoming Truly Human,' in *Theological Essays Vol. 2*
- 'Jesu Wort und Jesus als Wort Gottes. Ein hermeneutische Beitrag zum christologischen Problem, in Parrhesia, Karl Barth zum 80.' Geburtstag, edited by E. Busch, J. Fangmeier and M. Geiger (Zurich, 1966)

- 'Extra Christum nulla salus - als Grundsatz natürlicher Theologie? Evangelische Erwägun zur "Anonymität" des Christenmenschen,' in *Zeitschrift für Theologie und Kirche*, 72, 1975, pp.337-52
- 'Das dunkle Wort vom Tode Gottes,' *in Evangelische Kommentare*, 2,1969
- 'Karl Barth,' in *Evangelische Theologie*, 29, 1969
- 'The Mystery of Substitution,' in *Theological Essays Vol.2*

Works by Wolfhart Pannenberg

Pannenberg, W.

An Autobiographical Sketch, in *The Theology of Wolfhart Pannenberg* edited byBraaton and Clayton
- *Dogmatic Theses in the Doctrine of Revelation*, in *Revelation as History*
- *Anthropology in Theological Perspective*, English translation by M.J. O'Connell (Edinburgh: T&T Clark, 1985)
- *Basic Questions in Theology, Vols. 1&.2*, English translation by E.H. Kehm (London: SCM, 1971)
- *Die Pradestinationslehre des Duns Scotus im Zusammenhang der scholastischen Lehrentwicklung*, (G, 1954)
- *Human Nature, Election and History* (Philadelphia: Westminster, 1977)
- *Christian Spirituality*,(Philadelphia: Westminster 1983)
- *Jesus - God and Man*, 2nd.edition, English translation by L. Wilkins and D.Priebe, (London: SCM, 1968)
- *Metaphysics and the Idea of God*, English translation by P. Clayton, (Edinburgh: T&T Clark, 1988)
- *Revelation as History*, edited by W. Pannenberg , English translation by D. Granskou (New York, MacMillan, 1968)
- *Theology and the Kingdom of God,* (Philadelphia: Westminster, 1969)
- *An Introduction to Systematic Theology* (Edinburgh: T&T Clark, 1991)
- *Systematic Theology,* Volumes 1-3, English translation by G.W. Bromiley, (Edinburgh: T&T Clark, 1991-1998)
- *Theology and the Philosophy of Science*, English translation by F. McDonagh (Philadelphia: Westminster, 1976)

Secondary Sources

Achtemeier, P. *An Introduction to the New Hermeneutic* (Philadelphia, 1969)

Austin, J.L. *Philosophical Papers*, (Oxford: Clarendon. 1961)

Althaus, P. *The Theology of Martin Luther*, English translation by R. Schultz, (Philadelphia, 1966)

Altizer, T. and Hamilton, W. *Radical Theology and the Death of God*, (London, 1968)

Aquinas, T. *Summa Contra Gentiles*, (London, 1924)

Barth, K. *Church Dogmatics* I.1; IV.1-3, English translation by G.W. Bromiley & T.F. Torrance (Edinburgh T&T Clark, 1961)

- *The Humanity of God*, (London: Collins, 1961)

- *Letters, 1961-68*, English translation by G.W. Bromiley, (Edinburgh, T&T Clark 1981)

- *Come Holy Spirit*, (Edinburgh: T&T Clark, 1934)

Biggar, N. (ed.) *Reckoning with Barth*, (Oxford: Mowbray, 1988)

D. Bonhoeffer, *Letters and Papers from Prison*, English translation R. Fuller (New York, 1972)

Boyd, R. Come Holy Spirit. And we really mean come! , in *The Ecumenical Review*, 43.2, 1991.

Braaton and Clayton (eds) *The Theology of Wolfhart Pannenberg*, (Minneapolis, Augsberg, 1988)

Bradshaw, T. *Trinity and Ontology*, (Edinburgh: Rutherford House 1989)

'God's Relationship to History in Pannenberg,' in *Issues in Faith and History,* edited by N.M. de S. Cameron, (Edinburgh: Rutherford House, 1989)

Braun, H. 'The Problem of a New Testament Theology,' in *Journal for Theology and Church,* 1965, p.169

Bruce, F.F. *The Epistle to the Hebrews*, (Grand Rapids: Eerdmans, 1964)

Cobb, J. 'The meaning of pluralism for Christian self-understanding,' in *Religious Pluralism*, edited by L. Rouner (Notre Dame, 1984)

Cook, E.D., 'Truth, Mystery and Justice: Hick and the Myth of Christian Uniqueness,' in ,*One God, One Lord in a World of Religious Pluralism*, edited by A. Clark and B. Winter (Cambridge, 1991)

Cremer H. *Die christliche Lehre von den Eigenschaften Gottes*, (Gutersloh, 1897)

Dalferth, I. *Existenz Gottes end christlicher Glaube. Skizzen zu einer eschatologischen Ontologie*, (Munchen, 1984)

Dalferth, I. 'The Eschatological Roots of the Doctrine of the Trinity,' in *Trinitarian Theology Today*, edited by C. Schwöbel (Edinburgh: T&T Clark 1995

Doctrine Commission of the Church of England *We Believe in the Holy Spirit*, (London, 1991)

Dulles, A. *Models of Revelation*, (New York: Doubleday, 1983)

G. Ebeling, *The Nature of Faith* (London, 1961)

Fee, G. *God's Empowering Presence* (Massachusetts: Peabody, 1994)

Ford, D.F. *The Modern Theologians, Vol.1*, (Oxford: Blackwell, 1989)

Ford, D. 'Hosting a Dialogue: Jüngel and Levinas on God, Self and Language,' in *The Possibilities of Theology* edited by J. Webster

Fuller, D. *Easter Faith and History*, (Grand Rapids: Eerdmans, 1965)

Fuller, M. *Atoms and Icons*, (London, 1995)

Gadamer, H. *Truth and Method*, (London, 1979)

Garaventa, R. 'L'esito dell teologia: Dio e altro dall' uomo (intervesta a E. Jüngel,' in *Il Regno* 2, (Madrid, 1987)

Godsey, J. *The Theology of Dietrich Bonhoeffer* (London, 1960)

Gollwitzer, H. *The Existence of God as Confessed by Faith*, English translation by J. Leitch, (London, 1965)

Grenz, S.J. *Reason for Hope: The Systematic Theology of Wolfhart Pannenberg*, (Oxford: Oxford University 1990)

Grenz, S.J. 'The Irrelevancy of Theology: Pannenberg and the Quest for Truth,' in *Calvin Theological Journal*, 27, 1992

Gunton, C. *Becoming and Being: the Doctrine of God in Charles Hartshorne and Karl Barth*, (Oxford, 1978)

- 'The Spirit in the Trinity,' in B.C.C. Study Commission, *The Forgotten Trinity* edited by A. Heron (London, 1991)

- *The Three, the One and the Many*, (Cambridge: Cambridge University, 1993)

- *The Being and Attributes of God. Eberhard Jüngel's Dispute with the Classical Philosophical Tradition*, in *The Possibilities of Theology* edited by J. Webster

Hawking, S. *A Brief History of Time*, (London: Bantam, 1988)

Hegel, G. *The Phenomenology of Mind,* vol. 2, (New York: Harper Torchbooks, 1960)

Heidegger, M. *Being and Time*, (New York, 1962)

Unterwegs zur Sprache, (Neske, 1954)

Hesse, M. 'Retrospect,' in *The Sciences and Theology in the Twentieth Century*, edited by A. Peacocke (Stocksfield, 1981)

Hill, W. *The Three-Personed God*, (Washington: Catholic University of America Press. 1982)

Hinton, R. 'Pannenberg on the Truth of Christian Discourse: a Logical Response,' in *Calvin Theological Journal*, 27, 1992

Jenson, R. *The Triune Identity*,(Philadelphia: Fortress, 1982)

Systematic Theology, Vols. 1 and 2 (Oxford: Oxford University, 1997-99)

Jenson, R and Braaton, C.E. *Christian Dogmatics*, Vol.2 (Philadelphia, 1984)

Lampe, G. *God is Spirit*, (London, 1977)

Luther, M. *Weimar Ausgabe*, (Weimar, 1883 onwards)

- *Luther's Works*, edited by J. Pelikan (St Louis, 1957 onwards)

MacQuarrie, J.*Heidegger and Christianity* (London, 1994)

- *Principles of Christian Theology*, (London: Lutterworth, 1966)

McGrath, A.E. *Luther's Theology of the Cross*, (Oxford, 1985)

- *Iustitia Dei, Vol.2*, (Cambridge University, 1986)

- *Justification by Faith*, (Basingstoke: Marshall-Pickering, 1988)

- 'Barth on Jesus Christ, Theology and the Church,' in *Reckoning with Barth*, edited by N. Biggar, (Oxford: Mowbray, 1988)

McKenzie,D. *Wolfhart Pannenberg and Religious Philosophy*,(Washington: University Press of America, 1980)

Mazur, G. 'On Jüngel's Four-Fold Appropriation of Friedrich Nietzsche,' in *The Possibilities of Theology,*

Mohr, J. *Gesammelte Studien zum Neuen Testament und seiner Unwelt,* (Tübingen, 1962)

Molnar, P. 'The Function of the Immanent Trinity in the Theology of Karl Barth,' in *Scottish Journal of Theology*, 42, 1989

Molnar, P. 'Some Problems with Pannenberg's Solution to Barth's "faith subjectivism,"' in *Scottish Journal of Theology*, 48, 1995

Moltmann, J. *The Crucified God*, English translation by M. Kohl, (London: SCM, 1972)

- *The Trinity and the Kingdom of God*, English translation by M. Kohl, (London: SCM, 1981)

- *God in Creation*, English translation by M. Kohl, (London: SCM, 1985)

- *The Way of Jesus Christ*, English translation by M. Kohl, (London: SCM, 1990)

Newlands, G. 'The Love of God and the Future of Theology: A Personal Engagement with Jüngel's Work,' in *The Possibilities of Theology*

- *God in Christian Perspective*, (Edinburgh: T&T Clark, 1994)

Nicolin, F. *Unbekannte Aphorismen Hegels aus der Jenaer Periode*, (Bonn, 1967)

Nietzsche, F. *The Complete Works of Friedrich Nietzsche*, English translation by T. Common (London, 1930)

North, R. 'Pannenberg's historicizing exegesis,' in *Heythrop Journal*, 12, 1971

Obitts, S. 'Apostolic Eyewitnesses and Proleptically Historical Revelation,' in *The Living and Active Word of God,* edited by Inch and Youngblood (Eisenbrauns, 1983)

O'Donnell, J.J. *Trinity and Temporality*, (Oxford, 1983.)

Ogden, S. *The Reality of God*, (London: SCM, 1967)

Olson, R. 'Wolfhart Pannenberg's Doctrine of the Trinity,' in *Scottish Journal of Theology*, 43, 1990, pp.175-206

Olthus, J. 'God as True Infinite: Concerns about Wolfhart Pannenberg's Systematic Theology Vol.1,' in *Calvin Theological Journal*, 27, 1992

Otto, R. *The Idea of the Holy*, (New York, 1958)

Placher, W. 'The Present Absence of Christ,' in *Encounter*, 40, 1979

Polk, D. *On the Way to God: an Exploration into the Theology of Wolfhart Pannenberg*, (Lanham: University Press of America, 1989)

Prenter, R. *Spiritus Creator*, (Philadelphia, 1953)

Rahner, K. *The Trinity*, (New York, 1974)

Rendtorff, R. 'The Concept of Revelation in Ancient Israel', in *Revelation as History*

Ross, J.R. 'Historical Knowledge as a Basis for Faith,' in *Zygon*, 13, 1978, pp.209-224

Russell, D.S., *The Method and Message of Jewish Apocalyptic*, (London, 1964)

Schwöbel, C. 'Divine Agency and Providence,' in *Modern Theology*, 3:225-44, 1987

- 'Theology in Anthropological Perspective,' in *King's Theological Review,* X.2, 1987

- *Wolfhart Pannenberg, The Modern Theologians Vol.1*, edited by D. Ford

- *God, Action and Revelation*, (Kampen: Kok Pharos, 1992)

Spjuth, R. *Creation, Contingency and Divine Presence in the Theologies of Thomas F. Torrance and Eberhard Jüngel*, (Lund: Lund University, 1995)

Stroup, G. *The Promise of Narrative Theology*, (Atlanta, 1981)

Strobel, L. *Inside the Mind of Unchurched Harry and Mary*, (Grand Rapids, Michigan, 1993)

Thompson, J., 'Jüngel on Barth,' in *The Possibilities of Theology*

Torrance, A. *Persons in Communion. Trinitarian Description and Human Participation*, (Edinburgh: T&T Clark, 1996)

Troeltsch, E. *The Absoluteness of Christianity and the History of Religions,* English translation by Richmond (1971)

Tupper, E.F. *The Theology of Wolfhart Pannenberg*, (Philadelphia, 1973)

Venema, C.P. 'History, Human Freedom, and the idea of God in the Theology of Wolfhart Pannenberg,' in *Calvin Theological Journal*,, 1992, 17.

Ward, K. *God, Chance and Necessity*, (Oxford, 1996)

Watson, F. 'Is Revelation an Event?' in *Modern Theology*, 1994, 10.1, 383-399

Webster, J.B. *Eberhard Jüngel: An Introduction to his Theology*, (Cambridge: Cambridge University, 1986)

Webster, J.B. (ed.) *The Possibilities of Theology*, (Edinburgh: T&T Clark, 1994)

Welker, M. *God the Spirit*, English translation by J.F. Hoffmeyer, (Minneapolis: Fortress, 1994)

Whitehead, A. *Science and the Modern Mind*, (Cambridge, 1927)

- *Process and Reality: An Essay in Cosmology*, (New York, 1929)

Worthing, P. *God, Creation and Contemporary Physics*, (Oxford, 1996)

Wright, N.T. *Jesus and the Victory of God*, (London: SPCK, 1996)

Zizioulas, J. *Being as Communion*, (New York: St. Vladimir's, 1985)

- 'The Doctrine of God the Trinity today: Suggestions for an Ecumenical Study,' in BCC Study Commission *The Forgotten Trinity* (1991, pp. 19-32)

Theses and Unpublished Works

Colwell, J. 'Provisionality and Actuality: a study of the relationship between KarlBarth's Doctrine of Election and Eternity,' (PhD Thesis, King's College, London, 1985)

Gnanakan, K. 'God and Man in Universal History', (King's College, London, unpublished PhD thesis, 1982)

Kim, Y.S. 'Jesus and the Triune God: a Study of the Relationship between Christology and the Trinity in Wolfhart Pannenberg's Theology,' PhD (unpublished), King's College, London, 1992

McDermott, B. 'The Personal Unity of Jesus and God according to Pannenberg,' PhD (unpublished), (Nijmegan, 1973)

Mattes, M.C. 'Towards Divine Relationality: Eberhard Jüngel's New Trinitarian Postmetaphysical Approach,' PhD (University of Chicago, 1995)

Index of Names

Augustine, 45, 48, 137, 159
Austin, J.L., 11
Althaus, P., 178
Aquinas, T., 45

Barth, K., 3-14, 23, 29, 30, 31, 32, 38, 39, 40, 42, 43 44, 50, 51, 52, 54, 64, 65, 66, 67, 67, 68, 77, 78, 79, 89, 91, 98, 144, 155, 167, 168, 170, 171, 172, 177, 178, 182, 187, 190, 198, 201, 202, 203, 217
Bonhoeffer, D., 36, 38
Bultmann, R., 3, 4, 6, 78, 80
Braun, H., 4, 5, 6

Cobb, J., 100, 103
Cremer, H., 105, 107

Dalferth, I., 201, 209, 210, 211, 212
de Chardin, T., 186

Ebeling, G., 44, 186

Ford, D., 30
Fuchs, E. 44, 54, 168

Gollwitzer, H., 4, 5, 6
Gregory of Nyssa, 52, 100, 134
Grenz, S., 82, 88, 96, 113, 114, 115, 118, 120, 121, 133, 155
Gunton, C., 31, 32, 67, 118, 119, 161

Jenson, R., 12, 52, 53, 62, 63, 64, 115, 117, 119, 170, 215

Luther, M., 8, 22, 31, 36, 37, 38, 48, 49, 53, 54, 55, 69, 70, 114,

Hegel, G.W.F., 36, 37, 38, 78, 92, 100, 105, 118, 119, 124, 125, 134, 150, 155, 167
Hesse, M., 151, 67, 172, 173, 177, 178, 181, 182, 187, 188, 198

Macquarrie, J., 185
McGrath, A.E., 173
McKenzie, D., 120
Mazur, G., 28
Molnar, P.D., 67, 68, 153, 154, 155, 157
Moltmann, J., 54, 62, 63, 86, 87, 98, 132, 133, 203

Nietzsche, F., 26, 28

Obitts, S., 111
Olson, R., 89, 118, 120, 121, 158

Placher, W., 115
Polk, D., 116, 156, 157, 158
Prenter, R., 143

Rahner, K., 20, 98

Schwöbel, C., 103, 113, 148, 150
Scotus, D., 77, 100, 134
Spjuth, R., 195, 201

Thompson, J., 66, 67, 69
Torrance, A., 203, 204, 206, 207, 209, 212, 213
Troeltsch, E., 82

von Rad, G., 78

Watson, F., 29, 31
Webster, J., 3, 14, 28, 31, 32, 39, 49, 50, 73
Welker, M., 69, 70, 204, 205, 206, 207, 208, 212, 213

Whitehead, A.N., 10, 15, 16, 142, 151
Worthing, P., 152

Zizioulas, J., 20, 203

Subject Index

analogia entis, 171
analogy, 25, 72, 73, 100, 171, 189-193, 198
anthropology, 4, 49, 50, 51, 58, 67, 68, 73, 150
atheism, 23-27, 38-40, 77, 197

belief, 50, 111, 184

creation:
  and evolution, 186
  ex nihilo, 55, 56, 58, 61, 69, 195
  God's relation to, 11, 14, 15, 19, 41, 55, 87, 97, 99, 101, 104, 107-109
  future of, 62, 195
  and new creation, 55, 69, 72, 87, 193
  and the Spirit, 124-133, 171, 192
  suffering of, 74
Church, 29, 39, 64, 86, 207, 212
communion, 97, 159, 175, 176, 182-184, 187, 190, 199, 202-212, 213, 214
contingency, 110, 125, 131, 175
culture, 150

death, 12, 14, 17, 18, 26, 27, 72, 73, 87, 88, 139, 172, 180, 188-192
death of God, 28, 36-38, 41, 60, 94
doxology, 203, 206

economy of salvation, 4, 20, 89, 107
epistemology, 121, 150, 155, 170
eternity, 7, 52, 93, 97, 99, 102, 106, 110, 130-136, 139-141, 155, 162, 189, 193
evil, 121, 149, 158
eschatology, 23, 62-64, 83-85, 88, 95, 97, 98, 106, 117-120, 129, 131-134, 142, 149, 155-158, 160, 167-170, 179, 196, 195, 199-205, 210-214
existence of God, 25, 38, 40-42, 90, 101-105, 197
existentialism, 43, 168, 198
existentialist, 3.186
experience, 11, 13, 21, 30, 45, 47, 50, 72, 80, 81, 91, 101, 111, 113, 133, 154, 197, 205, 209
  as anticipation, 155
  historical, 88, 91, 98
  and participation, 206, 208, 210
  provisionality of, 83
  and revelation, 82
  self-transcendence, 48, 49, 51, 133, 159, 184, 186, 198
  subjectivity, 5, 7

faith, 173, 179, 181-185, 187-198, 206, 207, 209, 213, 214
fall of humanity, 111, 121, 149, 150
field theory, 102-104, 107, 109, 110, 121, 123-128, 129-138, 148, 151-153, 157, 159, 160-162, 171-173, 176, 185, 191, 192, 193, 196, 199, 202, 206-209, 213
filioque, 18, 95, 175
forgiveness, 71, 187
freedom, 7, 10, 14-16, 20, 23, 27, 43, 50, 51, 57, 63, 67, 69, 120, 125, 126, 147, 155-159, 170, 175, 177, 184, 193, 195, 196, 205, 213, 216

goodness of God, 110, 126, 175
Gospel, 12, 30, 47, 56, 57, 62, 68, 118, 187, 215
grace, 22, 49, 50, 67, 110, 121, 149, 177, 204, 207, 211, 216
hiddenness of God, 8, 32, 43, 172-174
history, 5, 12, 37, 40, 47, 50, 54, 59, 60, 65-67, 78-91, 98, 108, 110, 113, 116, 117-120, 127, 137, 140, 141, 148, 154, 155, 157, 168, 169-171, 179-184, 188, 198, 202, 212
hypostasis, 109, 145, 146, 159-162

image of God, 50, 186
immanence, 15, 27, 32, 42, 106, 107, 118, 126, 134, 150, 151, 158, 161
incarnation, 23, 39, 40, 68, 85, 108, 154, 156, 179, 182, 214, 215
infinity, 52, 100, 105, 107, 121, 123, 132-135, 148, 149, 150, 162, 196
inspiration, 114, 184, 202, 209, 211, 213
Israel, 78, 79, 82-84, 91, 169, 212

Jesus Christ:
  anhypostasia/enhypostasia 39, 40, 179
  ascension, 62, 68
  cross, 17-19, 23, 26-28, 31, 35, 36-38, 41-43, 47, 48, 51-53, 56, 58-61, 63, 65-68, 71, 73, 87, 94 98, 168-173, 176, 179-182, 185, 188, 189, 192, 193, 195, 198
  divinity, 85, 181
  humanity, 31, 37-40, 180, 181, 182
  resurrection, 12, 18, 40, 51, 52, 56, 58, 61-64, 68, 84-88, 94, 95, 112, 115-118, 131, 140, 154, 169, 172, 179, 180, 185, 188-190, 193, 194, 198, 202, 210-212, 215
  see also, incarnation and Trinity
judgement, 71, 72, 105, 184
justice, 29, 71, 205

justification, 4, 27, 35, 47-58, 61, 67, 69, 70, 72, 73, 151, 169, 184, 185, 187, 201

kenosis, 42
kerygma, 40
Kingdom of God, 11, 40, 54, 73, 91, 93, 94, 97, 120, 136, 140, 172, 179, 180, 187, 190, 194, 198

language, 3, 4, 9, 10-14, 16, 17, 23-25, 27, 30-32, 35, 37, 40, 41, 43-47, 51, 68, 72, 73, 88, 96, 103, 116, 119, 149, 152, 171, 172, 179, 189-191, 197, 201-203, 206, 208, 211, 212, 213, 216
Logos, 39, 40, 89, 161, 175, 176, 179, 180
love, 7, 10, 19-23, 29, 31, 32, 35, 37, 45, 52, 57, 61, 66, 67, 90, 94, 95, 108-111, 121, 125, 126, 143-148, 159, 160, 174, 175, 183, 188-190, 195-197, 206, 210, 211, 213-216

Marxism, 29
metaphor/metaphorical, 25, 43, 47, 64, 72, 73, 88, 116, 117, 151, 152, 171, 197, 202, 206, 207, 208, 212, 213, 214
metaphysics, 15, 54, 58, 59, 70, 103, 128, 134, 136, 186, 205
modalism, 89, 90, 169
monotheism, 93, 94, 173
mystery, 21-23, 25, 28, 31, 32, 35, 61, 67, 114, 174, 178, 201, 215

natural theology, 170
New Testament, 4, 11, 12, 21, 64, 78, 83-85, 106, 143

Old Testament, 78, 83, 125
omnipotence, 38, 41, 42, 106, 107, 108
omnipresence, 35, 37, 49, 106, 107
ontology, 37, 39, 49, 53-64, 68, 73, 120, 121, 136, 139, 148, 153, 155, 157, 158, 162, 171, 177, 185, 197, 198
openness, 80, 83, 111, 130, 199
otherness, 27, 103, 125, 134, 161, 178, 182, 185

pantheism, 199, 214
perichoresis, 107, 120, 208
person/personhood, 9, 15, 22, 30, 32, 45, 55, 56, 64, 89-95, 96-101, 104, 107, 109, 110, 114, 119, 121, 123-125, 128, 129, 135, 143-148, 152, 153, 158-162, 179, 185, 186, 190-193, 203-209, 213, 214
philosophy, 3, 10, 28, 29, 37, 46, 59, 77, 124, 127, 128, 141, 142, 147, 162, 185, 186
Process theology/philosophy, 10, 11, 15, 16, 120, 141, 142
proclamation, 40, 44, 47, 86, 140, 154, 179, 198
promise, 48, 62, 73, 188
providence, 189

realism, 80, 153, 187, 199, 207
reason, 78, 91, 103, 111, 133, 147
relativism, 24, 82
religion, 29, 36, 79, 81-84, 91, 101, 112, 113, 150
  history of, 154, 169

sacrament, 114, 215
salvation, 4, 20, 21, 39, 51, 60, 70, 71, 89, 98, 99, 107, 113, 120, 135, 181, 187, 194, 214
science, 24, 104, 128, 151
self-differentiation, 23, 92, 93, 118, 120, 174, 180, 202
self-realisation, 180
sin, 48, 51, 56, 61, 69, 71, 111, 121, 149, 150, 184, 205, 212

subordinationism, 92, 90, 117
substance, 26, 28, 53, 103, 124, 127, 128, 141, 161

theism, 23-26, 28, 29, 41, 53
theodicy, 74, 158
time, 46, 48, 59, 81, 106, 107, 110, 129-132, 136, 137-143, 152, 155, 156, 162, 169, 189, 193, 199
transcendence, 27, 42, 63, 106, 107, 133, 134, 150, 159, 178, 185-187

Trinity:
  Barth's doctrine of, 5, 6, 23, 91, 111, 113, 122, 177, 201, 203, 204
  correspondence (*ad extra*/*ad intra*), 5, 6, 18, 31, 42, 179, 197, 213
  and freedom of God, 127
  history of doctrine, 89-91, 118
  and the Holy Spirit, 31, 109, 121, 124, 128, 129, 135, 159, 160, 162, 188, 189, 194, 191, 192, 195, 202, 209, 211, 214, 215
  immanent/economic Trinity, 4, 5, 14, 20, 24, 66-68, 98-100, 106, 110, 111, 118-122, 155, 158, 195, 201, 204
  and the infinity of God, 148
  and Jesus Christ, 23, 67, 91, 185
  mutual relations, 9, 11, 16, 89, 95, 96, 107, 121, 143-145, 147, 158, 174, 190, 199
  and philosophy, 91, 118, 134, 163
  and salvation, 98, 99
  and the unity of God, 9, 91, 99-104, 113, 120, 147, 148, 152, 174
truth, 3, 56, 61, 65, 68, 72, 74, 81-83, 88, 112, 113, 141-142, 154, 155, 169, 178, 197, 198, 204, 213-216

universal history, 79, 118

wisdom, 110, 113

word of address, 13, 35, 43, 45-50, 52, 53, 168, 171, 183, 197

worship, 207, 215

Paternoster Biblical Monographs

(All titles uniform with this volume)
Dates in bold are of projected publication

Joseph Abraham
Eve: Accused or Acquitted?
A Reconsideration of Feminist Readings of the Creation Narrative Texts in Genesis 1–3

Two contrary views dominate contemporary feminist biblical scholarship. One finds in the Bible an unequivocal equality between the sexes from the very creation of humanity, whilst the other sees the biblical text as irredeemably patriarchal and androcentric. Dr Abraham enters into dialogue with both camps as well as introducing his own method of approach. An invaluable tool for any one who is interested in this contemporary debate.

2002 / 0-85364-971-5 / xxiv + 272pp

Octavian D. Baban
Mimesis and Luke's on the Road Encounters in Luke-Acts
Luke's Theology of the Way and its Literary Representation

The book argues on theological and literary (mimetic) grounds that Luke's on-the-road encounters, especially those belonging to the post-Easter period, are part of his complex theology of the Way. Jesus' teaching and that of the apostles is presented by Luke as a challenging answer to the Hellenistic reader's thirst for adventure, good literature, and existential paradigms.

2005 */ 1-84227-253-5 / approx. 374pp*

Paul Barker
The Triumph of Grace in Deuteronomy

This book is a textual and theological analysis of the interaction between the sin and faithlessness of Israel and the grace of Yahweh in response, looking especially at Deuteronomy chapters 1–3, 8–10 and 29–30. The author argues that the grace of Yahweh is determinative for the ongoing relationship between Yahweh and Israel and that Deuteronomy anticipates and fully expects Israel to be faithless.

2004 / 1-84227-226-8 / xxii + 270pp

Jonathan F. Bayes
The Weakness of the Law
God's Law and the Christian in New Testament Perspective

A study of the four New Testament books which refer to the law as weak (Acts, Romans, Galatians, Hebrews) leads to a defence of the third use in the Reformed debate about the law in the life of the believer.

2000 / 0-85364-957-X / xii + 244pp

Mark Bonnington

The Antioch Episode of Galatians 2:11-14 in Historical and Cultural Context

The Galatians 2 'incident' in Antioch over table-fellowship suggests significant disagreement between the leading apostles. This book analyses the background to the disagreement by locating the incident within the dynamics of social interaction between Jews and Gentiles. It proposes a new way of understanding the relationship between the individuals and issues involved.

***2005** / 1-84227-050-8 / approx. 350pp*

David Bostock

A Portrayal of Trust

The Theme of Faith in the Hezekiah Narratives

This study provides detailed and sensitive readings of the Hezekiah narratives (2 Kings 18–20 and Isaiah 36–39) from a theological perspective. It concentrates on the theme of faith, using narrative criticism as its methodology. Attention is paid especially to setting, plot, point of view and characterization within the narratives. A largely positive portrayal of Hezekiah emerges that underlines the importance and relevance of scripture.

***2005** / 1-84227-314-0 / approx. 300pp*

Mark Bredin

Jesus, Revolutionary of Peace

A Non-violent Christology in the Book of Revelation

This book aims to demonstrate that the figure of Jesus in the Book of Revelation can best be understood as an active non-violent revolutionary.

2003 / 1-84227-153-9 / xviii + 262pp

Robinson Butarbutar

Paul and Conflict Resolution

An Exegetical Study of Paul's Apostolic Paradigm in 1 Corinthians 9

The author sees the apostolic paradigm in 1 Corinthians 9 as part of Paul's unified arguments in 1 Corinthians 8–10 in which he seeks to mediate in the dispute over the issue of food offered to idols. The book also sees its relevance for dispute-resolution today, taking the conflict within the author's church as an example.

***2006** / 1-84227-315-9 / approx. 280pp*

Daniel J-S Chae

Paul as Apostle to the Gentiles

His Apostolic Self-awareness and its Influence on the Soteriological Argument in Romans

Opposing 'the post-Holocaust interpretation of Romans', Daniel Chae competently demonstrates that Paul argues for the equality of Jew and Gentile in Romans. Chae's fresh exegetical interpretation is academically outstanding and spiritually encouraging.

1997 / 0-85364-829-8 / xiv + 378pp

Luke L. Cheung

The Genre, Composition and Hermeneutics of the Epistle of James

The present work examines the employment of the wisdom genre with a certain compositional structure and the interpretation of the law through the Jesus tradition of the double love command by the author of the Epistle of James to serve his purpose in promoting perfection and warning against doubleness among the eschatologically renewed people of God in the Diaspora.

2003 / 1-84227-062-1 / xvi + 372pp

Youngmo Cho

Spirit and Kingdom in the Writings of Luke and Paul

The relationship between Spirit and Kingdom is a relatively unexplored area in Lukan and Pauline studies. This book offers a fresh perspective of two biblical writers on the subject. It explores the difference between Luke's and Paul's understanding of the Spirit by examining the specific question of the relationship of the concept of the Spirit to the concept of the Kingdom of God in each writer.

***2005** / 1-84227-316-7 / approx. 270pp*

Andrew C. Clark

Parallel Lives

The Relation of Paul to the Apostles in the Lucan Perspective

This study of the Peter-Paul parallels in Acts argues that their purpose was to emphasize the themes of continuity in salvation history and the unity of the Jewish and Gentile missions. New light is shed on Luke's literary techniques, partly through a comparison with Plutarch.

2001 / 1-84227-035-4 / xviii + 386pp

Andrew D. Clarke

Secular and Christian Leadership in Corinth

A Socio-Historical and Exegetical Study of 1 Corinthians 1–6

This volume is an investigation into the leadership structures and dynamics of first-century Roman Corinth. These are compared with the practice of leadership in the Corinthian Christian community which are reflected in 1 Corinthians 1–6, and contrasted with Paul's own principles of Christian leadership.

***2005** / 1-84227-229-2 / 200pp*

Stephen Finamore

God, Order and Chaos

René Girard and the Apocalypse

Readers are often disturbed by the images of destruction in the book of Revelation and unsure why they are unleashed after the exaltation of Jesus. This book examines past approaches to these texts and uses René Girard's theories to revive some old ideas and propose some new ones.

***2005** / 1-84227-197-0 / approx. 344pp*

David G. Firth

Surrendering Retribution in the Psalms

Responses to Violence in the Individual Complaints

In *Surrendering Retribution in the Psalms*, David Firth examines the ways in which the book of Psalms inculcates a model response to violence through the repetition of standard patterns of prayer. Rather than seeking justification for retributive violence, Psalms encourages not only a surrender of the right of retribution to Yahweh, but also sets limits on the retribution that can be sought in imprecations. Arising initially from the author's experience in South Africa, the possibilities of this model to a particular context of violence is then briefly explored.

***2005** / 1-84227-337-X / xviii + 154pp*

Scott J. Hafemann

Suffering and Ministry in the Spirit

Paul's Defence of His Ministry in II Corinthians 2:14–3:3

Shedding new light on the way Paul defended his apostleship, the author offers a careful, detailed study of 2 Corinthians 2:14–3:3 linked with other key passages throughout 1 and 2 Corinthians. Demonstrating the unity and coherence of Paul's argument in this passage, the author shows that Paul's suffering served as the vehicle for revealing God's power and glory through the Spirit.

2000 / 0-85364-967-7 / xiv + 262pp

Scott J. Hafemann

Paul, Moses and the History of Israel

The Letter/Spirit Contrast and the Argument from Scripture in 2 Corinthians 3

An exegetical study of the call of Moses, the second giving of the Law (Exodus 32–34), the new covenant, and the prophetic understanding of the history of Israel in 2 Corinthians 3. Hafemann's work demonstrates Paul's contextual use of the Old Testament and the essential unity between the Law and the Gospel within the context of the distinctive ministries of Moses and Paul.

2005 / 1-84227-317-5 / xii + 498pp

Douglas S. McComiskey

Lukan Theology in the Light of the Gospel's Literary Structure

Luke's Gospel was purposefully written with theology embedded in its patterned literary structure. A critical analysis of this cyclical structure provides new windows into Luke's interpretation of the individual pericopes comprising the Gospel and illuminates several of his theological interests.

2004 / 1-84227-148-2 / xviii + 388pp

Stephen Motyer

Your Father the Devil?

A New Approach to John and 'The Jews'

Who are 'the Jews' in John's Gospel? Defending John against the charge of antisemitism, Motyer argues that, far from demonising the Jews, the Gospel seeks to present Jesus as 'Good News for Jews' in a late first century setting.

1997 / 0-85364-832-8 / xiv + 260pp

Esther Ng

Reconstructing Christian Origins?

The Feminist Theology of Elizabeth Schüssler Fiorenza: An Evaluation

In a detailed evaluation, the author challenges Elizabeth Schüssler Fiorenza's reconstruction of early Christian origins and her underlying presuppositions. The author also presents her own views on women's roles both then and now.

2002 / 1-84227-055-9 / xxiv + 468pp

July 2005

Robin Parry

Old Testament Story and Christian Ethics

The Rape of Dinah as a Case Study

What is the role of story in ethics and, more particularly, what is the role of Old Testament story in Christian ethics? This book, drawing on the work of contemporary philosophers, argues that narrative is crucial in the ethical shaping of people and, drawing on the work of contemporary Old Testament scholars, that story plays a key role in Old Testament ethics. Parry then argues that when situated in canonical context Old Testament stories can be reappropriated by Christian readers in their own ethical formation. The shocking story of the rape of Dinah and the massacre of the Shechemites provides a fascinating case study for exploring the parameters within which Christian ethical appropriations of Old Testament stories can live.

2004 / 1-84227-210-1 / xx + 350pp

Ian Paul

Power to See the World Anew

The Value of Paul Ricoeur's Hermeneutic of Metaphor in Interpreting the Symbolism of Revelation 12 and 13

This book is a study of the hermeneutics of metaphor of Paul Ricoeur, one of the most important writers on hermeneutics and metaphor of the last century. It sets out the key points of his theory, important criticisms of his work, and how his approach, modified in the light of these criticisms, offers a methodological framework for reading apocalyptic texts.

***2006** / 1-84227-056-7 / approx. 350pp*

Robert L. Plummer

Paul's Understanding of the Church's Mission

Did the Apostle Paul Expect the Early Christian Communities to Evangelize?

This book engages in a careful study of Paul's letters to determine if the apostle expected the communities to which he wrote to engage in missionary activity. It helpfully summarizes the discussion on this debated issue, judiciously handling contested texts, and provides a way forward in addressing this critical question. While admitting that Paul rarely explicitly commands the communities he founded to evangelize, Plummer amasses significant incidental data to provide a convincing case that Paul did indeed expect his churches to engage in mission activity. Throughout the study, Plummer progressively builds a theological basis for the church's mission that is both distinctively Pauline and compelling.

***2006** / 1-84227-333-7 / approx. 324pp*

David Powys

'Hell': A Hard Look at a Hard Question

The Fate of the Unrighteous in New Testament Thought

This comprehensive treatment seeks to unlock the original meaning of terms and phrases long thought to support the traditional doctrine of hell. It concludes that there is an alternative—one which is more biblical, and which can positively revive the rationale for Christian mission.

1997 / 0-85364-831-X / xxii + 478pp

Sorin Sabou

Between Horror and Hope

Paul's Metaphorical Language of Death in Romans 6.1-11

This book argues that Paul's metaphorical language of death in Romans 6.1-11 conveys two aspects: horror and hope. The 'horror' aspect is conveyed by the 'crucifixion' language, and the 'hope' aspect by 'burial' language. The life of the Christian believer is understood, as relationship with sin is concerned ('death to sin'), between these two realities: horror and hope.

***2005** / 1-84227-322-1 / approx. 224pp*

Rosalind Selby

The Comical Doctrine

The Epistemology of New Testament Hermeneutics

This book argues that the gospel breaks through postmodernity's critique of truth and the referential possibilities of textuality with its gift of grace. With a rigorous, philosophical challenge to modernist and postmodernist assumptions, Selby offers an alternative epistemology to all who would still read with faith *and* with academic credibility.

***2005** / 1-84227-212-8 / approx. 350pp*

Kiwoong Son

Zion Symbolism in Hebrews

Hebrews 12.18-24 as a Hermeneutical Key to the Epistle

This book challenges the general tendency of understanding the Epistle to the Hebrews against a Hellenistic background and suggests that the Epistle should be understood in the light of the Jewish apocalyptic tradition. The author especially argues for the importance of the theological symbolism of Sinai and Zion (Heb. 12:18-24) as it provides the Epistle's theological background as well as the rhetorical basis of the superiority motif of Jesus throughout the Epistle.

***2005** / 1-84227-368-X / approx. 280pp*

Kevin Walton

Thou Traveller Unknown

The Presence and Absence of God in the Jacob Narrative

The author offers a fresh reading of the story of Jacob in the book of Genesis through the paradox of divine presence and absence. The work also seeks to make a contribution to Pentateuchal studies by bringing together a close reading of the final text with historical critical insights, doing justice to the text's historical depth, final form and canonical status.

2003 / 1-84227-059-1 / xvi + 238pp

George M. Wieland

The Significance of Salvation

A Study of Salvation Language in the Pastoral Epistles

The language and ideas of salvation pervade the three Pastoral Epistles. This study offers a close examination of their soteriological statements. In all three letters the idea of salvation is found to play a vital paraenetic role, but each also exhibits distinctive soteriological emphases. The results challenge common assumptions about the Pastoral Epistles as a corpus.

***2005** / 1-84227-257-8 / approx. 324pp*

Alistair Wilson

When Will These Things Happen?

A Study of Jesus as Judge in Matthew 21–25

This study seeks to allow Matthew's carefully constructed presentation of Jesus to be given full weight in the modern evaluation of Jesus' eschatology. Careful analysis of the text of Matthew 21–25 reveals Jesus to be standing firmly in the Jewish prophetic and wisdom traditions as he proclaims and enacts imminent judgement on the Jewish authorities then boldly claims the central role in the final and universal judgement.

2004 / 1-84227-146-6 / xxii + 272pp

Lindsay Wilson

Joseph Wise and Otherwise

The Intersection of Covenant and Wisdom in Genesis 37–50

This book offers a careful literary reading of Genesis 37–50 that argues that the Joseph story contains both strong covenant themes and many wisdom-like elements. The connections between the two helps to explore how covenant and wisdom might intersect in an integrated biblical theology.

2004 / 1-84227-140-7 / xvi + 340pp

Stephen I. Wright

The Voice of Jesus

Studies in the Interpretation of Six Gospel Parables

This literary study considers how the 'voice' of Jesus has been heard in different periods of parable interpretation, and how the categories of figure and trope may help us towards a sensitive reading of the parables today.

2000 / 0-85364-975-8 / xiv + 280pp

Paternoster
9 Holdom Avenue,
Bletchley,
Milton Keynes MK1 1QR,
United Kingdom
Web: www.authenticmedia.co.uk/paternoster

July 2005

Paternoster Theological Monographs

(All titles uniform with this volume)

Dates in bold are of projected publication

Emil Bartos

Deification in Eastern Orthodox Theology

An Evaluation and Critique of the Theology of Dumitru Staniloae

Bartos studies a fundamental yet neglected aspect of Orthodox theology: deification. By examining the doctrines of anthropology, christology, soteriology and ecclesiology as they relate to deification, he provides an important contribution to contemporary dialogue between Eastern and Western theologians.

1999 / 0-85364-956-1 / xii + 370pp

Graham Buxton

The Trinity, Creation and Pastoral Ministry

Imaging the Perichoretic God

In this book the author proposes a three-way conversation between theology, science and pastoral ministry. His approach draws on a Trinitarian understanding of God as a relational being of love, whose life 'spills over' into all created reality, human and non-human. By locating human meaning and purpose within God's 'creation-community' this book offers the possibility of a transforming engagement between those in pastoral ministry and the scientific community.

2005 */ 1-84227-369-8 / approx. 380 pp*

Iain D. Campbell

Fixing the Indemnity

The Life and Work of George Adam Smith

When Old Testament scholar George Adam Smith (1856–1942) delivered the Lyman Beecher lectures at Yale University in 1899, he confidently declared that 'modern criticism has won its war against traditional theories. It only remains to fix the amount of the indemnity.' In this biography, Iain D. Campbell assesses Smith's critical approach to the Old Testament and evaluates its consequences, showing that Smith's life and work still raises questions about the relationship between biblical scholarship and evangelical faith.

2004 / 1-84227-228-4 / xx + 256pp

Tim Chester

Mission and the Coming of God

Eschatology, the Trinity and Mission in the Theology of Jürgen Moltmann

This book explores the theology and missiology of the influential contemporary theologian, Jürgen Moltmann. It highlights the important contribution Moltmann has made while offering a critique of his thought from an evangelical perspective. In so doing, it touches on pertinent issues for evangelical missiology. The conclusion takes Calvin as a starting point, proposing 'an eschatology of the cross' which offers a critique of the over-realised eschatologies in liberation theology and certain forms of evangelicalism.

***2006** / 1-84227-320-5 / approx. 224pp*

Sylvia Wilkey Collinson

Making Disciples

The Significance of Jesus' Educational Strategy for Today's Church

This study examines the biblical practice of discipling, formulates a definition, and makes comparisons with modern models of education. A recommendation is made for greater attention to its practice today.

2004 / 1-84227-116-4 / xiv + 278pp

Darrell Cosden

A Theology of Work

Work and the New Creation

Through dialogue with Moltmann, Pope John Paul II and others, this book develops a genitive 'theology of work', presenting a theological definition of work and a model for a theological ethics of work that shows work's nature, value and meaning now and eschatologically. Work is shown to be a transformative activity consisting of three dynamically inter-related dimensions: the instrumental, relational and ontological.

2005 / 1-84227-332-9 / xvi + 208pp

Stephen M. Dunning

The Crisis and the Quest

A Kierkegaardian Reading of Charles Williams

Employing Kierkegaardian categories and analysis, this study investigates both the central crisis in Charles Williams's authorship between hermetism and Christianity (Kierkegaard's Religions A and B), and the quest to resolve this crisis, a quest that ultimately presses the bounds of orthodoxy.

2000 / 0-85364-985-5 / xxiv + 254pp

Keith Ferdinando

The Triumph of Christ in African Perspective

A Study of Demonology and Redemption in the African Context

The book explores the implications of the gospel for traditional African fears of occult aggression. It analyses such traditional approaches to suffering and biblical responses to fears of demonic evil, concluding with an evaluation of African beliefs from the perspective of the gospel.

1999 / 0-85364-830-1 / xviii + 450pp

Andrew Goddard

Living the Word, Resisting the World

The Life and Thought of Jacques Ellul

This work offers a definitive study of both the life and thought of the French Reformed thinker Jacques Ellul (1912-1994). It will prove an indispensable resource for those interested in this influential theologian and sociologist and for Christian ethics and political thought generally.

2002 / 1-84227-053-2 / xxiv + 378pp

David Hilborn

The Words of our Lips

Language-Use in Free Church Worship

Studies of liturgical language have tended to focus on the written canons of Roman Catholic and Anglican communities. By contrast, David Hilborn analyses the more extemporary approach of English Nonconformity. Drawing on recent developments in linguistic pragmatics, he explores similarities and differences between 'fixed' and 'free' worship, and argues for the interdependence of each.

***2006** / 0-85364-977-4 / approx. 350pp*

Roger Hitching

The Church and Deaf People

A Study of Identity, Communication and Relationships with Special Reference to the Ecclesiology of Jürgen Moltmann

In *The Church and Deaf People* Roger Hitching sensitively examines the history and present experience of deaf people and finds similarities between aspects of sign language and Moltmann's theological method that 'open up' new ways of understanding theological concepts.

2003 / 1-84227-222-5 / xxii + 236pp

John G. Kelly

One God, One People

The Differentiated Unity of the People of God in the Theology of Jürgen Moltmann

The author expounds and critiques Moltmann's doctrine of God and highlights the systematic connections between it and Moltmann's influential discussion of Israel. He then proposes a fresh approach to Jewish–Christian relations building on Moltmann's work using insights from Habermas and Rawls.

2005 */ 0-85346-969-3 / approx. 350pp*

Mark F.W. Lovatt

Confronting the Will-to-Power

A Reconsideration of the Theology of Reinhold Niebuhr

Confronting the Will-to-Power is an analysis of the theology of Reinhold Niebuhr, arguing that his work is an attempt to identify, and provide a practical theological answer to, the existence and nature of human evil.

2001 / 1-84227-054-0 / xviii + 216pp

Neil B. MacDonald

Karl Barth and the Strange New World within the Bible

Barth, Wittgenstein, and the Metadilemmas of the Enlightenment

Barth's discovery of the strange new world within the Bible is examined in the context of Kant, Hume, Overbeck, and, most importantly, Wittgenstein. MacDonald covers some fundamental issues in theology today: epistemology, the final form of the text and biblical truth-claims.

2000 / 0-85364-970-7 / xxvi + 374pp

Keith A. Mascord

Alvin Plantinga and Christian Apologetics

This book draws together the contributions of the philosopher Alvin Plantinga to the major contemporary challenges to Christian belief, highlighting in particular his ground-breaking work in epistemology and the problem of evil. Plantinga's theory that both theistic and Christian belief is warrantedly basic is explored and critiqued, and an assessment offered as to the significance of his work for apologetic theory and practice.

2005 */ 1-84227-256-X / approx. 304pp*

Gillian McCulloch

The Deconstruction of Dualism in Theology

With Reference to Ecofeminist Theology and New Age Spirituality

This book challenges eco-theological anti-dualism in Christian theology, arguing that dualism has a twofold function in Christian religious discourse. Firstly, it enables us to express the discontinuities and divisions that are part of the process of reality. Secondly, dualistic language allows us to express the mysteries of divine transcendence/immanence and the survival of the soul without collapsing into monism and materialism, both of which are problematic for Christian epistemology.

2002 / 1-84227-044-3 / xii + 282pp

Leslie McCurdy

Attributes and Atonement

The Holy Love of God in the Theology of P.T. Forsyth

Attributes and Atonement is an intriguing full-length study of P.T. Forsyth's doctrine of the cross as it relates particularly to God's holy love. It includes an unparalleled bibliography of both primary and secondary material relating to Forsyth.

1999 / 0-85364-833-6 / xiv + 328pp

Nozomu Miyahira

Towards a Theology of the Concord of God

A Japanese Perspective on the Trinity

This book introduces a new Japanese theology and a unique Trinitarian formula based on the Japanese intellectual climate: three betweennesses and one concord. It also presents a new interpretation of the Trinity, a co-subordinationism, which is in line with orthodox Trinitarianism; each single person of the Trinity is eternally and equally subordinate (or serviceable) to the other persons, so that they retain the mutual dynamic equality.

2000 / 0-85364-863-8 / xiv + 256pp

Eddy José Muskus

The Origins and Early Development of Liberation Theology in Latin America

With Particular Reference to Gustavo Gutiérrez

This work challenges the fundamental premise of Liberation Theology, 'opting for the poor', and its claim that Christ is found in them. It also argues that Liberation Theology emerged as a direct result of the failure of the Roman Catholic Church in Latin America.

2002 / 0-85364-974-X / xiv + 296pp

Jim Purves

The Triune God and the Charismatic Movement

A Critical Appraisal from a Scottish Perspective

All emotion and no theology? Or a fundamental challenge to reappraise and realign our trinitarian theology in the light of Christian experience? This study of charismatic renewal as it found expression within Scotland at the end of the twentieth century evaluates the use of Patristic, Reformed and contemporary models of the Trinity in explaining the workings of the Holy Spirit.

2004 / 1-84227-321-3 / xxiv + 246pp

Anna Robbins

Methods in the Madness

Diversity in Twentieth-Century Christian Social Ethics

The author compares the ethical methods of Walter Rauschenbusch, Reinhold Niebuhr and others. She argues that unless Christians are clear about the ways that theology and philosophy are expressed practically they may lose the ability to discuss social ethics across contexts, let alone reach effective agreements.

2004 / 1-84227-211-X / xx + 294pp

Ed Rybarczyk

Beyond Salvation

Eastern Orthodoxy and Classical Pentecostalism on Becoming Like Christ

At first glance eastern Orthodoxy and classical Pentecostalism seem quite distinct. This ground-breaking study shows they share much in common, especially as it concerns the experiential elements of following Christ. Both traditions assert that authentic Christianity transcends the wooden categories of modernism.

2004 / 1-84227-144-X / xii + 356pp

Signe Sandsmark

Is World View Neutral Education Possible and Desirable?

A Christian Response to Liberal Arguments

(Published jointly with The Stapleford Centre)

This book discusses reasons for belief in world view neutrality, and argues that 'neutral' education will have a hidden, but strong world view influence. It discusses the place for Christian education in the common school.

2000 / 0-85364-973-1 / xiv + 182pp

Hazel Sherman

Reading Zechariah

The Allegorical Tradition of Biblical Interpretation through the Commentary of Didymus the Blind and Theodore of Mopsuestia

A close reading of the commentary on Zechariah by Didymus the Blind alongside that of Theodore of Mopsuestia suggests that popular categorising of Antiochene and Alexandrian biblical exegesis as 'historical' or 'allegorical' is inadequate and misleading.

***2005** / 1-84227-213-6 / approx. 280pp*

Andrew Sloane

On Being a Christian in the Academy

Nicholas Wolterstorff and the Practice of Christian Scholarship

An exposition and critical appraisal of Nicholas Wolterstorff's epistemology in the light of the philosophy of science, and an application of his thought to the practice of Christian scholarship.

2003 / 1-84227-058-3 / xvi + 274pp

Damon W.K. So

Jesus' Revelation of His Father

A Narrative-Conceptual Study of the Trinity with Special Reference to Karl Barth

This book explores the trinitarian dynamics in the context of Jesus' revelation of his Father in his earthly ministry with references to key passages in Matthew's Gospel. It develops from the exegeses of these passages a non-linear concept of revelation which links Jesus' communion with his Father to his revelatory words and actions through a nuanced understanding of the Holy Spirit, with references to K. Barth, G.W.H. Lampe, J.D.G. Dunn and E. Irving.

***2005** / 1-84227-323-X / approx. 380pp*

Daniel Strange

The Possibility of Salvation Among the Unevangelised

An Analysis of Inclusivism in Recent Evangelical Theology

For evangelical theologians the 'fate of the unevangelised' impinges upon fundamental tenets of evangelical identity. The position known as 'inclusivism', defined by the belief that the unevangelised can be ontologically saved by Christ whilst being epistemologically unaware of him, has been defended most vigorously by the Canadian evangelical Clark H. Pinnock. Through a detailed analysis and critique of Pinnock's work, this book examines a cluster of issues surrounding the unevangelised and its implications for christology, soteriology and the doctrine of revelation.

2002 / 1-84227-047-8 / xviii + 362pp

Scott Swain

God According to the Gospel

Biblical Narrative and the Identity of God in the Theology of Robert W. Jenson

Robert W. Jenson is one of the leading voices in contemporary Trinitarian theology. His boldest contribution in this area concerns his use of biblical narrative both to ground and explicate the Christian doctrine of God. *God According to the Gospel* critically examines Jenson's proposal and suggests an alternative way of reading the biblical portrayal of the triune God.

***2006** / 1-84227-258-6 / approx. 180pp*

Justyn Terry

The Justifying Judgement of God

A Reassessment of the Place of Judgement in the Saving Work of Christ

The argument of this book is that judgement, understood as the whole process of bringing justice, is the primary metaphor of atonement, with others, such as victory, redemption and sacrifice, subordinate to it. Judgement also provides the proper context for understanding penal substitution and the call to repentance, baptism, eucharist and holiness.

***2005** / 1-84227-370-1 / approx. 274 pp*

Graham Tomlin

The Power of the Cross

Theology and the Death of Christ in Paul, Luther and Pascal

This book explores the theology of the cross in St Paul, Luther and Pascal. It offers new perspectives on the theology of each, and some implications for the nature of power, apologetics, theology and church life in a postmodern context.

1999 / 0-85364-984-7 / xiv + 344pp

Adonis Vidu

Postliberal Theological Method

A Critical Study

The postliberal theology of Hans Frei, George Lindbeck, Ronald Thiemann, John Milbank and others is one of the more influential contemporary options. This book focuses on several aspects pertaining to its theological method, specifically its understanding of background, hermeneutics, epistemic justification, ontology, the nature of doctrine and, finally, Christological method.

***2005** / 1-84227-395-7 / approx. 324pp*

Graham J. Watts

Revelation and the Spirit

A Comparative Study of the Relationship between the Doctrine of Revelation and Pneumatology in the Theology of Eberhard Jüngel and of Wolfhart Pannenberg

The relationship between revelation and pneumatology is relatively unexplored. This approach offers a fresh angle on two important twentieth century theologians and raises pneumatological questions which are theologically crucial and relevant to mission in a postmodern culture.

***2005** / 1-84227-104-0 / xxii + 232pp*

Nigel G. Wright

Disavowing Constantine

Mission, Church and the Social Order in the Theologies of John Howard Yoder and Jürgen Moltmann

This book is a timely restatement of a radical theology of church and state in the Anabaptist and Baptist tradition. Dr Wright constructs his argument in dialogue and debate with Yoder and Moltmann, major contributors to a free church perspective.

2000 / 0-85364-978-2 / xvi + 252pp

Paternoster
9 Holdom Avenue,
Bletchley,
Milton Keynes MK1 1QR,
United Kingdom
Web: www.authenticmedia.co.uk/paternoster

July 2005

www.ingramcontent.com/pod-product-compliance
Lightning Source LLC
LaVergne TN
LVHW050615100826
845148LV00011B/1594

* 9 7 8 1 5 9 7 5 2 7 7 0 5 *